Walking—
for Health, Fitness and Sport

PENN HILLS PUBLIC LIBRARY
240 ASTER STREET
PITTSBURGH, PA. 15235

ENTERED FEB 1998

613.717
CAR

Walking—
for Health, Fitness and Sport

Bob Carlson

Fulcrum Publishing
Golden, Colorado

Copyright © 1996 Bob Carlson
Cover photograph copyright © 1996 Greim/Stock Imagery
Interior illustrations by Wayne J. Tirone, copyright © 1996
Book design by Bill Spahr

All rights reserved. No part of this book may be reproduced or transmitted in any form or by any means, electronic or mechanical, including photocopying, recording or by any information storage and retrieval system, without permission in writing from the publisher.

Library of Congress Cataloging-in-Publication Data

Carlson, Bob.
    Walking for health, fitness and sport / Bob Carlson.
        p.   cm.
    Includes bibliographical references and index.
    ISBN 1-55591-236-2 (pbk.)
    1. Fitness walking. I. Title.
    RA781.65.C373   1996
    613.7'176—dc20
    96-27829   CIP

Printed in the United States of America

0 9 8 7 6 5 4 3 2 1

Fulcrum Publishing
350 Indiana Street, Suite 350
Golden, Colorado 80401-5093
(800) 992-2908 • (303) 277-1623

Dedicated to all the great and loyal friends I have acquired in the past 11 years in the Front Range Walkers; racewalkers all over the United States; and my five children—Tina, Bob, Doug, Glenn and Jim— for their moral support in all my endeavors.

Contents

PART 3
Walking for Sport   79

PART 4
Appendices   141

Acknowledgments

I am indebted to the following experts who I have consulted for advice on named subjects during the writing of this book: Bob Anderson of Palmer Lake, Colorado, stretching expert (Flexibility Training, chapter 19); Bob Bowman of Oakland, California, Head of World Racewalk Judges (Racewalk Judging, chapter 24; Olympic records, appendix 5); Tina Braet-Thomas, R.D., M.S. of Cody, Wyoming, and Lynn Umbreit, R.D. of Denver, Colorado (Nutrition and Health, chapter 4); Philip Howell of Atlanta, Georgia, Walking Club of Georgia (Racewalking History and Records, appendix 5); Leonard Jansen, biomechanist in Hershey, Pennsylvania, for information on training (chapters 17–21); Beverly LaVeck of Seattle, Washington, and keeper of world masters racewalk records (appendix 5); former national racewalk coach and author, Martin Rudow of Seattle, Washington, for assistance on racewalking technique (Technique Training, chapter 17); Rob Sweetgall of Clayton, Missouri, president of Creative Walking, Inc., for information on innovative physical education for children (Children Are Our Future, chapter 9); and Elaine Ward of Pasadena, California, for supplying the racewalking regional ladder system (Racewalking Speed, appendix 4).

Acknowledgements

Preface

Why another book on walking? I was compelled to write this book because there are precious few books on the market that cover almost *all* the reasons people should walk with good form, posture and efficiency. Recent research indicates that more people in the United States—at least 75 million U.S. citizens—use walking as their primary mode of exercise. However, only a tiny percentage of these people know how to get the most benefit and enjoyment out of the activity by using the natural biomechanics of the body at its maximum efficiency.

The American public needs all the encouragement it can get in alleviating the great health care financial crisis facing the United States today. All of us should realize that taking care of ourselves is vital if the efforts of the surgeon general, the American Medical Association and the U.S. Congress are to be successful at pulling in the reins before our economy is ruined. If each of us would consider it our patriotic duty to take charge of our own health and well-being to prevent sickness or decrepitude, then we would not need to ask our physicians and health professionals to cure us of the many illnesses that plague us. Great progress could be made in the cost of health care and personal well-being. The word *prevention* should become the most important one in our vocabularies. Why not lessen the risk of contracting some catastrophic illness that would, if not kill you quickly, cause ruination of the quality of the rest of your life—both financially and physically? A prudent lifestyle is the main road to success.

One of the main things that must change in the present health care system is the fact that health insurance companies will pay huge sums for such procedures as heart bypass operations yet will pay nothing for the many less costly steps people can take to prevent such disasters in the first place. A consistent walking for exercise program, eschewing tobacco in all its forms and healthy eating habits can go a long way in reducing health care costs. Proposed universal health care plans do not dwell enough on preventive measures. The emphasis seems to be on early detection of diseases instead of prevention of these first stages from the beginning. It is strange that our society spends billions of dollars on insurance against our death. When the time comes, it is the beneficiaries of these "death insurance" policies who receive monetary benefits, not the deceased. Yet, oddly enough, most of us don't bother to spend thought, money and effort on our true life insurance, that is, good diets, exercise and other healthy lifestyle habits. Aren't our health and well-being the most precious things we have on earth—far outstripping any material possessions? My fondest hope is that somebody who reads this book will take heed and improve their knowledge of how to attain some health and fitness goals.

The human body has remarkable recuperative powers if it is given half a chance. The late Dr. Walter Cannon once said: "When you understand a great deal about the human body and its resources for health, you wonder why anyone is ever sick. Any physician knows that if given rest, proper food and ease of mind, 90 percent or more of his patients get well. As a ship rights herself after a squall has keeled her over, so the body rights itself after the minor squalls that strike it daily in health and after the tempests of disease." The trouble is that some of our habits are so bad that the human body's immune system becomes overwhelmed. What we can do is adopt healthy habits that will help to boost the body's built-in immune system.

Walking for health, fitness and sport are the three main topics that need addressing. Few books are exclusively about racewalking. Many others are about walking for health and/or fitness. Consequently, I have divided the book into three sections, three topics that have differences but are nevertheless close relatives and complement each other.

The biomechanics of walking at whatever speed are generally misunderstood. Biomechanics simply means how all the body's muscles, bones and tendons function in relation to each other as nature intended. Any time that the principles of biomechanics are violated, walking efficiency and enjoyment are compromised, an issue that is further explained in the walking for sport section. As far as the health and fitness sections are concerned, many believe that health and fitness are one and the same. Not so! You can be healthy and not fit, and fit but not healthy. If we wish to live our lives optimally, we must strive to become both fit and healthy.

The purpose of this book is to provide a deeper understanding of the many principles of walking with the hope that such understanding will give you confidence that you are doing something that can have a profound influence on your well-being throughout the rest of your life. More and more physicians and health care providers now recommend walking as the ideal aerobic exercise for improved health and fitness, as well as being one with an extremely low injury rate. Everyone who is interested in improving or maintaining their present health, both physically and mentally, should have at least a rudimentary knowledge of the human body, how it works and what is good or bad in diets and exercise methodology. In this book, I will offer recommendations about how much walking is necessary to make a positive impact on your health and physical fitness.

Questions Often Asked about Walking

In my fifteen-plus years as a championship racewalker and walking instructor, I have conducted well over a hundred three-week classes on walking technique in the 1980s and first half of the 1990s and have fielded practically every question imaginable on the activity. The following questions are the ones that seem to be asked most often:

- Is walking as effective as running or jogging for weight loss?
- How do you choose the proper footwear?
- Where is the best place to get walking shoes?
- What is the price range for good footwear?
- How much walking must a person do to get into shape?
- How fast should a person walk to get the most benefits?
- Why do my shins hurt after walking faster than normal?
- Is it true that walking is nearly injury-free and is easy on the legs?
- Which muscles are toned in rapid walking that are not in running?
- What are your diet considerations for increasing strength and endurance?
- Where can I learn efficient walking technique?
- What are the main health benefits I can expect to get from walking?
- How do I find out about and get into races?
- Should I carry hand or ankle weights to get in shape faster?
- Sometimes my right side hurts. What can I do to help this?
- How fast do the world champions walk?
- Does air pollution have much effect on exercising outdoors?
- How important are warm-up and stretching exercises?
- What are the advantages of joining an organized walking club?
- How do you know when you've overdone it?
- What is a good way of monitoring your progress?
- Are there age or medical limitations?

These questions and many others will be addressed in this book as you read along. I will also address the following points in detail to convince you that your walking program can be enjoyable, and may even become a positive addiction:

1. Do not set unrealistic goals for yourself. Goals that are too hard to reach can be very discouraging.
2. Be prepared for your walking sessions. Get adequate rest. Eat properly and not too soon before exercise bouts. Stay well hydrated especially in the warmer parts of the year.
3. Keep your equipment in top shape, especially your shoes.
4. Be flexible in your routine and try to keep it from becoming boring. Vary the route, time, place, companions, etc.

5.   Plan ahead and dress properly for the weather conditions. If the weather is unpleasant, plan to get out at another more pleasant time.

6.   Adopt a relaxed attitude about your walking program so that it does not become too rigid or demanding. In other words go with the flow—but don't get lazy. You will discover that walking will be very relaxing for the mind and body.

My intent is to convince you that this perfectly natural activity can become a part of a healthy lifestyle if you follow a regular, consistent program. You can lose weight, increase lung power, muscle tone, strength, endurance and, best of all, feel super about yourself.

PART 1

Walking for Health

1 A Definition of Health

"She who has health has hope, and she who has hope has everything."
—Arabian Proverb

The dictionaries define "health" as "the sound condition of a living organism" and "the absence of ailments or defects." However, one can be healthy but also unfit. Some young sedentaries can be completely free of disease, yet also be completely unfit in a physical sense.

For the purposes of this book, "fitness" is the ability to do physical work and to use the principles of exercise physiology. Embracing a fitness program improves muscle tone and function. A healthy person may have a heart and lungs good enough for most ordinary daily activities, but be unable to sustain exertion. Every muscle in the body has a purpose, but we must make a conscious effort to use them all. Unused muscles become weak and flabby and may even atrophy.

If you are unhealthy, it may be even more difficult to achieve fitness, yet it should be a top priority. Prior to starting an exercise program, get a physical exam, including a full-spectrum cholesterol-level test and tests for blood pressure, clotting tendency, diabetes, stress factors and waist-hip ratio.

Sedentarianism is a dangerous condition and we should work to counteract it. Whether you are walking for health, fitness or both, make sure you get out and do it on a regular basis. A *total* healthy lifestyle provides us with the optimum health and fitness combination.

A Position Statement

In recent years the International Federation of Sports Medicine developed the following health and fitness position statement, entitled *Physical Exercise: An Important Factor for Health.* This august body of fitness experts say what I would like to and in far better terms.

> The human body has great potential for functional and structural adaptation to vigorous physical exercise. Humans have been nomads and hunters throughout thousands of years of evolution. During recent history, however, a drastic reduction has occurred in the amount of physical activity performed in daily life because of the use of labor-saving devices and motorized transport.

One result of this reduction in physical exercise has been a decrease in physical fitness levels in the populations of the industrialized world with a simultaneous increase in the prevalence of cardiovascular disease as a cause of death and disability. This suggests that the change to a sedentary lifestyle may be both detrimental to the individual's health and potentially expensive for society. Studies have not demonstrated a direct cause-and-effect relationship between the lack of exercise and cardiovascular morbidity and mortality.

However, epidemiologic evidence strongly suggests the beneficial effects of exercise in the prevention of coronary artery disease and in the reduction of all causes of mortality when exercise constitutes an integral part of occupational and leisure-time activities. Moreover, physical exercise can alter other risk factors by improving the blood lipid profile, maintaining blood pressure within safe limits and controlling body weight. In addition, exercise can contribute to the control of diabetes mellitus and the maintenance of bone density in the elderly.

Although physical health, as appraised by morbidity and mortality rates, has been steadily improving throughout the world, epidemiologic and experimental evidence indicates that it is important for a person to engage in a program of regular physical exercise as a part of a healthy lifestyle. Adherence to a regular program of aerobic exercise involving large muscle groups can enhance the physiologic systems that support such activity and concomitantly improve the capacity for such exercise. This phenomenon is commonly referred to as physical fitness. A physically fit person has greater ability to tolerate the physical challenges of daily life whereas an unfit person would terminate activity because of fatigue.

Physical fitness and good health are not synonymous but are complementary. While good health merely means the absence of illness, physical fitness implies ample vigor to reach for life's rewards and not be physically dependent on others. In sports medicine, preventing or remedying the effects of a sedentary lifestyle or of aging is of paramount importance. Therefore, appropriate physical activity is a valuable component in the therapeutic regimen to control and treat coronary heart disease, systemic hypertension, obesity, musculoskeletal disorders, respiratory diseases and depression. Physical fitness can also contribute to feelings of well-being and self-esteem.

It is the recommendation of the International Federation of Sports Medicine (IFSM) that each person should engage in a regular program of aerobic exercise consisting of three to five exercise sessions of 30 to 60 minutes' duration each week. The aerobic exercise may consist of such activities as walking, running, hiking, swimming, cycling, rowing, skating or cross-country skiing. Racquet sports and team sports can also be employed if the intensity is regulated and bursts of high activity are avoided. The intensity of the exercise should routinely elicit a heart rate within 50 percent to 80 percent of the individual's maximum. The choice of activity for each individual should depend on such factors as physical condition, age, access to facilities and interest. A preparticipation screening exam performed by a medical doctor is advised, especially for older adults (e.g., age 35 and older) and for those with known risk factors.

Regular physical exercise can enhance health and can provide an individual with a more productive and enjoyable life.

Exercise and Health

When Jim Fixx, the author of several books on running, died on a training run on July 20, 1984, at the age of 52, the running community was shocked. How could a runner who was so superbly fit die of a heart attack? Well, simply stated, Fixx was fit but not healthy. Authorities blamed his early death on his unhealthy diet and undiagnosed heart disease.

Can exercise keep us well? There are two sides to this question. According to some authorities, a moderate amount of an exercise such as walking can relieve stress and help us avoid getting sick. Alternatively, excessive exercise can increase stress on the body and lower resistance to illness. Level of exercise is relative—moderate exercise to an elite athlete could be an extreme overstress to someone who has had sedentary habits.

A program of personal fitness—such as a good consistent walking program—conditions the body. For young people, conditioning means strength, speed and dexterity. For adults, it relates to endurance, coping with mental stress and preventing cardiovascular disease and cancer. Walking can also condition the mind, leading to mental satisfaction and feelings of accomplishment and increased self-esteem.

The World Health Organization has stated: "Health is a state of full *physical, psychological* and *social* well-being, not simply the absence of diseases or incapacity." This is the new holistic philosophy. Therefore, total wellness will necessarily enter into the equation along with physical wellness.

Perhaps when we are saying good-bye to friends we should say "Take care of yourself" or "When I see you again, be healthy—health is priceless." After all, what is the most important thing that we have? Life is no fun without good health, and neither money nor fame can have the same impact on our daily lives. Being healthy and fit makes life more pleasant. Health and fitness, although they do have their differences, should be thought of as reinforcing each other and each should be strived for on a consistent basis.

2 Taking Charge of Your Health

"Unless you try to do something beyond what you have already mastered, you will never grow."
                                          —Ronald E. Osborne

As the ancient Greeks realized and wrote about more than 2,500 years ago, physical activity is one of the main roads to a sound mind and body. Today's technological society places a heightened responsibility on each of us to take charge of our own physical fitness and health. Many years ago, physical fitness was a natural by-product of people's efforts to provide for their daily needs. In fact, an inactive lifestyle was impossible for most people. In the past century, labor-saving devices have had a profound impact on the average lifestyle, and little physical activity is required to survive. This being the case, physical fitness must be consciously pursued, and we must make exercise a consistent part of our daily routine.

Trouble in Unfit America

Let's look at some eye-opening figures about our unfit America. The following figures from the American Medical Association are current estimates of how many Americans die annually of diseases that could in many cases be prevented through prudent lifestyles:

heart attacks—550,000
strokes—170,000
diabetes, adult onset—136,000
lung cancer—130,000
colon cancer—60,000
breast cancer—40,000
prostate cancer—26,000

These figures add up to 1,112,000 deaths a year, representing about 65 percent of all deaths. Many of these deaths—particularly the cancers—are preceded by long periods of suffering and financial expense. Another 50 to 60 million citizens are affected by high blood pressure, the so-called "silent killer," which, if untreated, can lead to cardiovascular disease and stroke.

Think of the effect on this country and its overburdened health care system if we could prevent even half of these disorders through vigorous exercise, prudent diet and giving up smoking and alcohol. The more astute among us don't need a life-threatening emergency to realize that we need to care for our bodies with the same diligence that we do a new automobile. Think about it—the automobile can be replaced with a new one. If your body is destroyed, where do you turn?

Infectious disease treatments and emergency care have vastly improved in recent years. This being the case, the next great medical breakthrough must come from people who strive for personal health through healthy lifestyles. Those who do not exercise at all are doing their bodies (and, I might add, their country) a great disservice. It could rightfully be called an act of patriotism to take care of yourself to such an extent that the poor taxpayers don't need to subsidize the attempts to ameliorate your health problems in your middle or old age.

Hypokinetic Disease

There is another sickness in this country called hypokinetic disease (defined as "lack-of-movement disease"). Another name for this dread disease is "sedentarianism." Credit for this idea goes to doctors Hans Krause and Wilhelm Raab, who wrote a book on this subject years ago. Sedentarianism stems in part from Newton's law of inertia, which states that "a body at rest tends to stay at rest." The comfort of the couch is so appealing for many that it is hard to overcome. Most of us lead lives vastly inferior to our potentials and too often we settle for a comfortable mediocrity. As Jean Giraudoux once said, "Only the mediocre are always at their best."

Those who choose to lead a sedentary lifestyle are taking great risks with their mental and physical well-being. Sedentarianism is a disease. Anyone who has been confined to a bed for several weeks knows what lack of movement can do to weaken the body. Sedentarianism causes lower back pain and leads to poor circulation. Our two legs are superior pumps for coursing the blood through the system but only if they are used in rhythmic motions on a regular basis. Be your own doctor by prescribing a daily dose of exercise for yourself, and get out and avoid this disease.

Health Benefits of Walking

Now let's review the health benefits that can result from a walking program:

1. Walking improves circulations by increasing blood flow and the size and tone of the blood vessels, reducing the risk of cardiovascular and cerebrovascular disease.
2. Walking strengthens the muscles of the body, including the heart muscle, and makes them work more efficiently.
3. Walking slows the resting heart rate by increasing stroke volume, or the volume of blood the heart pumps with one contraction.

4. Walking tends to reduce the height to which arterial pressure rises during exercise and stress.
5. Walking encourages collateral circulation to the heart muscle. This can dramatically increase your chance of surviving a coronary.
6. Walking reduces the risk of obesity.
7. Walking improves digestion and elimination of body wastes.
8. Walking increases the oxygen supply to the brain and mental sharpness, increasing the potential for creative thought.
9. Walking tends to retard the aging process and provide a more youthful appearance.
10. Walking aids lymphatic circulation.
11. Walking stimulates the metabolism both during and after exercise.
12. Walking increases respiratory capacity and aerobic power.
13. Walking benefits body growth and recovery from trauma.
14. Walking reduces blood fat (triglycerides) levels.
15. Walking reduces insomnia and provides for better relaxation.
16. Walking reduces the incidence of minor illness, allergies, headaches and abdominal problems.
17. Walking improves coordination by activating neurotransmitters and training the muscle fibers.
18. Walking increases the flexibility of the joints and muscles and reduces aches and pains in the back, neck and other body joints.
19. Walking circulates more oxygen to all body tissues, restoring the balance between oxygen required by the tissues and that made available through exercise.
20. Walking tones up the glandular system and increases thyroid gland output.
21. Walking increases the production of red blood cells by the bone marrow.
22. Walking increases the ability to store and utilize nutrients, increasing endurance.
23. Walking augments the alkaline reserves of the body, which can be significant in an emergency requiring extended effort.
24. Walking gives a feeling of muscular strength by toning major muscles.
25. Walking counteracts feelings of fatigue.
26. Walking causes muscles to move vital fluids throughout the body, which lessens the work done by the heart.
27. Walking has a stabilizing affect on blood pressure.
28. Walking releases the flow of endorphins, which are the body's own natural tranquilizers.
29. Walking has a hardening and strengthening effect on the bones.
30. Walking provides a reserve of body strength and physical efficiency.
31. Walking improves the ratio between high-density and low-density components of cholesterol, which lessens the risk of artery disease and cancers.
32. Walking greatly improves mental outlook, optimism, morale and self-esteem.

Feeling Less than Your Best

Although you might be in the greatest shape of your life, that does not necessarily mean that you will never experience fatigue, weakness or a general lack of energy. These disturbing symptoms can come from many sources and may or may not be related to illness. If the symptoms persist, you might investigate the following possible causes.

Food, Drink and Drugs

Check your eating habits. You may be taking in too few calories to maintain your level of training. Many active people watch their weight too carefully and don't eat enough to maintain strength and energy, compromising endurance.

Conversely, overeating is also a contributor to sluggish fatigue. When you eat too much, the digestive system steals blood needed to provide energy to do other things. In addition, extra body weight often makes exercise less pleasant, keeping you from a regular exercise routine. It can become a vicious cycle as your strength and energy declines, making exercise a chore. Remember that the proper amount of exercise will keep your energy reserves high if your food intake is prudent.

Another cause of general fatigue may be caffeine intake. If you drink more than two cups of coffee or caffeinated soft drinks each day, you may become addicted to this drug. Caffeine withdrawal can lead to symptoms such as nervousness, skipped heartbeats, trembling hands, insomnia and headaches. Researchers have found that while mild doses of caffeine (100 to 200 mg.) can act as a stimulant and aid performance in endurance events, overdose can lead to chronic fatigue and dehydration.

Alcohol, tranquilizers, antihistamines, sleeping pills and blood pressure medicine all have side effects including fatigue. While a beer or a glass of wine now and then are unlikely to cause problems (some researchers say small amounts of alcohol may even be beneficial), too much can prevent deep sleep, reduce your motor and mind control and drain your energy reserves.

Depression

Many times the stresses of modern living are underestimated and can lead to depression. Depression can cause loss of interest in many things, fitness included, and lead to feelings of dissatisfaction, lack of motivation and profound fatigue. Other symptoms include a sense of worthlessness, insomnia, insecurity, changes in appetite and weight, chronic pains and the inability to make logical decisions. Exercise normally helps relieve mild depression, but more severe depression may need professional treatment. For some people, the right exercise can have the same antidepressant effects as prescription drugs, and with beneficial side effects as well.

Sometimes overtraining causes depression. If you've dramatically increased your workouts, you may need more sleep than usual. Too much sleep can make you feel fatigued, as can undertraining muscles used to exercise. If you get too little sleep, you may find yourself sleeping very late on weekends, snoozing during the day or feeling groggy in the morning. Moderation in all things seems to be the best road to stability.

Illness

Illness can also lead to fatigue. If you have been ill, it may take longer to get back to normal than you anticipate. Flu and the common cold are obvious culprits, but some hidden infections and endocrine disorders can also cause unexplained tiredness. For example, infectious hepatitis, a viral infection of the liver, and infectious mononucleosis both drain personal energy.

The thyroid gland, which regulates the body's metabolic processes, can be either underactive or overactive. Hyperthyroidism burns up calories too fast causing weakness and irritability while an underactive thyroid causes fatigue and puffiness, weight gain, dry skin, coarse hair, constipation and chills.

Other culprits causing energy deficiency are diabetes, in which the pancreas does not produce enough insulin (the hormone that delivers glucose to the cells for energy), and anemia, in which there is a deficiency of red blood cells.

If you feel under par for any reason for an extended period of time, you should make every effort to find the cause and address it in a positive fashion. See a physician, who will be able to diagnose any of the problems mentioned here. Above all, though, keep walking and eating well.

Taking Personal Charge of Your Health

In the past we have relied on personal physicians to take charge of our health. If we got sick, the doctor would supposedly have a magic pill or remedy to make us healthy or at least get us back to a state of out-of-shape semihealth. These days, we all must take personal charge of our quality of life and take action to accomplish good personal health habits for the remainder of our lives. The key is taking measures to prevent health problems ourselves. We can determine our future well-being to a far greater extent than previously realized.

There are times, however, when we may be faced with a serious illness or life-threatening emergency, and we must get to an emergency room in a hospital to take advantage of the best allopathic (traditional) medical care possible. Doctors are well trained to handle acute cases of all kinds of ailments with expert skill.

Unfortunately, most modern medicine doesn't concentrate enough on prevention and alternatives to traditional medicine. Medical schools have paid superficial attention to the effects of nutrition and exercise in the prevention of ailments and they often don't adequately address the personal patient-doctor relationship. Modern medicine has become so technologically complicated that just learning how to practice "crisis medicine" more than fills up the years of medical school, internships and residencies. Many natural healing methods that have been effective for centuries are ignored in favor of powerful drugs, many of which have deleterious side effects.

There are very few medical students who learn to counsel patients adequately about exercise and diet. Fortunately, there are a few dedicated souls who make the time to learn about preventive medicine and the other aspects of human health that need addressing.

Alternative Health Professionals

There are many other health professionals who spend many years studying the things that physicians don't have time to master. These health professionals include:

- Dietitians, nutritionists and naturopathic doctors, who have expert knowledge of the effect of foods on the body—both good and bad. Look for the title "R.D." or "N.D." after their names.

- Chiropractors, who study the nervous system and spine and learn how to apply alternatives to surgery and drugs.

- Osteopaths, who are similar to chiropractors but place more emphasis on the circulatory system than the nervous system.

- Exercise physiologists, psychologists and kinesiologists, who study how exercise affects the body both physically and psychologically.

- Physical therapists, who help patients restore mobility after injury.

- Massage therapists, who are experts in manipulating the body to keep it flexible, loose and relaxed, especially from middle age on. Find one who has a degree from an accredited school.

There are other specialties, such as homeopathy, biofeedback, herbalism, acupuncture–acupressure and reflexology. No matter what type of health professional you consult, find one in whom you trust and who comes recommended by other patients.

The patient must become an active partner in the quest for healing, and a good rapport with the health care professional is a vital element in the process. Often, the enthusiasm of the professional and the patient's faith in the treatment can have a positive influence on the final result. The mind is a powerful tool for healing. As many wise healers of the past and present have stated, the mind and body cannot be separated and mutually reinforce each other.

3 | Addressing the Aging Process

"The secret of staying young is to live honestly, eat slowly and lie about your age."

—Lucille Ball

Exercise walking should be started early and be kept up for the rest of your days. Unless you die accidentally or kill yourself at a young age with a miserable lifestyle, old age is something that must be anticipated. One of the biggest oversights of young people today is that they regard old age as being too far in the future to be important to them. In reality, they should start building a foundation for their future life. Young people need to take into account that what they do to their bodies now can come back to haunt them in future years. Autopsies performed on American soldiers killed in Vietnam showed a shocking amount of plaque buildup in the coronary arteries. This made the medical profession sit up and take notice. Military doctors found these problems in so many young men as a result of excessive fat intake and smoking.

Some Basic Precepts about Aging

1. There is no "normal" rate of aging. Aging is related to personal lifestyle, and one's physiological age might be vastly different than someone else of the same chronological age.
2. Chronological age is a poor predictor of a person's physical capacity or fitness. It is related to the body's capacity for processing oxygen. The average sedentary person's capacity declines about 8 percent per decade, but living a prudent, active lifestyle can reduce that by about 2 percent. A rise in body fat is the main cause for the decline in physical fitness, that is, if you are not a smoker.
3. The process of aging of the working parts of the body is perfectly natural.
4. Genes have a substantial affect on the aging process and to some degree on life span. Lifestyles, however, can change life span by as much as 20 to 30 years.
5. It has been estimated that nearly 60 percent of diseases are preventable through prudent lifestyle. Aging can be a painful process if one does nothing to prevent these diseases.

6. Everyone's body breaks down eventually, but if the consequences of all the harmful things that happen to us can be avoided by adopting optimum lifestyle habits, then we could live out a potential maximum human life span of approximately 120 years.
7. Practically no one dies of old age any more. Unless accidentally, one is almost sure to die of heart attack, stroke, cancer, pneumonia or other type of disease.

Maintaining Independence

Most adults don't take into account what might happen if they think of retirement as a time to rest and sit around watching television. They don't understand that physical exercise should be a lifelong proposition. Nursing homes are not pleasant places to wind our lives down, yet many of us become too decrepit to live anywhere else. Compared to the United States, the rest of the world has few elderly people living in nursing homes. In Europe, most elderly are taken care of in their own homes by relatives. The best thing to do is to avoid this dilemma entirely by staying is good shape for life. Exercise can provide independence in the retirement years that might not be possible for an infirm oldster. Walking on a regular basis can provide people 60 years of age and older with increased functioning of the heart, muscles and most of the organs of the body. Activity begets activity, and those who are active can do many of the same things that young people do. We must remain young at heart and body!

Exercise and Life Expectancy

The main reason so many elderly people must resort to an awkward shuffle, portable walkers or wheelchairs is that they have lost most or all of the mobility in their hips. Walking throughout life using a health walking technique, a slow version of racewalking, with its wider range of motion is the most obvious antidote to this common problem.

A body can be reconditioned at any age through exercise such as brisk walking. Eula Weaver and Ivor Welch, both famed for their endurance exploits, began their exercise programs in their early eighties with outstanding results in their nineties. According to the prominent exercise researcher Ralph Paffenberger, M.D., a person adhering to a prudent exercise program can increase life expectancy by an average of two years. Of course, this varies according to a person's other lifestyle habits or genetic traits. But probably more important than the length of life is the quality of life.

Gerontologist authority Dr. Alex Comfort of England says it is quite possible to extend life spans as much as 10 to 20 percent if the present trends in lifestyle improvement continue. But most scientific authorities think that the maximum possible human life span may never exceed 120. The oldest authenticated person on earth with a valid birth certificate is Mme. Calmet of France who attained the age of 121 in 1996.

Walking does not provide an absolute fountain of youth, but it is the next best thing. It will allow you to extend your middle age, slow the aging process and even make you middle-aged physiologically for the rest of your life. Perhaps middle age, which can vary widely from person to person, can best be defined as that stage in life when the narrow waistline and the broad mind are likely to change places.

As we age our senses tend to dull. This seems to be one of the laws of aging. But our senses are enhanced by aerobic exercises at any age. Our central nervous system, through which we perceive the world by sight, sound, smell and touch, performs below par if we are unfit. Impulses generated in the muscles through walking stimulate the nose, eyes, ears, mouth and skin surface. This results in an entirely different and vital perspective on life.

Your Potential Is Greater than You Think

The potential for improving all aspects of health and fitness with systematic use of proper conditioning methods is great regardless of age. In general, the earlier you start, the higher the potential level of health and fitness. Children must be taught at an early age to prepare for a vigorous old age. Many infirmities of old age stem directly from lack of conditioning. The human body is a unique machine. Unlike an automobile or other mechanical contrivance, the more it is used the stronger it gets and the more energy it can produce. The more energy you expend in aerobic activities, the more you have to engage in other activities.

Keep that Heart Muscle Strong

The heart is just another of the body's muscles, albeit the most important one related to health. Just like any other muscle, if the heart is not exercised, it tends to wither and become weak. We all know what happens when arms and legs are encased in plaster casts—they shrink and become much weaker. By not exercising and not using the heart muscle, we are in effect immobilizing it. Recent research has shown that passive lifestyles can give even a young person many of the symptoms that the elderly experience. In Sweden, Dr. Bengt Saltin and his researchers put five healthy young men in bed for 20 days and kept them there. At the end of this period, the average decrease in cardiac output was 26 percent. The young men also had a significant decrease in lean body tissue. Although resting in bed for this period of time may seem extreme, it is not far different from what is experienced in the old age of inactive people.

Heart Rate Is Significant

There have been some theories espoused that we all have a finite number of heartbeats to last us for a lifetime. If there is any truth to these theories, then lowering our resting heart rates through conditioning could be a real boon to each of us. A resting heart rate of 80 beats per minute (bpm) means 115,000 beats in a 24-hour period. If the resting bpm rate is only 50, then the total is 72,000 beats. The extra rest between the stronger beats means less work on the heart. During a workout you may expend an extra 2,000 heartbeats, but you are conditioning your heart, so for the rest of the day you may save 20,000 to 30,000 beats.

Importance of Circulation

When we settle for a sedentary life, we fail to give the circulatory system the push it needs through exercise, and the blood tends to pool in the belly and feet. The rate of the return blood flow slows, and its volume decreases. The heart must work harder to keep the decreased supply of blood moving faster to maintain the circulation of life-giving oxygen and the removal of cellular wastes. Though the heart is the main circulator of the oxygenated blood, it can receive great assistance from other pumps, such as briskly moving legs and arms.

One main reason many older people do not like cold weather is that poor circulation makes them very uncomfortable in the cold and susceptible to illness. Aerobic exercise would go a long way in overcoming the difficulties that the elderly experience in the cold.

Importance of Diet

The elderly are notorious for neglecting a healthy diet, and this is often the cause of irregularity. Colon cleansers such as oat bran and psyllium husk swell to many times their original size in the intestines and create bulk in the diet, and if eaten regularly can lead to a regular bowel movement every day. A judicious balanced diet with plenty of fresh fruits, vegetables and fiber has been shown to reduce greatly the risk of diseases and cancers of the colon.

Older people do not need as many calories as younger people and must cut back on the amount of food they consume. Moderation in eating can be a favorable factor for vigorous later years if brisk walking is used to burn off some of the excess calories.

Keep the Brain Ventilated

Senility has been associated with hardening of the arteries and the poor circulation to the brain that results. The elderly are at the mercy of their own oxygen delivery systems. The stronger the oxygen delivery system, the better the quality of life. Oxygenation of the brain has been shown to delay or decrease senility. Controlling hypertension is a major factor in atherosclerosis, which, if unchecked, can cause an intellectual decline after the age of 65. Memory deficit has also been linked to oxygen shortage in the brain. However, logical thinking can continue into very old age if people are active and continue to challenge their minds and muscular systems. Brisk walking has been shown to be instrumental in strengthening the blood and oxygen delivery systems throughout the entire body. Dr. Carl Eisdorfer, Director of Aging Research at Duke University, has said that, "Some of our recent work on blood pressure and intelligence has pretty well demonstrated what a lot of people have accepted as a normal process of aging. That the loss of intelligence between 65 and 75 years of age is largely related to hypertension. In groups of subjects without elevated blood pressure or where it has been controlled, there is no intellectual drop."

Places Where Centenarians Abound

Studies have been done in three areas of the world where people seem to live long lives in vigorous good health: the Caucasus Mountains that form the border between Russia and Georgia (in the former USSR), northern Pakistan and in the high mountains of Ecuador. Even though many of these people exaggerate their age by using a parent's name, there are still many healthy and vigorous oldsters, many from their eighties to more than 100 years old. It is unlikely that any exceed 120 years of age, widely considered to be the maximum at this period in history. These selected groups of people have the following characteristics in common:

1. These people engage in many hours of physical exertion daily, carrying heavy objects up and down hills.
2. Their diets are low in calories, protein, animal fats, cholesterol and salt, but are high in complex carbohydrates and fiber.
3. They are generally slender, well muscled and have a vigorous youthful appearance.
4. High blood pressure and cardiovascular diseases are virtually unknown.
5. Total cholesterol counts are much lower than the average found in the United Sates.
6. The elderly are revered by the young in these cultures, and there is a general expectation of living to 100 or more years.
7. Studies on subjects in the Caucasus Mountains showed some evidence of heart or blood vessel disease, but the subjects' collateral circulation was so good that minor heart attacks actually went unnoticed and did them little harm.

A Study on Aging

Following is a summary of conclusions of a three-day conference on exercise and aging held at the National Institutes of Health in Bethesda, Maryland, a few years ago. The conclusions reached include the following:

1. Walking is the most efficient form of exercise and the only one that a person can safely follow for a lifetime.
2. As people get older, their bones begin to demineralize and weaken. Exercise such as walking slows the demineralization process particularly in the legs, and stimulates bone-growing cells—bones can remain tougher and harder to break. Walking also affords greater range of motion.
3. As people get older, particularly those who smoked or worked in high-pollution areas, they develop emphysema-like symptoms. Individuals who exercise may still exhibit such changes, but they maintain greater lung capacity than sedentary people.

4. As people age, their cardiovascular function loses its elasticity and vigorousness. However, the cardiovascular systems of older Americans who exercise preserve much of their function.
5. As people get into their forties, fifties and sixties, their weight and percentage of body fat normally escalate, greatly affecting health. However, aerobic exercise is a strong deterrent to obesity.
6. Closely related to obesity is the fact that as people get older they tend to eat less in an effort to control their weight. Nutrition often suffers when this happens. Daily exercise permits greater food intake and better blood circulation, which improves each cell's nourishment while preventing obesity.
7. Many overweight older Americans fear adult-onset diabetes. This disease can be controlled, although it can still have serious effects. Late-onset diabetes related to obesity is almost entirely reversible by exercise.
8. Rheumatoid arthritis and osteoarthritis are common in older people. It has been estimated that more than 90 percent of Americans over 60 have some form of osteoarthritis. The studies from this conference showed that people with arthritis can benefit the most from exercise, provided the level of exercise is increased gradually.
9. Many Americans fear aging, afraid that they will be "turned out to pasture" and become unwanted. This increases stress, depression and fear. However, walking improves the quality of life. Research comparing exercise to a widely prescribed tranquilizer, Valium, found exercise to relax people more and elevate their moods more effectively—with none of the drug's detrimental side effects.

Other Aging Considerations

The principal law of aging is that any function, skill or tissue that is not used continuously throughout life will gradually be lost. Disuse is the greatest cause of the deterioration of physical and mental powers as we age. As Dr. Fred Schwartz, Director of the AMA Committee on Aging, said, "Many so-called infirmities of old age stem directly from lack of conditioning. Great numbers of people after leaving high school or college settle into a sedentary life. In these circumstances it is easy to understand why the physical horizons have become cramped and why hands shake and why the gait becomes uncertain and tottery."

Aging Americans often experience an increase in body fat, loss of muscle and bone mass, decline in physical and mental vigor, increase in triglycerides and cholesterol, increase in high blood pressure and increased instance of cardiovascular disease and cancer. Other common effects of aging include fatigue, reduced joint flexibility, changes in bowel and bladder habits, decline in sex drive, failing sight and hearing, decrease in mental agility and general lack of endurance and stamina. These unpleasant changes are so common in America's older population group that they have become "normal" conditions for older people. Most of these conditions, however, can be reduced or eliminated through a well-designed walking exercise program.

Unfortunately, all parts of the human body do not age at the same rate. We become victims of our weakest links, so we should identify our weaknesses and address them in a positive manner. A heart weak from lack of exercise may kill you even if everything else is in good shape. Lack of oxygen to the brain caused by inactivity and hardened arteries can produce senility in an otherwise well-functioning body.

When Are We Old?

Old age is not defined by the number of birthdays observed, but in how a person acts and thinks. Old age starts in the forties or earlier for those who are not young at heart or who have neglected their health. The process of aging varies so much from person to person that it is impossible to generalize the point at which old age occurs. Someone who has been active throughout life can be younger physiologically and psychologically at 70 than a person of 40 with unhealthy habits. At age 70, Clive Davies of Oregon could still run a marathon (26.2 miles) in about three hours. Ed Benham of Maryland at age 80 ran one in about three and three-quarters hours and Dr. Paul Spangler of California ran marathons at over age 90. The most amazing person may be Larry Lewis of San Francisco. In 1971, at age 104, he was still running 6 miles each morning in Golden Gate Park before walking 5 miles to work as a waiter. Dr Ernest Jokl, authority on aging from the University of Kentucky, has stated that: "There is little doubt that proper physical activity as a part of a way of life can significantly delay the aging process."

We are old when we think we are. If we get out and walk and participate in some of the vigorous activities that young people do, we will tend to think young as well. At 72 years of age I have found that when I participate in walking events, either as participant or judge, I maintain a youthful mentality. I am interacting with younger generations, which gives me a positive and optimistic attitude that I would not otherwise have.

Plan for Retirement

How about investing in life so you can enjoy your golden years? Consider it a sort of lifestyle IRA. Invest a little time for a consistent walking program and reap the benefits later. The active elderly should fear being relegated to a nursing home.

People commonly plan for their retirement years with the idea that financial resources can ensure health and happiness. More often than not, though, they neglect their physical resources, then cannot enjoy a vigorous retirement anyway. The stories of people who die soon after retirement are legend. These people may have traded their health for wealth, which in the end is of no value to them but to their heirs instead. However, it is never too late for most people if a sensible walking program is undertaken. The Metropolitan Life Insurance Company states that: "Exercise does not have to be either laborious or time consuming. One of the simplest ways is to walk when you do not absolutely have to ride. Walking is a good way to keep yourself in fine shape."

Renowned cardiologist Dr. Paul Dudley White said that most physicians do not realize how tough and resilient the human body is. It can bounce back from even massive heart attacks through the judicious use of a progressive walking program. People facing retirement have two choices—lie around waiting for the Grim Reaper or get up, get moving and get into shape.

Today, many well-conditioned oldsters seem to have more stamina than the average teenager. Television sets, fast foods and fast wheels have robbed young people of their vitality. These habits, continued throughout life, will inevitably result in large numbers of people entering their retirement years in horrible shape unless preventative measures are taken to maintain a healthy lifestyle.

Reducing the Hazards of Aging

Good health is not a commodity that you can buy at a store, health club or from a high-priced doctor. Being in excellent condition is a do-it-yourself activity and cannot be attained through the use of pills or elixirs. Much of the deterioration blamed on old age is actually the result of diseases—many of them self-inflicted. An example is arteriosclerosis, once thought to be a normal part of the aging process. It is now clear that arteriosclerosis is a disease that afflicts both young and old and is brought on primarily by an unhealthy lifestyle. Scientists and medical researchers have found that many diseases come with old age—but not because of age.

Modern allopathic medicine has not yet developed a drug that slows the aging process appreciably. There is, however, a nearly magic formula that many researchers say is the closest thing to an antiaging pill—movement of the human body as it was designed to move, using all its muscles. Persistent, regular aerobic exercise such as brisk walking can be the key to a vigorous lifestyle as the body grows old chronologically, slowing physiological aging to a remarkable degree.

Take a look at the miseries commonly associated with old age discussed earlier in this chapter. Then make a list of the maladies caused by a sedentary lifestyle. The parallel nature of the two lists is striking. Most of the things thought to be the normal effects of aging are actually the effects of disuse of the body. A great number of scientific studies show aerobic exercise to be a super antidote to all these ailments. When active people in their seventies and even older are studied, they have the same cardiovascular capacity as sedentary people in their thirties.

We can control our own destinies to a large degree. We can make up our minds that in the years to come we are going to be self-sufficient and not a burden to others as so many sedentary people seem to be. If at the age of 70 you exercise regularly, you will be in better overall condition than 95 percent of the people your age. Here are some ways to prepare for a healthy, vigorous retirement:

1. Walk aerobically at least four times a week so that it will become an ingrained habit that will be sorely missed if you don't do it.

2. Take full responsibility for your own health. Doctors are available for crisis situations, but don't look to them to give you pills to correct your indiscretions.
3. Eat natural foods as much as possible. Much modern food processing lessens the nutritional value of foods and destroys the natural enzymes our bodies require.
4. Make sure you get enough sleep.
5. Develop creative, fun hobbies to carry on after you retire. Continue to expand your knowledge and interests throughout life. Make life a constant learning process.
6. Develop the optimistic attitude that your "golden years" will be just that. Remember, you can walk away from old age and maintain a body far younger than your chronological age.
7. Cultivate your sense of humor and don't worry unnecessarily about things you can do nothing about.
8. Think of each day as an opportunity to contribute something and make the world a better place. A sense of self-worth is important in avoiding depression.
9. Set realistic goals, then get into the habit of attaining them. Life should be filled with constant growth and achievement.
10. Develop a sense of independence so that the loss of a loved one will not destroy your life. Always think about living your life to the best of your own unique ability.
11. Obtain a quality treadmill so you can walk when the weather is bad.
12. Above all, don't become a spectator of life, watching what could be some of your best years pass by without participating in them.

4 Nutrition and Health

"I've been on a diet for two weeks, and all I've lost is two weeks."
—Totie Fields

It has been said many times that you are what you eat. If you eat sensible amounts of healthy, energy-efficient foods, you can affect a higher level of body tone and general health. The principles of excellent nutrition apply to everyone, regardless of the condition of their bodies.

The bookshelves of America are literally jammed with advice on how to eat or not eat your way to health with many different theories about what constitutes a healthy diet. Some provide sound advice, but many plans are patently ridiculous—such as "eat lots of grapefruit and melt away fat." Diets that severely restrict calories can be dangerous, and any that promise weight loss of more than two pounds per week should be regarded with skepticism—they usually never work. Starvation diets cause your body to think it is experiencing famine, so that it must conserve calories to stay alive. Your metabolism slows so that fewer calories are needed to maintain your current weight. Soon, your body's metabolism will slow so much that you will not lose much weight even on very few calories.

Food, water and oxygen are the fuels we need to survive. As Hippocrates, the ancient Greek father of medicine, said: "Thy food shall be thy remedy." It is important that we know how to eat healthy if we are to optimize our lives.

What Should We Eat?

Some health professionals say that we are all too often digging our graves with spoons, knives and forks. There is still confusion about what foods are truly good for us. What kind of a diet should we have to optimize everyday performance and health? But most professionals agree that the best diets include breads and cereals; vegetables and fruits; dairy products such as low fat milk, yogurt and cheese; and lean meat, poultry, fish and beans. Vegetarian diets can be very healthful if planned correctly, but you should get the advice of a registered dietitian (R.D.) or research healthy vegetarian eating thoroughly before you start.

Through creative and knowledgeable planning, balanced diets can be both tasty and nutritious. Here are some general dietary suggestions to keep in mind:

1. Decrease sugar consumption. The typical American eats about 150 pounds of sweeteners per year. Exercisers find it easy to become "sugar junkies," but an excess raises fat and cholesterol levels. Go easy on empty calories, that is, simple sugars that have little or no nutritive value. This includes candies, soft drinks, desserts and other sweet-tooth treats.

2. Think of your body as an engine fueled by food and oxygen. High-octane fuels, such as complex carbohydrates and other unprocessed foods (e.g., fresh fruits, vegetables, etc.), will provide a higher level of performance and improve energy. These unprocessed foods have more of their original minerals, fiber and other nutrients.

3. Reduce your fat intake. The average American diets have traditionally been overloaded with fats, constituting about 45 percent of the total calories consumed. This is well above the 30 percent recommended for good health. There are three kinds of fat in foods, but only one—saturated fat—is highly detrimental. Saturated fats are solid at room temperature. Monounsaturated and polyunsaturated fats, which remain liquid at room temperature, are not considered dangerous. But even these should not be eaten in large amounts. For health's sake everyone should limit daily intake of fat to between 10 and 30 percent of their total calories. If your daily intake is 1,500 calories, this means around 45 grams of fat. The typical American diet contains more than 100 grams of mostly saturated fat per day. A healthy diet should not include more than 10 percent saturated fat, with another 10 percent worth of polyunsaturated fats and 10 percent monounsaturated fats. To determine fat percentage in packaged foods by using the new USDA food labels, which tell how many grams of fat the food has per serving, multiply grams of fat by 9 to figure fat calories. The labels also provide the percentage of total calories from fat.

4. Do not overdo protein intake. The typical American diet has too much protein as well as fat. Excess protein is not easily metabolized and thus can add to your fat stores. A normal person's need for protein will not exceed 56 to 60 grams per day—or about 10 percent of total calories. There are about 7 grams of protein in one ounce of meat, fish or poultry, but protein can also be supplied from certain vegetables, grains and dairy products.

5. When shopping for groceries, do what can be called "perimeter shopping." Concentrate on the outside walls where most unprocessed foods such as fresh fruits and vegetables are normally placed. You will then be purchasing natural nutrients, vitamins, minerals and dietary fiber in abundance. The middle sections of markets are filled with highly processed foods stripped of much of their original nutritional value. Look at the sugar and chemical content of foods on the required ingredient labels. You may be amazed at the composition of some manufactured foods.

6. Dietary fiber is an important component of a healthy diet. Fiber keeps the body regular and cleans the digestive system, keeping the body functioning properly. Fresh fruits and vegetables and whole grain products are good sources of dietary fiber. Oat bran has been touted as an antidote for

elevated cholesterol levels. Psyllium husk, recommended as a fibrous colon cleanser, is also effective in reducing cholesterol.

7. Calcium is important to keep bones strong. Milk and dairy products are good sources. If you are lactose-intolerant, try a cultured dairy product such as yogurt. Remember that most cheeses have a lot of fat, so choose low-fat varieties.

8. Control caffeine intake. A cup or two of coffee or regular tea a day is probably okay, but more may be counterproductive and make you nervous. Experiments on endurance athletes have shown that caffeine facilitates fat burning and is a stimulant. But it is also a diuretic and can cause dehydration. It can also be addictive, leading to headaches and fatigue during withdrawal.

9. Limit extra salt in your diet. Many foods have a natural amount of sodium in them and many processed foods are loaded with salt. Excess salt can cause fluid retention, a condition called edema, which results in swelling that causes the blood oxygen exchange to be reduced between cells and capillaries.

10. Make sure you get enough iron. Iron helps restore red cells, but can cause problems if overconsumed. If you supplement your diet with vitamins, remember that vitamins are essentially the same, whether they are natural or manufactured.

11. Maintain a healthy level of fluid intake. Many of us neglect adequate fluid intake. A person should normally consume about 2 $1/2$ quarts of fluids every day (or at least eight large glasses of water) and much more when exercising and sweating in hot weather. A mere 2 percent loss in body fluids causes a noticeable loss in the body's ability to cool itself. A 4 percent loss results in about 30 percent less muscle endurance. Heat exhaustion can occur at a 5 percent loss, and a 7 percent loss of body fluids can result in hallucinations and heat stroke. Fluids, especially water, aid in regularity and flush poisons out of the body. Many people have a delayed thirst response, and this can cause chronic dehydration. Athletes may be too slow in replacing sweat losses and should force themselves to drink well in excess of their thirst reaction. Muscles do not work properly when the body is dehydrated, and recovery time from exercise sessions is substantially increased. Develop the habit of having a glass of water, herbal tea or diluted fruit juice (soft drinks are not recommended) handy whenever you are sitting around for any length of time.

12. Eat lightly during the three to four hours before a competition or any prolonged exertion. Digestion draws blood needed for the muscles to the stomach. The food will be digested anyway, and so will not provide energy to the muscles.

The previous guidelines are general principles that should help you think of eating healthy. While it is okay to reward yourself with favorite foods, just use common sense. You'll know when you are cheating.

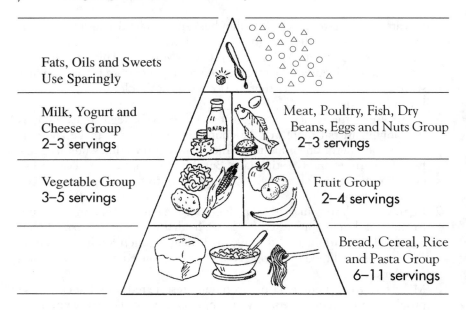

Fats, Oils and Sweets
Use Sparingly

Milk, Yogurt and
Cheese Group
2–3 servings

Meat, Poultry, Fish, Dry
Beans, Eggs and Nuts Group
2–3 servings

Vegetable Group
3–5 servings

Fruit Group
2–4 servings

Bread, Cereal, Rice
and Pasta Group
6–11 servings

The USDA Food Pyramid

I would like to dispel the rumor that the traditional basic four food groups are Wendy's, Burger King, McDonald's and Pizza Hut. The U.S. Drug Administration (USDA) has developed a more powerful guide to good nutrition—the Food Guide Pyramid—to replace the former basic four food groups model. After years of research, advances in the nutrition field and the concern of dietary excesses versus dietary deficiencies, many nutrition experts, the USDA and the Department of Health and Human Services realized the Basic Four was no longer suitable for the American population.

The Food Guide Pyramid incorporates "The Dietary Guidelines for Americans" with consideration of food portions necessary to meet nutrient needs; moderation to avoid excess fat, sugar, sodium and alcohol and selecting a variety of foods—all essential ingredients for a fit body. The five major food groups are: breads, cereals, rice, pasta; vegetables; fruit; milk, yogurt, cheese; and meat, poultry, fish, dry beans, eggs, nuts.

Emphasis is placed on whole grain breads and cereals, fresh fruits and vegetables, and low-fat milk and meat products. The division of fruits and vegetables into separate categories favors an increased intake of fiber and encourages cancer-fighting nutrients such as vitamins A, C and E. The other food category of less importance is the fats, oils and sweets group, which includes foods that are high in calories but provide few vitamins and minerals.

In the graphic of the pyramid, dots represent naturally occurring and added fats, and triangles represent added sugar. The top of the pyramid signifies foods that are particularly high in fat and sugar. Examples of these foods are salad dressings, butter, margarine, oils, all sugars (white, brown, honey, molasses, etc.), cream, soda pop, candy and many desserts.

Although many food groups contain products that are high in fat, there are still items in these categories that are low fat, nonfat and lean. Avoiding the foods represented by dots and triangles is one key to healthy eating.

Food Guide Suggestions at Three Calorie Levels:

	Older Adults	Active Women	Active Men
CALORIE LEVEL	1,600	2,200	2,800
bread servings	6	9	11
vegetable servings	3	4	5
fruit servings	2	3	4
milk servings	2–3*	2–3*	2–3*
meat (ounces/day)	5	6	7
Total Fat = # grams[1]	53	73	93
Added sugar (tsp.)[2]	6	12	18

*3 servings required if under 24 years old or pregnant or breast feeding.

[1]One teaspoon of pure fat (i.e., butter, oil) = 4 grams of fat.
[2]One teaspoon = 4 grams of sugar.
(Source: USDA. *The Food Guide Pyramid.* USDA Bulletin 252, August 1992.)

What Constitutes a Serving Size?

- Breads, cereals, rice, pasta: 1 slice of bread; 1 oz. ready-to-eat cereal; 1 cup cooked cereal, rice, pasta
- Vegetables: 1 cup raw leafy vegetables; $\frac{1}{2}$ cup other cooked or chopped raw vegetables; $\frac{3}{4}$ cup vegetable juice
- Fruits: 1 medium apple, banana, orange; 1 cup chopped, cooked or canned fruit; $\frac{3}{4}$ cup fruit juice
- Milk, yogurt, cheese: 1 cup milk or yogurt; $1\frac{1}{2}$ oz. natural cheese; 2 oz. processed cheese
- Meat, poultry, fish, dry beans, eggs, nuts: 2 to 3 oz. cooked lean meat, fish or poultry; $\frac{1}{2}$ cup cooked dried beans; 1 egg or 2 Tbsp. peanut butter count as 1 oz. of lean meat

To maintain a healthy, balanced diet, select foods from the bottom of the pyramid up, so the majority of foods you eat come from the bread, cereal, rice and pasta group. Continue up the pyramid, choosing from a wide range of vegetables and fruits for increasing fiber and important vitamins such as vitamins A, E, C, K and folic acid and minerals such as potassium. The best sources of protein, iron, zinc and calcium are found in the meat and dairy groups. Don't be swayed by the many "nonexperts" who claim that meat and milk products aren't good for you, but beware of overdoing them and minimize saturated fat.

Many athletes' nutrient needs are increased because of the wear and tear that exercise can place on the body. Choose low-fat or nonfat foods, and those with low saturated fat, sugar and sodium contents. Remember to use the power of the pyramid to nourish the body.

Eating for Better Performance and Health

Tina Braet-Thomas, a registered dietitian and racewalker in Cody, Wyoming, says, "If you are one of those who use exercise as a justification for eating whatever you wish, believing that it will be 'burned off' in the course of your workout—think again!" Reduction of food intake is the biggest key to success in maintaining or losing weight. You only need a slight calorie deficit each day to lose weight over the long term. You can burn a lot of calories by racewalking. In a study Dr. Robert Gutin and his associates at Columbia University concluded that racewalking can burn up even more calories than running. They found that at 5 miles per hour, running uses 480 calories/hour but walking uses 530. At 6 mph, running burns 660 calories/hour, walking 734. At 7 mph, running burns 690 calories/hour, walking 960. The higher calorie count undoubtedly comes from the more dynamic movements of more muscles required to move fast while maintaining contact with the ground.

Body Weight

Forget those insurance "ideal weight" charts. Percent of body fat is the true indicator of your ideal body weight. Muscle weighs more than fat, so if you have well-developed muscles, you could weigh more than someone who has few muscles but a lot of body fat. We all need some body fat—about 3 percent of total body weight is called "essential fat" and is found in cell membranes, bone marrow, nerve tissue and in and around the heart and other vital organs.

In addition to essential fat, men and women each need a certain amount of storage fat to allow for energy needs—about 10 to 15 percent of total body weight. If you have fat to lose, the best method is a combination of diet and exercise. If you can either burn 500 calories more a day or eat 500 fewer calories, you can lose a pound a week, as 3,500 calories equals a pound of fat. If you keep it up, that means 50 pounds in a year. However, trying to lose too much weight at once can be foolish and even dangerous. There are no shortcuts to effective weight loss short of amputation or liposuction. Do not attempt to lose more than 1 to 2 pounds per week through a combination of a prudent diet and lots of walking.

Lowering Cholesterol Naturally

Cholesterol is the main villain in artery disease. Everyone should be checked to see if their cholesterol level is too high. If your total cholesterol count is over 200, you should take some sort of action to lower it. Although cholesterol is necessary for the human body to function, this waxy substance collects in our arteries if there is an excess.

The ratio between total cholesterol and high density lipoprotein (HDL), or "good cholesterol," is a good indicator of whether you have potential problems. Even if your total cholesterol total count is below 200 and you have a low HDL count, the ratio can still be higher than 4.5, the accepted top healthy standard for this ratio.

There has been a great deal of hoopla and controversy about the benefits of oat bran for lowering cholesterol, but there are many other common foods that have beneficial effects as well. Dr. Earl Mindell, a nationally known authority on nutrition, believes that natural means should be tried before resorting to drug therapy to lower cholesterol. Here are some of the foods that Dr. Mindell's research has shown to lower cholesterol levels:

1. Eat more onions, garlic and raw carrots. If you don't like raw onions or garlic, you may cook them. Garlic is especially helpful in raising the HDL levels.
2. Eat more eggplant. Eggplant breaks down into components that bind excess cholesterol and promote its excretion.
3. Eat more beans (pinto, navy and kidney). An experiment at the University of Kentucky lowered cholesterol levels 20 percent in three weeks after subjects ate 4 ounces of beans daily.
4. Eat more soybeans. While they may not have much of a beneficial effect on lowering LDLs, "the clogging type" of cholesterol, they are an excellent source of protein for those who do not eat much meat.
5. Eat more water-soluble fiber. Oat bran and psyllium husk help speed the passage of food wastes through the small bowel, which means that less cholesterol is absorbed by the system. Psyllium may be the most water-soluble fiber readily available commercially. Barley also has been shown to be beneficial.
6. Eat more pectin. Pectin is found in many vegetables and fruits, especially apples. Pectin slows the digestion of fatty foods and has a gel-forming property that apparently converts cholesterol into a form not easily absorbed by the body.
7. Use polyunsaturated or monounsaturated fats instead of saturated fats when cooking. These fats are liquid at room temperature. Examples are canola, soy, corn, sunflower and olive oils. Avoid hydrogenated fats, too.
8. Eat more yogurt. The best is plain nonfat yogurt, which can be flavored with natural fruits, and flavored nonfat yogurt that is not heavily sugared.
9. Eat more seafoods rich in Omega 3 fatty acids. Salmon is one of the best sources of this type. Be aware that some seafoods, especially shellfish, are high in cholesterol.
10. Supplement vitamins and minerals beneficial in the cholesterol-lowering process; for example, lecithin, choline, insitol, chromium (found in yeast), vitamin C, vitamin E, niacin (in carefully prescribed doses). Of course, these vitamins and minerals are also found in natural foods.

On Keeping a Sugar Balance

Sugar is the great seductress in our diets. Glucose (blood sugar) is the most available source of energy to our bodies, but not many of us know how to maintain the best balance to avoid the "sugar blues." When we consume refined sugars, the body counteracts this infusion with an insulin reaction to protect it from too much sugar in the blood. This lowers our energy level, causing hunger for more sugar or other food. The name for this reaction is "rebound hypoglycemia," and there can be a yo-yo effect as one sugar fix after another causes the rapid rise of sugar in the blood stream only to be counteracted by the insulin response.

Refined sugar has practically no nutritive value. When exercising, we need vitamins and minerals, and sugar is devoid of these. For this reason, as we prepare to exercise we should concentrate on eating complex carbohydrates (e.g., pasta, fruits, vegetables, etc.), which are absorbed into the system much more slowly and do not activate the insulin response as rapidly.

5 | Overcoming Problems

"Treat the reason, not the result. Treat the cause, not the effect."
—George Sheehan, M.D.

Walking is a safe and practically injury-free form of exercise. That is not to say, however, that soreness and pain will never occur, especially if you have not put in very much distance. Some reasons for discomfort are doing too much too soon, bad shoes, bad feet, bad technique, walking soon after eating or walking on uneven surfaces.

Practically all of the body's muscles will become conditioned as you walk briskly along, but stretching and flexibility exercises often will prevent or reduce muscle strain and soreness. Nearly everyone will experience some muscle soreness and pain at first, no matter what shape they are in. Soreness may begin immediately or not show up for 24 to 48 hours.

Types of Problems

Let's discuss some of the problems that might occur when you first embrace a walking program.

Chest Pain
The most worrisome pains occur in the chest. Most chest pains are not serious, but they should never be ignored, especially if they persist. The cause of pain may be heartburn, which very closely mimics heart pains and is often relieved by an antacid. If the pain feels like pressure on the chest and subsides abruptly after cessation of exercise, seek medical advice. It could be angina, caused by an insufficient supply of blood to the heart muscle. If the pain is not specific, it will probably test out to be negative by your physician.

Sciatica
Sciatica, or injury to the sciatic nerve, can cause pain anywhere from the upper buttocks to the bottom of the foot. The main causes of sciatica are structural weakness due to bony or ligamentous malalignments in the spine, and postural weakness caused by the overdevelopment of the lower back muscles and the relative weakness of the opposing stomach muscles. Walking

has actually been used as a cure for sciatica, especially racewalking, which tends to strengthen the muscles of the back and abdomen. Treatment should be aimed at flattening the spine and rotating the hips backward and forward. Bent leg sit-ups are very good for sciatica. Other suggestions are to go without shoes at home to stretch the hamstrings. Chiropractic or osteopathic adjustments can provide temporary relief in many cases.

Hip Pain

Hip pain is fairly common early in a fitness walking program, because previously little-used muscles are being brought into play. These pains will soon disappear as the walker gets into better shape, but don't overdo it. Hip pain can come from a variety of sources—weak or high-arched feet, leg length discrepancy, tight hamstrings and weak abdominals, overstriding and going up and down too many hills. Hip stretching exercises and bent leg sit-ups are often helpful in alleviating and preventing hip pains. Get sufficient rest after long walks.

Side Stitch

Beginning walkers will often get pains or cramps in the upper abdomen, commonly on the right side. These are often caused by a pressure on the diaphragm from the lungs and the stomach muscles, which restricts the blood supply to the diaphragm. Gas can also cause cramping. It is prudent not to eat particular foods known to produce gas before exercising. Stitches are far less common in experienced aerobic exercisers who are in good condition.

If a stitch occurs, breathe deeply using your stomach muscles and slow your pace. Often pressing on the painful spot with your fingers will relieve the pain. Bend forward and exhale hard while pursing your lips. Acupuncture books suggest rubbing the front center of your rib cage, pressing vigorously to get relief. Probably the best preventive measure is to do exercises designed to strengthen the diaphragm and belly muscles such as bent leg sit-ups.

Cramps and Spasms

Cramps and spasms are common for beginning exercisers. The circumstances under which cramps occur may be the best indication of their cure. If you experience leg cramps while walking, you are probably dehydrated. Should you experience leg cramps frequently at night, see your physician or other knowledgeable health professional to rule out mineral abnormalities or other problems. If these tests are negative, a stretching regimen prior to going to bed may help. Stand facing the wall with your feet about 4 feet from the baseboard. Put the palms of your hands against the wall at shoulder height. Keeping your back straight, bend the elbows and lean your upper body toward the wall. Keep your heels on the floor as you do this, stretching the calf muscles. Repeat this 10 to 20 times.

Although some people believe that vitamin E may be a remedy for leg cramps, this claim seems to be unsubstantiated in any scientific experiments. Acupressurists suggest that firmly grasping your upper lip between your thumb and forefinger can give temporary relief.

The occurrence of cramps can be reduced by eating a well-balanced diet with adequate salt and potassium, drinking plenty of fluids, warming up before strenuous exercise and stopping before becoming too fatigued. Usually cramps can be relieved by stretching or massaging the affected muscle. Apply heat afterward to aid in circulation.

Sprains and Strains

Sprains and strains are caused by the overstretching or tearing of muscles, ligaments or tendons. Small blood vessels are broken, causing pain when the surrounding area swells up and affects the adjacent nerve endings.

Sprains and strains are not as common among walkers as runners. The biggest danger in this type of injury is the possibility of misdiagnosis of a simple fracture. It is therefore wise to get X-rays of all strains or sprains. Measures to prevent further injury and expedite healing include:

1. Remember the word RICE—Rest, Ice, Compression, Elevation.
2. Do not put weight on the injury.
3. Use cold packs to reduce swelling for the first 24 hours after injury. Avoid heat, which increases swelling.
4. Keep the injured part elevated as much as possible.
5. If you must walk, use an elastic bandage wrapping for support.
6. Let a health professional examine the injury.

Lower Back Pain

Millions of Americans suffer from lower back pain each year. More productive work hours are lost because of this injury than almost any other ailment. Sedentarianism and sitting in chairs all day long take their toll on us by causing all sorts of miseries associated with lack of tone in the muscles that support the back.

There are a large number of causes of back pain, but the most prevalent ones are precipitated by strain and herniated disks in the spine. Strain can be defined as injury caused by stresses on muscles and ligaments that surround the spine. Some doctors say that degenerative and traumatic changes in the disk of the vertebrae are a main culprit causing susceptibility to strains and resultant pain. It is believed that at least 70 percent of those suffering lower back pain get well if the back is rested properly, and that they are left with few or no symptoms.

The real problem, however, is lack of fitness and muscle tone. The back muscles are among the strongest in the entire body. The culprits are the opposing muscles at the front—the abdominals. Most people have notoriously weak abdominal muscles (e.g., men have pot bellies). Therein lies an imbalance and added strain on the back muscles.

Being in good physical condition is the best antidote to back injury and pain, and brisk walking is the safest and most logical way to achieve this conditioning. The jarring caused by jogging makes it a poor mode of exercise when the miseries of back pain strike. If you experience severe lower back pain, seek professional advice on how to alleviate it.

How do we tone those muscles to keep them strong enough to avoid muscle imbalances and painful back injuries? Dr. Will Evans, a noted back specialist in Englewood, Colorado, suggests that brisk walking is a good exercise for your back. Abdominal strength can also go a long way in preventing back problems.

The Vulnerable Knee

The knee is one of the most vulnerable parts of the body for a person involved in weight-bearing exercises. Problems are far more common in running than walking. The knee is vulnerable because of a poor bone arrangement, and the fact that tendons and ligaments provide the main support. The causes of knee pain are almost always the feet. Weak arches, poor foot structure, improper foot plant and walking on slanted surfaces are the most common causes of knee pain. If the foot collapses while walking, the lower leg rotates inward and the kneecap moves to the inside. Repeated steps cause the kneecap to move back and forth constantly. The knee may become irritated and swollen.

If you have knee pain, make a special effort to walk with the toes pointed in a straight line. If your footprints are visible, you should see a straight line with one foot straight in front of the other. If the pain persists, professional orthotics may be the best solution.

Shin Pain

Walkers often suffer from tenderness and pain in the shin and calf or on the front and back of the thigh. This type of soreness will usually last only a few days. If the pain occurs immediately, it is probably due to waste products such as lactic acid in the muscles. Delayed soreness usually means muscle tears or localized contractions of the muscles. Other causes include walking with your toes pointed out, causing muscle imbalance and inflamed tendons or irritated membranes. You can avoid much soreness if you build up the intensity of the exercise very gradually, do some appropriate stretching exercises and taper off at the end of your exercise.

True "shin splints" are seldom caused by walking. This is normally a running injury. Walking at faster than normal speeds often causes shin pain because the muscles are being used harder and with a wider range of motion than usual. In addition to conditioning the affected parts, wearing good footwear with a padded sole and walking on soft surfaces may help alleviate shin pains.

Building the intensity of exercising slowly and exercises to flex the foot up and down, either with weights for resistance or lifting the whole body up and down, are very helpful for this condition. Cold compresses can be of some benefit to reduce swelling and pain.

Achilles Tendonitis

Injuries to the Achilles tendon are extremely painful and debilitating. This tendon controls the hinging action of the ankle joint with every step and is a workhorse in the walking process. Once injured, it does not heal easily, and injuries often start with microscopic tears, causing inflammation, or tendonitis.

This is far more common in running than walking. Tendonitis is usually caused by unaccustomed changes in walking routines or footwear. Women can have a real problem if they wear high-heeled shoes, which results in the shortening of the tendon and destroying much of its flexibility.

The Achilles tendon must be kept stretched and flexible to avoid injury. Do not stretch it after it has been injured because overstretching caused the injury in the first place. To reduce pain use ice or cold water applications after mild exercise. Use pain as an indicator as to whether the Achilles tendon should be exercised or rested—if it hurts, stop. Walking barefoot helps you become resistant to Achilles tendon injury. Tendons can be strengthened by standing on the toes on a two-by-four or a thick book (a phone book works well) and stretching the heels down and up.

Heel Pain

Some walkers experience heel pain caused by bone bruises or bony growths called heel spurs. These are far more common from running because of the greater degree of pounding, but can also be caused by walking on concrete with unpadded shoes, stepping on sharp objects hard enough to cause a bruise or just wearing unsuitable footwear. Often a foam pad over the tender spot will relieve pressure and pain.

Blisters

The most common ailment experienced by walkers is blisters. The best prevention for blisters is good-fitting, dry footwear. Always wear comfortable, high-quality shoes with no pressure points. Maintain the shoes so that they don't become brittle, and break them in before walking long distances. Wear shoes and socks that breathe and move with your feet by holding them snugly—folds in socks are among the worst offenders.

Sometimes people get blisters even under the best conditions. First aid for blisters can be summed up in three words—KEEP THEM CLEAN! The main danger is infection. Use a sterilized needle to release the fluid, but do not remove the skin. Soap and water are the best medicine and clean socks are the best dressing. If there is any sign of infection—pus or extreme redness and heat—let your physician take care of it.

The Agony of Defeet

If your toes hurt or are cramped, the most likely cause is poor-fitting shoes. It is very important to select a walking shoe that matches the shape of the foot as closely as possible for maximum comfort. Keep the toenails trimmed to avoid ingrown toenails. The metatarsals, the bones immediately behind the toes, are subject to small stress fractures, but this occurs more frequently in runners than walkers since it involves more pounding of the feet on the ground. Although painful, they will heal themselves in a month or two unless aggravated. The only cure for these fractures is to cut back on the duration and intensity of walking and walk only on soft surfaces such as grass.

Sore and Tired Feet

If you have just finished a long walk and your feet are tired and sore, get a golf ball and massage your foot with the ball as an aid. The little ridges on the golf ball help stimulate the nerve endings in the foot, break up microspasms in the muscles and warm and stretch the plantar fascia, a fan-shaped band of connective tissue that extends from the heel to the ball of the foot. This tissue can become inflamed and develop plantar fascitis, a painful condition that can seriously limit your fitness walking or racewalking activity. Stretching and self-massage of the feet feels good, promotes muscle tone and flexibility and counteracts much of the fatigue and soreness caused by a long walk.

Bob McAtee, who runs ProActive Massage Therapy in Colorado Springs, recommends the following exercises for relieving sore feet:

1. Sit comfortably in a chair or on the floor. Grab your foot with both hands, placing your thumbs on the sole of the foot. Begin by squeezing, stretching and twisting your foot.
2. Use your thumbs, knuckles or fist to methodically massage the entire bottom of the foot, including the heel. Use circular strokes, go back and forth or use long strokes along the length of the foot. Do whatever feels good. If you find sore spots, spend extra time working on them. This may "hurt good" but should not cause real pain. If your hands tire, break out the golf ball and use it as a massage tool. Use the palm of your hand to roll the ball around on the bottom of the foot with a fair amount of pressure.
3. Sit in a chair, place the golf ball on the floor and put the sole of your foot on it. Use your body weight to apply moderate pressure, then roll your foot around on the ball. If you apply this technique on a regular basis, you can eventually stand up and place most of your weight on the golf ball.

Once you've squeezed, twisted, kneaded and "golf-balled" your feet, spend a few minutes stretching your feet and legs. You'll be amazed how good you feel. Adding this simple massage and stretching routine to your training schedule will help keep your feet healthy and happy and increase your walking pleasure immeasurably.

Foot Pronation and Related Problems

Pronation is a common word these days in both running and walking. As one leg swings forward during each stride, it rotates inward until it contacts the ground. Once the foot is solidly flattened after heel strike, the kneecap faces inward and the arch is lowered, preventing side-to-side motion. This activity is what we call pronation, and it is necessary for the foot to adapt to varying types of surfaces. After contact, the rotation reverses and external rotation occurs. The foot must then become a rigid lever so that a powerful push-off can be attained. The kneecap points to the outside, the foot becomes rigid as the arch raises and then the whole process begins again.

If the walker is lucky enough to have a neutral foot structure—that is, if everything is in perfect alignment and balance—then the stride can be very efficient. If not, imbalances and strain in the foot, leg and hip can occur.

Walkers must be wary of running shoes, which have a lot of spongy padding in the heel and sole because the foot may roll excessively, causing excessive rotation and lack of power. Firm contact with the ground is important when pushing for a powerful stride. If a walker has a marked imbalance and excessive pronation takes place, injuries can result.

It may help to describe some basic foot types so you can determine which most closely approximates your own.

Neutral Foot

A "neutral foot" is the ideal foot type with the heel perpendicular to the ground, a normal arch and all the metatarsal heads resting on the ground at once—which means intrinsic stability when both feet are on the ground. This stability means that the joints are in a neutral position and that muscles do not need to support the arch or body weight.

Forefoot Varus

A forefoot varus means that the inner metatarsals do not contact the ground when the rest of the foot is in a neutral position, so the inner foot rotates to the floor, causing strain in the arch and the leg.

Forefoot Vulgus

Forefoot vulgus means that the outside metatarsal heads do not touch the ground when the heel is in a neutral position. The foot tries to compensate by supinating toward a neutral position. In this case, the arch becomes high and more rigid and the leg rotates externally. This action can strain or tear the plantar fascia, the connective band of tissue beneath the skin of the arch. Calluses can form beneath rigid metatarsal heads, and the big toe may have limited flexibility. This type of foot does not absorb strain well because of all this rigidity, so ankle sprains are more common, and the legs, knee and hip may be more prone to injury.

Abnormal foot conditions should be corrected, but a knowledgeable professional should decide which corrections are needed. If the foot is in imbalance and a neutral position cannot be attained naturally, orthotics can allow the foot to reach this normal position and effect essential changes in the foot motion.

Morton's Foot

Morton's foot is when the second toe is longer than the big toe. This upsets the normal balance and too much weight falls on the inside arch, straining the leg. This somewhat common condition should be treated by a podiatrist, who may design a suitable orthotic.

Other Potential Problems

Frostbite

Unless you live in an area of extreme cold, frostbite is unlikely. However, if you walk on very cold days, dress adequately. Several layers of thin materials work better than a heavy one. Frostbite usually affects exposed skin, append-ages and extremities and is a greater risk if you get wet. Accordingly, make sure your fingers, ears and nose are covered with dry protection. Try to keep your shoes and socks as dry as possible. You may need to cut your walk short if your clothing becomes wet during freezing weather. Recognizing frostbite is important because it occurs in small degrees. It may manifest with a feeling of extreme coldness leading to numbness or tingling of the affected part. A blu-ish or ashen color may develop in the skin.

Heat Exhaustion and Heatstroke

Perhaps the most dangerous weather for the walker is the beautiful, hot day with just enough breeze to keep you from realizing just how hot the sun is. It is this kind of day that can bring on heat exhaustion or potentially fatal heat-stroke. Days of 90° F are potentially more dangerous than cold winter days, so caution must be exercised. Walk in shaded areas if possible. Drink a lot of liquids; dehydration is the worst enemy. Carry water with you and drink more often than you think you need to. The feeling of thirst often has a delayed reaction. Wear cool, loose-fitting clothing that will let air circulate around your body. In extreme conditions (either hot or cold) it is best not to exercise alone.

Symptoms of heat exhaustion or heatstroke include weakness, lightheadedness, clammy or very hot skin, nausea, headache, extreme thirst and faintness to unconsciousness. Symptoms such as these may occur in any combination or to any degree. If you suspect either heat exhaustion or heat-stroke, begin first aid as follows:

1. Get the victim out of the sun into a cool place as quickly as possible.
2. Lay the victim face up with the head elevated slightly.
3. Cool the victim with cool damp cloths as quickly as possible.
4. Have the victim sip cool liquids. Do not let the victim drink great quan-tities of liquid in too short a time, as this may cause vomiting or choking.
5. Take the victim to the nearest medical facility as quickly as possible and continue cooling him or her during transportation.

Insect Bites

Prevention is the best remedy against insect bites. Repellents are usually quite effective, so make sure to spray some onto exposed skin areas if necessary. If you do get bitten, clean the bite with soap and water. Most bites are not dan-gerous unless you are allergic to them, in which case you need to seek medical help. Some bites can get infected if you scratch them too much. Over-the-counter medications can counter the itching effect.

Dog Bites

If this happens and the skin is broken, stop the bleeding with direct pressure to the injured area and get the victim to a medical facility so that the wound can be properly cleaned. Even an insignificant-looking animal bite can cause severe infection (and rarely rabies), so always err on the side of caution and get medical attention as soon as possible.

Scratches

If you get into scratchy plants or brush or slip and fall, scratches may result. Soap and water are the best remedies. If any signs of infection follow (pus or redness and heat), get medical attention.

Oxygen-Free Radicals

There is increasing scientific evidence that oxygen-free radicals, particularly reactive molecules and atoms, are damaging to human health. These scavengers rob the body of oxygen at the cellular level, creating a chemical reaction known as oxidation at the wrong place and time. These reactions damage healthy tissue repair and impair immune function.

Although the human body provides antioxidant enzymes, an excess of free radicals can lead to excessive oxidation. Therefore, active exercisers should supplement their antioxidant levels with vitamins C and E, beta carotene and proanthocyanadin, a derivative of grape seeds or pine barks.

Should We Exercise When under the Weather?

If you are suffering from tension, worry or fatigue, walking can make you feel better. Exercise can have a calming and beneficial effect. Beware, however, of overexercising if suffering physical illness or injury. The whole basis of getting stronger and healthier through exercise is to do it in such a way that the muscles and tissues tired by exercise have time to recover before the exercise is again undertaken. In this case, muscle tone and strength will gradually increase. Tissue protein must be replaced to effect the rebuilding and strengthening process.

If you're sick, the tissue-repairing ability of the body is decreased. If you have a sore throat, you must decide whether or not it is from yelling at a sporting event, too much time in a smoke-filled room or actually a symptom of flu. The first two will not preclude your normal exercise, but the third definitely should. The flu will retard tissue regeneration. Emotional stress can also reduce recuperative processes.

Think before You Walk

Remember that prevention is better than first aid. A little forethought, planning and common sense will take care of practically all walking injuries. Be careful about where and how you walk and watch your step. Practically all of the conditioning that is needed will come automatically from just getting out and walking. As for the unlikely injuries and various pains discussed in this chapter, I have some overall suggestions:

1. Take good care of your feet and use high-quality, well-fitted socks and shoes.
2. Do plenty of flexibility stretching exercises for the whole body.
3. Concentrate on strengthening the muscles, ligaments, tendons and joints of the feet, legs and trunk.
4. Be consistent with your exercise walking and avoid doing it in spurts of frenzied activity.
5. Most of all, build up the intensity and duration of your walking program gradually to keep it pain-free and enjoyable.

6 Memory and Emotional Health

"Recollection is the only paradise from which we cannot be turned out."
—Jean Paul Richter

Have you ever laid down a set of keys one minute and then forgotten where they are the next? Research has demonstrated that you can minimize memory loss by supplying the brain with plenty of oxygen through physical exercise—that means brisk walking.

No organ is more sensitive to oxygen deprivation than the brain—even a few minutes without oxygen can irreversibly damage brain function. Initial studies seem to indicate that even if sedentarianism doesn't block the memory process, it can nevertheless slow the response time, so that it takes longer to remember things.

There is another way in which aerobic exercise can be an aid to memory. Sedentary people are far more susceptible to fatigue than active people. If you are very tired, you probably won't listen as carefully as when you are alert and will tend to remember less. Being in shape will promote more alertness in cases where a fitness factor lessens fatigue.

The Mental Side of Health

It is now well known that the physical aids the mental. In 1553 Spanish writer Cristobal Mendez said in his book on exercise that, "The easiest way to preserve health and with greater profit than with all other measures put together is to exercise well."

The New York Times wrote, "As long ago as 1911, Santiago Ramon y Cajal, a pioneering neurobiologist, proposed that cerebral exercise could benefit the brain." These concepts are in concert with the holistic attitude, called *arete*, of the ancient Greeks, who went to great lengths to develop the mind and body simultaneously through exercise.

Great thinkers throughout history have used long walks as a thinking aid. Thoreau once said, "The moment my legs begin to move, my thoughts begin to flow." With all these centuries of experience behind us in which walking has been used so successfully to aid thinking and memory, we would be very foolish indeed if we did not take advantage of this very convenient and inexpensive panacea.

Your Emotional Health

Exercise experts are now realizing what an impact regular exercise programs have on a person's emotional health. One of the most important things that happens as a result of exercise is increased blood flow. Muscles attuned to exercise become more efficient and the heart muscle pumps more oxygenated blood throughout the body. Normally 20 percent of the blood supply is directed to the brain—the organ of personal behavior and emotions—but during moderate to intense exercise, this flow is increased in proportion to the intensity. The more the brain is oxygenated, the higher the quality of life and well-being. There is a dramatic effect on how you feel and think. The rest of the body becomes superoxygenated as well.

Scientific studies and empirical evidence show that stress decreases as the body and mind meld during exercise. According to a study done by Dr. John Greist, a Wisconsin psychiatrist writing in *Physician and Sports Medicine,* exercise proved to lower depression more effectively than psychotherapy in a large majority of cases. Another psychiatrist, Dr. Robert Brown of the University of Virginia, found similar results as he tested 101 depressed college students over a ten-week period. However, Dr. Brown doesn't think exercise cures depression as much as lack of exercise causes it. Dr. Austin Gontang, director of the San Diego Marathon Clinic, says that bad posture can also lead to depression. He says, "When people are depressed they assume a depressed posture—a slouching, tense, contracted pose. But this pose can also be the cue that causes depression. A person with chronically poor posture gets tired, starts having negative thoughts and *then* gets depressed." Interestingly, one of the main factors in teaching people to walk correctly and efficiently is to correct their postural defects.

Dr. Thaddeus Kostrubala, another noted psychiatrist, says that depression can also be engendered by a lack of the hormone norepinephrine. As he says, "A current theory of depression says that it's caused by a deficiency of norepinephrine in the synapses of the brain. The spaces between the nerve cells across which messages are relayed. Norepinephrine increases during a run, and there's a surge right afterward. So just as doctors treat diseased organs with drugs, you could think of running as a self-induced pharmacological treatment of the brain, which is the organ of behavior." Of course, fast walking will bestow the same benefits because the effort is similar.

The Body's Own Chemicals

During moderate to intense exercise, a marvelous transformation takes place in the brain. The pituitary gland releases natural morphinelike substances called endorphins, which act as natural pain killers. Endorphins are actually far more potent than morphine and can cause a feeling of euphoria, a natural "high" and a feeling of relaxed power. Sometimes participants in the longer endurance events report an altered state of consciousness as these chemicals act on the brain.

Addressing Stress and Sex

It is thought that undue stress accelerates aging. Dr. Hans Selye, the world's most prominent authority on human stress, has stated that every stress leaves an indelible scar, and that the organism pays for its survival after a stressful situation by becoming a little older. However, brisk walking is proven to reduce stress. Dr Herbert deVries, a former gerontologist at the University of Southern California, demonstrated that a brisk 30-minute walk has roughly the same tranquilizing effect as the commonly prescribed dose of Xanax, Valium or Prozac.

The stresses of life are well known for causing depression and other disturbing symptoms such as lowered testosterone levels, which affects sex drive in both men and women. It is well documented that exercise is a superb stress reliever, but it can improve sex life in several other ways as well. It improves a person's self-esteem and physical attractiveness. It improves blood circulation, which not only improves potency but energy levels, self-confidence, outlook on life and practically every other bodily function. "Sexperts" say that a good self-image is a giant turn-on for the opposite sex, and that it may be the most important of all. Exercise, including brisk walking, of course, is truly the "Rx for sex."

Nine Ways Walking Can Benefit Emotional Health

Emotional health and physical health go hand in hand. Dr. Bob Conroy, a psychiatrist in Topeka, Kansas, says that "Exercise is emotional aerobics. Any aerobic routine that speeds up heart and breathing rates carried on a minimum of three times a week for 30 minutes per session pays big dividends." Some of those dividends include:

- feelings of exhilaration and well-being
- reduction in depression
- reduction in insomnia
- rejuvenation of energy levels
- improvements in self-image and confidence
- reduction in tension and anxiety
- reduction in hostile behavior
- increased ability to counteract life's daily stresses
- increased thinking and memory powers

After discovering all the benefits that a walking program can bestow upon you, I can't imagine why you would not want to rush out the front door and get started walking for health without delay.

PART 2

Walking for Fitness

7 The Importance of Fitness

"No one ever attains very eminent success by simply doing what is required of him; it is the amount and excellence of what is over and above the required that determines the greatness of ultimate distinction."
—Charles Kendall Adams

I have already addressed the basic differences between health and fitness. Now it is time to discuss why personal fitness is so important. Using exercise to improve fitness is not only a twentieth-century phenomenon. Historians have documented that the ancient Greeks advocated fitness as a key to a sound mind and body more than 2,500 years ago. In 1553 a Spanish gentleman named Dr. Cristobal Mendez published a book on exercise in which he said that "The conditions of exercise are three—it should be done of our own free will, the movement should be such as to have the breathing shorter and more frequent and we should have pleasure and enjoy." These principles still hold true today.

Technology vs. Fitness

In modern times, the technological revolution has had a profound impact on the importance of physical fitness. Most of our daily needs can now be obtained with little or no physical activity on our part, unlike a century ago when most people had to work hard physically to earn a living. Today, physical fitness must be consciously pursued. It is the responsibility of each of us to make exercise a consistent part of our daily routine. We all walk during the day to accomplish our necessary daily activities, but most of us will need to increase the intensity and duration of our walking to truly get the benefits that come from aerobic exercise.

Aerobic and Anaerobic Exercise

Aerobic fitness is the body's ability to take in, process and utilize oxygen to serve the body's vital needs. When your aerobic fitness is high, your physical health and mental health are enhanced. Aerobic fitness increases the total number of capillaries for a given cross section of muscle, thereby increasing blood circulation into the muscles. Many psychiatrists and psychologists prescribe aerobic exercise as a therapeutic tool to their patients. Aerobic exercise is a "steady state" of exercise that can be carried out for long periods of time without distress. Exercise physiologists have determined that a 20-minute session of constant rhythmic exercise three days a week is the minimum amount of time needed to attain a reasonable fitness goal. The body can recover from all but the most strenuous exercise bouts in about 48 hours.

Anaerobic exercises, which include most popular sports, are those with explosive bursts of speed and power that use fast-twitching muscle fibers. "Anaerobic" means without oxygen. Anaerobic exercise increases mucle strength, as opposed to aerobic exercise, which increases endurance. It is helpful to competitive walking and running athletes who use a technique called "interval training." These are repeated sessions with short recovery periods designed to teach the body to move as fast as possible for a short time.

A Big Boom

The great fitness boom, which started for a number of different reasons in the 1970s, promoted a variety of exercises for the improvement of physical health. Running was among the more prominent of these, with vast numbers taking up the sport. Walking, on the other hand, was generally considered by more active people to be something that only the aged, weak, obese or infirm needed to do. Walking was for the dog's daily outing or just to get a little fresh air. Now that faulty notion is being changed, and health authorities agree that brisk walking is a beneficial and healthy exercise regardless of age or weight. Of course, many people have used walking all their lives as their principal mode of exercise, but its true benefits were greatly underrated.

Conventional wisdom has been that if you aren't in shape enough to run, then walk until you can run. Practically every running book out there offers this sage advice. Even the President's Council on Physical Fitness and Sports in its published walking booklet recommends walking as a springboard to jogging, an interim activity to get in shape for the "real" exercise of jogging. However, walking is in itself an effective exercise method, providing all the cardiopulminary benefits of running with less risk of physical injury. As you walk faster, employing fitness walking, or its faster counterpart, racewalking, you will feel more of the body's musculature come into the action. In truth, you will be exercising practically every muscle in your body, from the neck right down to your toes.

Walking and a Feeling of Well-Being

Sometimes when we are somewhat nervous and edgy and don't feel like going for a walk, we suddenly remember how great we felt after a previous walk. So we take charge of our bodies and head out. Invariably we are glad we did afterward. The exercise improves mood, eases stress and tension and has an exhilarating effect.

Probably the most prominent researcher in the relationship of exercise to mental well-being was Dr. Herbert deVries, former gerontologist and physiologist from the University of Southern California. DeVries conducted five separate studies of the mental effects of exercise in women and men of all ages, and in each aerobic exercise improved the ability to relax both immediately and over a sustained period. DeVries found that a 15-minute walk was more effective in relieving nervous tension than a single dose of Valium. He also found that tension headaches were greatly reduced as a consequence of exercise. Dr. deVries wrote about the experiments in his book *Vigor Regained*.

Strive for Flexibility

You don't need to exercise strenuously to achieve desirable effects. The most important thing is to stay flexible. As we age our muscles shorten, causing pressure on the nerves within them. The best way to accomplish flexibility and mobility is to stretch after exercising, when muscles and tendons are warm and pliable. Stretching cold muscles and tendons before exercise is unwise as they are stiffer and more susceptible to injury.

Remember when stretching to avoid bouncing, called "ballistic stretching." Stretch things out gradually. Don't try to stretch muscles while they are bearing weight. There are literally hundreds of ways to stretch out, and you can devise your personal routine. A yoga class, for example, is a good way to learn how to stretch without injury.

All things considered, a good exercise walking program and continued maintenance of our flexibility and mobility is our best insurance against the miseries of old age—to keep us feeling relaxed and great at the same time. See appendix 2 for loosening and flexibility exercises.

Getting High on Exercise

During extended exercise, the body produces certain chemicals that can give a euphoric effect. These natural opiates produce the "highs" described by so many aerobic exercisers (mainly long-distance, endurance exercisers). It is sometimes described as a trancelike state accompanied by seemingly effortless movement and creative thoughts. It is sort of like shifting into "overdrive."

Researchers say that this effect, called the "second wind," does not normally occur until the exercise has been constant and rhythmic for at least 30 or 35 minutes. It may be that this natural high is why long-distance runners can become obsessive about their exercise and even run right through pain until injuries hurt so much that continued exercise becomes impossible. These people become so addicted to running that they keep on going when common sense tells them to rest their body and its muscular systems. Maybe the reason you rarely hear of such problems in walkers is that true, nagging injuries are very seldom incurred in the first place.

Personal Commitment to Exercise

Even the busiest people make time for exercise and fitness programs ranging from modest to rigorous. A good evidence of this in Colorado is two of the state's most dedicated local exercise and fitness buffs: former Governor Richard

Lamm and former Denver Mayor Federico Pena, who was appointed by President Clinton as secretary of transportation. President Clinton himself gets out to jog regularly. We are hard pressed to find people with more demanding schedules and time commitments than these "jocks," yet somehow, almost every day, they find or *make* the time to keep their bodies and souls together with rigorous aerobic training—even if it means getting up at 5 A.M.

Do Your Own Planning

For your own exercise regimen, plan ahead on your calendar and stick to it unless some emergency prevents you from doing otherwise. It is easy for unexpected things to interfere if this personal time is not blocked out. If you must cancel make an effort to find another time. It is easy to let things slide by and avoid exercising. When exercise must be cut back, make sure the reduction is a temporary aberration. The most important thing when starting out with a modest walking program is to build the intensity and duration gradually as you go along. Take a walking break during your lunch hour. Walk the stairs instead of using the elevator. Park a mile from your place of work and walk the remaining distance before and after work. One little step at a time can cumulatively result in giant steps in your fitness level later on. Those who can't take at least half an hour out of each day for their personal health should reassess their lifestyle priorities. Just making time for exercise not only is worth the effort but gives you an excellent return on your investment.

8 Designing a Personal Exercise Program

"Physical activity must be considered a lifetime pursuit. The benefits of a sound exercise program are rapidly lost once that program is discontinued."
—Jack Wilmore, Ph.D.
and David L. Costill, Ph.D.

Brisk walking is undoubtedly the safest and most sensible type of exercise program you can design for yourself. One is never too old to start. I have seen people in their sixties and seventies work their way very successfully into walking for exercise, even though they had paid little attention to fitness exercise in their earlier lives. If you have been sedentary much of your life and want to improve your quality of life, I suggest getting a fitness evaluation and exercise stress test at a physical education or physiology department at a major university. These tests are also available through hospitals and sports medicine doctors, but the cost may be triple that of those offered in a university.

The main reason for a stress test is to uncover any silent coronary artery disease that may need addressing before you enter a world of unaccustomed exertion. Complete evaluation tests should include blood analysis for cholesterol, triglycerides, glucose, blood pressure, a history of family and personal health, a stress test electrocardiogram to determine your ideal level of exercise, a dietary evaluation and body composition analysis. All these tests, which are well supervised and safe, tell a health professional just how much exercise you can safely tolerate. They also provide enough information for either you or a professional to document your current fitness level and design a walking program best suited for your personal fitness improvement.

Attaining and Measuring Fitness

Most fitness experts say that a half hour of rhythmic nonstop exercise, performed at least three times a week, improves the heart and circulatory system and gets the heart pumping large quantities of blood so that large muscle groups can function at their optimum level. Your pulse rate is the best indicator of the effort you expend while exercising. As the intensity of exercise increases, your heart rate speeds up and your perceived effort follows. There are certain heart rate ranges that are considered the most beneficial if one is to get the best training effect. If the effort is too mild, the training effect might be quite minimal. If it is too intense, the heart rate approaches maximum effectiveness and the exercise must either slow down or cease. Overexertion may be dangerous for an untrained person. Some exercise trainers recommend that exercisers stop during and after workouts to count heartbeats by feeling the pulse, counting 10 beats and multiplying by 6 to get the rate per minute (bpm). This formula is only an approximation of the actual rate.

Pulse Rate Monitors

Some recently developed pulse rate monitors are very useful for providing an accurate assessment of your heart rate during exercise. These devices are not only great training devices but are also helpful for anyone with a heart problem who must carefully stay within a certain heartbeat range. The pulse rate monitors I have found to work best for serious racers and those exercisers who must be careful not to get overstressed because they are on a controlled, prescribed exercise program is made by Polar CIC, Inc. of Port Washington, New York. This company has several models, but the two most popular are the "Favor," which displays heart rate only, and the "Pacer," which can be set to personal target zone settings and has a beeping alarm that goes off when you go out of your desired range. For instance, if you want to stay within the range of 120 to 150 bpm, you could set the monitor to beep either below 120 or above 150. In this way you can either speed up or slow down if the device beeps. For many exercisers it is well worth the investment to have one of these monitors to keep track of your current conditioning and to measure your improvement. If you train consistently, you may experience a dramatic decrease in heart rate for a certain amount of work accomplished at a certain heart rate.

Get to know how your body operates under various levels of exertion so that you know whether your exercise is too intense or too mild to provide a training effect. As your condition improves, your basic range will remain the same—it's just that your better-conditioned heart can do more work within the range.

The Best Time to Exercise

There is no single recommended best time to exercise because everyone's lifestyle is different. The best time for vigorous exercise is when you can fit it into your busy schedule. One bit of advice is not to do your brisk walking right after eating a large meal because the digestion process demands part of the blood supply that normally would go to the muscles. Nevertheless the muscles must still draw blood to function. This causes an uncomfortable bloated feeling as partially undigested food sits in the stomach. For this reason the timing of your meals should have a direct correlation with the timing of your exercise program. It may take as much as 4 hours for a large, heavy meal to pass through the stomach and upper intestines and a small one in 90 minutes to 2 hours. However, mild exercise, such as strolling slowly immediately after eating, is actually thought to aid digestion by increasing the speed of passage of food through the digestive tract.

Climatic conditions are also a factor. Midday in the summer in southern Arizona is definitely not the time to be outdoors, but it might be perfectly delightful in the winter. Under humid conditions, coupled with heat, early morning before breakfast is probably the best time to exercise. In northern climates, at certain times of the year, it may be too cold to exercise in the morning or evening, so the noon lunch hour may be the best choice. There are some good indoor exercise machines that you can use at home when the weather is unfavorable. Most experts on fitness and exercise agree that an excellent indoor exercise machine is the Nordic Track, which exercises the large leg muscles as well as the upper body. See chapter 12 on environmental considerations.

All humans and animals have built in 24-hour rhythms called "circadian," meaning "daily." These rhythms vary according to a person's own physiological systems that control the body's internal activities and can determine the response to exercise at any time of day. This phenomenon explains why some people are "early birds" and others "night owls." Because most people know where their highs and low occur, some feel better exercising in the early morning while others prefer to exercise in the evening. The time of day when you feel most energetic will have an influence on your motivation to exercise.

If weight loss is in your plans, walking in the evening may be the best time. Because eating in the evening has been known to be associated with weight gain, some fitness authorities believe that exercise in the evening may counteract a tendency toward weight gain. Since the body's metabolic rate stays elevated after exercise and the rate is increased in proportion to the intensity of the exercise, a good brisk walk in the evening could be a very good weight loss technique. But remember that going to bed immediately after exercising is not conducive to falling asleep. Rather, eat your evening meal after exercising and allow a couple of hours to allow your body to settle down before going to bed.

Find a regimen that you like, and then decide that you are going to improve and maintain your fitness level. Perseverance is the key. You will find that the time and effort are well spent.

9 | Children Are Our Future

"Mankind owes to the child the best it has to give."
—U.N. Declaration

Aren't problems such as clogged arteries and high cholesterol normally associated with middle-aged or elderly people? This is not always so. It is now being realized that the habits of a person's life are primarily formulated in the very early years. High blood lipid (cholesterol) levels and hypertension are being found in children as young as four years old. According to *Walking* magazine, approximately 35 percent of American children are overweight and have poor cardiovascular efficiency by the age of six. About the same percentage acquire heart disease risk factors such as obesity, high cholesterol and hypertension by the time they reach second or third grade. The number of obese children between the ages of 6 and 11 has risen about 54 percent since the 1960s.

Why Are Children in Such Bad Shape?

Many children in the United States are out of shape for several reasons. The greatest childhood treat seems to be going to McDonald's, Burger King or other "fat" food outlets. Heavily sugared foods are also a big part of their diets. Children eat an average of over 120 pounds of sugar a year. These are empty calories that could otherwise be devoted to healthy foods that aid in their development. Fat cells develop the most during the formative years up to puberty, and these cells might remain with a person forever. A fat child will generally become a fat adult. Television also can add to a child's poor health. When overconsumed, it takes time away from participating in imaginative play so necessary for a person in their formative preschool years. With the exception of such excellent educational programs as *Sesame Street,* excessive TV viewing is not a healthy influence on children. The more TV children watch, the more they become dependent on it for their recreation and the less time they spend outdoors playing with others in normal activities.

Our bodies were designed to thrive on a certain amount of daily movement and exercise. Few children are told that aerobic exercise, such as brisk walking, is the most practical way to get into an exercise habit that will keep their bodies trim and that they can use for the rest of their lives. The truth is that children are normally not educated about the facts of a healthy life either at home or at school. Many elementary schools have had to drop physical education and health classes from their curriculum as a result of budget restraints. Some of the schools that do not have them provide poor information to the students. The sad fact is that some teachers aren't very good role models. When adults exhibit unhealthy practices such as overeating fatty food, drinking too much alcohol or smoking, children tend to think that such behaviors are the norm and often emulate them. In these cases, they often grow up without the understanding that healthy habits learned at a young age can have a profound effect on the outcome of their later lives.

Physical Education for Kids

What are children being taught in the typical physical education classes these days, if indeed they even have access to them? They are often pushed into competitive team sport activities. They are not told that hardly anyone dies from lack of strength, or that, conversely, there *are* epidemics of people who die from the inability to breathe or to circulate vital fluids through the body. Schoolkids are tested mainly for speed, strength and agility. The trouble is that the genetically gifted athletes shine in every test while those with lesser abilities are continually disappointed to see that they will never catch up. Why not set up programs that are noncompetitive, in which the child's personal improvement is duly noted and rewarded accordingly? An aerobic walking program is the ideal way to accomplish this goal. Rob Sweetgall, noted expert on elementary physical education, says that there are growing numbers of physical educators embracing sensible programs all across the country, but there is still a long way to go.

Why not have them run? Some children don't like to run and others are simply not biomechanically suited to do it. Jogging throws a lot of weight, up to four times the body weight on young bones and joints. If the weight is distributed unevenly on these body parts due to imbalance, it could distort the layered buildup of a young person's bone tissue. Get them walking aerobically and imbue them with ideas of this lifelong activity.

A Great Program to Get the Kids Started

How can specific programs that teach America's youth the benefits and joys of lifetime personal fitness through aerobic exercise be instituted in the schools? Rob Sweetgall has designed an ongoing innovative program for the school systems of several states.

Rob himself is quite a remarkable person. Motivated by the fact that some of his own family members died of cardiovascular disease in a short period of time, Rob left a high-paying job as a chemical engineer at DuPont in 1981 to institute his program. Now, through his organization Creative Walking, Inc. headquartered in Clayton, Missouri, he devotes his entire life to informing others of the vital need to remain active for life. Creative Walking is designed to address people of all ages from kindergarten through middle school. I strongly recommend this program to all school administrators and teachers as well as concerned parents. See a listing of his books in appendix 12.

In 1984 Rob decided to take a solo walk across all 50 U.S. states, carrying only a small fanny pack for survival supplies. In one year Rob walked 11,608 miles, visiting over 200 schools along his route. The University of Massachusetts Medical School flew him back to their facility for extensive testing every 7 weeks to find out what happens to a human body averaging 31 miles of walking every day for a year. Every calorie eaten as well as other aspects of what he had done each day were meticulously recorded on computers for study. He enjoyed a trip that most would consider the ultimate in self-torture and agony, and he finished in better health than when he started. It became the most involved study of a person's physiology in history.

The Walking Wellness School Program

Rob's long walk was designed around the scheduling of school assemblies along the route he took through parts of every state. He lectured to thousands of children and educators during his walk. Ideas were collected from all parts of the country for a new concept of physical education and developed into a comprehensive curriculum called "Walking Wellness" that incorporates a lifetime fitness manual for each child who must keep track of his/her aerobic fitness throughout the year. The program educates students before peer pressure becomes a problem. Homework assignments and workshops, numbering 16 half-hour sessions per year, cover the major aspects of personal fitness and health. During each Walking Wellness session students walk, talk, write, read, reason, calculate, plan, analyze, cooperate and discover. Half the course entails physical walking exercise, and the other half is "walking for the mind." No workshop is complete without the homework, and the principles of healthy lifestyle are thus put firmly into the students' minds. This concept addresses each student's needs and encourages *all* students regardless of ability level. Each student competes with only him- or herself as personal improvements are noted. Students are encouraged to keep written records all through their school years to refer to and reinforce their commitment to a lifetime of healthy habits. Initiating and engraving preventive ideas deeply into students' minds at an early age can have a huge impact on health care in the United States in the future years. The future health of our nation depends upon what the children of today learn and believe regarding healthy lifestyles.

Why Children Should Walk

Rob has suggested 20 reasons why children should use walking as a beneficial exercise, taken from the book *Walking for Little Children* and reprinted here with permission of Creative Walking, Inc. Walking …

- builds self-esteem
- builds strong bones
- increases attentiveness
- increases muscle mass

- controls disruptive behavior
- controls fat cell growth
- diminishes stress
- reduces hyperactivity
- strengthens the heart
- strengthens communication skills
- develops a good wellness attitude
- stabilizes friendships
- stabilizes blood pressure
- develops good blood pressure
- encourages use of senses
- encourages drug-free living
- promotes language development
- promotes physical coordination
- lets everyone participate
- lets everyone have fun

Improving Attention Spans

Rob notes that children have short attention spans and tend to get restless in school classrooms. As the temperature in the room and the level of carbon dioxide rises, a decrease in breathing rate occurs, which results in a mental dullness, inattentiveness and impaired learning caused by oxygen deficiencies in the brain. He says, "Walking pumps fresh oxygen into their brains to refill their 'think tanks.' It wakes kids up for the next lesson."

The New System's Advantages

Competition has been the heart of past physical education programs with the star athletes excelling. The "nonstars" begin to get their training for becoming the spectators of life—those sitting in the stands desperately in need of exercise, while they watch a few athletes on the field desperately in need of rest. Most sports require equipment and fields that must be maintained. Taking kids out for an aerobic walk costs nothing except a half hour of their time. They can also learn many things on a walk that they would normally learn in the classroom.

The great majority is not very good at the popular sports and do not enjoy participating in them. Many young people are forced to participate in little league programs by their parents, sometimes because their parents were made to do the same thing when they were young. Let's get children walking at a young age and encourage them to continue this exercise throughout their life with vigor and robust good health. Children are great imitators and they love to mimic adults if they look up to them as role models. If their mentor can demonstrate an aerobic walking technique to them instead of just talking about it, a more rapid development will follow. Practically every kid in school can benefit at some level by engaging in aerobic walking.

In summary, the basic objectives of Rob's program provide:

- lifelong aerobic exercise in a noncompetitive win-win environment;
- a way to use walking as a medium to support reading, writing, math and science;
- walking as a support for healthy lifestyles in workshops where students think about and discuss stress, tobacco, drugs and nutrition while walking;
- encouragement through teamwork, communication, respect and honesty in fun outdoor walking situations;
- students with the idea that they can observe nature and their environment on foot at 3 mph instead of through car windows;
- involvement of family members in walking workshops and lifestyle planning;
- students a method to develop realistic walking wellness action plans that make walking a regular and lasting habit and to follow up with them on those plans;
- a means to avoid unhealthy habits before they ever occur;
- students with the knowledge that if they are somewhat competitive in nature that there are great opportunities to get involved in the kinder, gentler sport of racewalking.

The Little Publicized Avenue to Athletic Success

For the athletic and competitive kids in middle school and high school, walking can be an avenue to athletic success. Most people do not know that competitive walking is now starting to become very popular in the United States. Youth camps are now being conducted to develop racewalking athletic talent. In the past, only a handful of high schools in New York State and several NAIA colleges have had competitive walking as part of their athletic programs. Now the state of Maine has a fledgling high school program. Since racewalking is a technique-intensive sport, as much so as pole vaulting, high jumping, javelin, basketball, soccer, etc., it takes a lot of dedication to become an elite walker. But it is fun to learn because participants can feel their efficiency rise and speed improve steadily. They get into fantastic shape by training and can still run with the other athletes. If some of the gifted athletes would take up the sport, they would have a vastly greater chance of getting on a national team. If we could get youngsters into walking early, then we could get a pool of good athletes interested in working to do it well.

Our U.S. Olympic Committee and USA Track & Field team would like to see a large improvement in our development of youth and competitiveness in racewalking compared to the rest of the world. Even our smaller neighbor Mexico has concentrated on the sport with greater success than us, ever since the 1968 Olympics with their great imported Polish coach Jerzy Hausleber. Many European countries give walking equal importance with other track events, and their racewalking stars are revered as much as their other prominent track athletes. As a country, the United States has a lot of catching up to do, not only in competitions, but in getting more of our young generations into improved fitness.

10 Oxygen—The Staff of Life

"Faulty breathing is almost universal. Most of us breathe backward."
—Dr. George Sheehan

Of course, we all know that without oxygen our bodies will wither and die within minutes. What many people do not know is that the more oxygen our body can be trained to process, the better off it will be in practically all aspects of life. There are so many older people who have not taken proper care of themselves, as is evident by the oxygen bottles they must carry around with them in order to breathe. Their faces have a distinctive pallor. This is no way to spend your golden years. What better way to prevent the possibility of this sort of personal tragedy than by taking a few pleasant brisk walks each week.

Walking and Breathing

Oxygen is the vital fuel of the muscles and the brain. The yogis of the Far East have understood the beneficial effects derived from the principles of deep breathing for many centuries. It is an integral part of their meditation techniques. They have known that breath is the staff of life—the real life force in our bodies.

Without food, some people have been known to survive up to two months before starving to death. Without food *and* water a person may last a week. But without oxygen, brain damage and ensuing death can occur in as little as four minutes. This makes breathing our most important bodily function. The fact is that the more breathing we do and the deeper we breathe, the better it is for our mental and physical health.

Exercise works its magic in rejuvenatory powers not by making us hurt but by making us breathe deeply—a process that oxygenates all of the cells of our bodies. "Belly breathing" is the key when we walk for aerobic conditioning. This means breathing in deeply into the bottoms of the lungs until they are fully inflated and forcibly exhaling as much air as possible on each breath, but with resistance as through pursed lips. This type of breathing facilitates taking in more oxygen to fully inflate the lungs. Studies have shown that after the age of 20, when we are at our maximum powers, we begin to lose an average of 1 percent of our oxygen processing capacity per year. This results in a decline in cellular activity and our bodies start a long, slow decline toward suffocation—that is, unless we undertake a program to do some form of aerobic exercise, such as fast walking, for the rest of our lives to slow the deadly process.

Through aerobic exercise our hearts and lungs remain strong enough to supply an amount of oxygen equal to what our bodies processed when we were young. Some people who are chronologically old can maintain breathing capacities similar to sedentary people who are 40 years younger. In one experiment, exercise physiologists found that a group of previously unconditioned men and women from 60 to 83 years of age were able to increase their breathing capacities by an average of almost 30 percent in a year's time by doing light calisthenics and walking consistently several times per week. According to the physiologists, those gains in aerobic capacity compared favorably to what might have been expected from people much younger. Staying active is truly the key to remaining vigorous throughout life.

Lung Inflation

One of the greatest physical deficiencies in modern-day life is underinflation of the lungs. For the sedentary lifestyle, very shallow breathing is all that is necessary to get by. The lungs of a sedentary person are almost always in a collapsed state, which often results in lung disease, drooping shoulders, sunken chests, headaches and undue fatigue. What must be done to avoid these less-than-pleasant conditions? We can sit around practicing deep breathing all we want, but we won't get the full depth of respiration that we do from aerobic exercise such as brisk walking. What we must seek is complete breathing and breath control that can make countless improvements in our overall health and fitness. Proper deep breathing is essential if any semblance of endurance is to be attained.

How We Should Breathe

Let's look at some specifics of the breathing process. The respiratory muscles of the diaphragm and the ribs create a vacuum in the lungs by expanding them in size. The more strenuous the exercise, the more the lungs expand and the more oxygen drawn into the body for use. There are three types of breathing, all of which become incomplete unless aided by aerobic exercise.

1. Abdominal, or belly, breathing, which results from lowering the diaphragm and the extension of the abdomen.
2. Intercostal breathing in the middle of the chest is produced by the contraction of the intercostal muscles between the ribs.
3. Clavicular breathing, in which the very tops of the lungs are ventilated by the muscular elevation of the collarbones during inhalation.

These individual patterns aid in the breathing process, but they are incomplete in themselves as each one only partially fills the lungs with air. Yogis concentrate on each of these breathing patterns, starting with the abdominal, which attempts to fill the lower lobes completely, then concentrating on filling the middle lungs and finally raising the shoulders to fill the upper lobes. The great Australian running coach, Percy Cerutty, taught his athletes to pull their shoulders up and raise their arms periodically while running in order to get the lungs completely full to the top of the lobes. He understood that this action added to their aerobic power, and thus increased their strength, endurance and speed.

Increase Your Resistance

Yogis claim that when the vitality of the lungs is improved by deep breathing, the lining of the lungs is better able to resist the invasion of bacteria and viruses. As a result, the incidence of flus, colds and pneumonia can be dramatically reduced. In addition, the quality of the blood is greatly improved by added oxygen in the system, which ultimately benefits all the organs and muscles in the body. Also, the up and down movement of the diaphragm massages the digestive system, causing food to be propelled along faster and providing additional blood to aid in the digestion process. The benefits of deep breathing have been proven over the centuries. By walking briskly and breathing deeply, we expand our capillary network, exercise the heart muscle, stimulate the enzyme system and burn calories.

Find Your Ideal Breathing Pattern

Practice using all the three breathing patterns while walking. Think about filling the diaphragm, then the middle lungs and finally the upper lobes as you move along. This is a slow and methodical breathing process and you may find it helpful to use a certain number of steps—possibly six or eight—for each complete breath. If you breathe in a shallow, rapid fashion, you may experience the discomforting sensation of hyperventilation caused by the excessive exhalation of carbon dioxide. It is essential that you experiment to find your own ideal breathing pattern. When you do find it stick with it until the breathing becomes automatic.

Maximum Oxygen Uptake—
A Standard Measurement of Fitness

There are several ways to assess physical fitness. Maximum oxygen uptake (VO_2 max), is an excellent indicator of a person's level of conditioning and cardiovascular fitness. The maximum volume of oxygen that can be processed by the lungs and body per minute while engaging in strenuous exercise, VO_2 max can be measured on a treadmill or bicycle ergometer by a trained technician. A low reading, such as 30 milliliters of oxygen per kilogram of body weight per minute (ml/kg/min) or lower, means an unfitness level that does not allow the body to process oxygen in adequate quantities to sustain a quality lifestyle. On the other hand, high readings such as 50 up to the mid-90s (the maximum amount attainable by the world's best athletes) denote excellent personal aerobic fitness. Those readings with values above 60 are usually achieved by trained athletes who have worked very hard to attain such high levels of aerobic capacity. One of the highest readings achieved by an American was Steve Prefontaine, a middle-distance runner who died in an auto crash in the mid-1970s, with a VO_2 of 86. A Norweigian cross-country skier has been measured at 94—the highest ever recorded in the world. Too many people fall in the 20 to 35 range, which is typical of living in a semi-health state devoid of exercise and good breathing capacity.

Walking Can Raise Your Fitness Score

Walkers may use only a fraction of potential aerobic power, but endurance training can cause impressive increases in this regard. It will facilitate the absorption of oxygen more readily and use it more efficiently by converting food into the energy necessary to keep it going for extended periods. Increased endurance will manifest itself in two ways: a lower resting pulse rate and faster recovery of the pulse rate after bouts of training.

The body expends 5 kilocalories of energy for every liter of oxygen consumed. If VO_2 max is done according to approved protocols, there should be an error of 3 percent or less, which can be a good indicator of your present fitness level. The larger the muscle masses used in the test, the greater the oxygen consumption. Running or walking on a treadmill as the speed and incline are gradually increased until exhaustion occurs is considered to be the standard test. A bicycle ergometer gives a maximum reading of about 10 percent less, probably because the exercise is nonweight bearing. Take this into account in case you get an ergometer test.

Body size enters into the measurement picture because a large person can consume more oxygen than a small one. A normal person's resting oxygen uptake is approximately 3.5 ml/kg/min, but during a maximal test the measurement can increase from 10 to 20 times depending on the person's fitness level. As intensive exercise is undertaken, cardiac blood flow increases to several times the resting rate. The heart pumps more blood per beat and the stroke rate rises. The efficiency of the muscle cells determines how rapidly the rate of oxygen feeds into the muscles for energy production.

Your potential for a high oxygen uptake can be genetic, but training has the most dramatic effect on oxygen consumption. Such aerobic exercises as racewalking and cross-country skiing are excellent for increasing a person's oxygen-carrying and cardiovascular capacity. During this process more oxygen becomes available to the muscles and increases their ability to use oxygen, which nearly doubles your oxygen uptake no matter what age you are.

An average person just starting a training regimen can expect to make quick gains early in training—10 to 20 percent gains are common in the first 10 weeks of dedicated exercise. From this point on, VO_2 max increases are harder to come by as one gets closer to his or her genetic limit. But even if gains are no longer able to be made, the decline due to aging can be slowed significantly over time. The secret is to keep up your walking program for life.

11 Energy's Basic Fuel

"The habits of a nutritional diet and physical fitness should be established during childhood and maintained throughout life."
—American Dietetic Association
Position Statement

Should you eat sugars just before exercising? How does exercise affect blood sugar levels? People who exercise heavily know that they must fuel the body to maintain the exercises they do. They tend to learn from experience what and when to eat. Let's look at the pertinent factors to give those who have not had such experience a better understanding.

Glucose for Energy

The body and brain are dependent on sugar (glucose) as a primary source of energy, along with oxygen. As glucose molecules in the blood are linked together in a chain, they are stored in liver and muscle cells and become glycogen. Although glucose is the main factor for providing energy, it is not the only one. During low levels of exercise, some fat is also metabolized. As the energy level increases, more and more glucose is used until at maximum effort it becomes the sole source of energy. In normal training exercising of up to two hours in which maximal or even 80 percent effort cannot be sustained unless you are a well-trained athlete, the supply of glycogen will be sufficient to sustain the exercise. After that, fat becomes a very important source. But the length of time glucose can supply energy is dependent on how much glycogen was stored in the muscles and liver beforehand. Eating many complex carbohydrates, especially those found in many natural foods, helps in increasing the stored supplies of glycogen. As you start exercising, a process occurs whereby adrenaline reacts with the muscle glycogen, breaking it down into glucose and making it immediately available for muscle contractions.

If muscle glycogen becomes depleted or reaches a low level, the liver comes to the rescue and delivers its stored glycogen through the bloodstream. This comes about as the pancreas releases the hormone glaucagon, which is instrumental in breaking down liver glycogen to glucose. When liver glycogen levels become too low, the next source is the hormone cortisol from the adrenal gland, which breaks down some protein into amino acids that the liver can convert into glucose. Body tissues need these proteins to function properly, and their use is a sort of last resort before you completely run out of energy.

Glucose is so important in its function to prevent hypoglycemia that the body tries to use it judiciously. Hypoglycemia is the condition when the blood becomes deficient in glucose, thus causing nausea, confusion and dizziness. Carried to its extreme, it can even cause convulsions, loss of consciousness and coma. Considering the fact that low glucose can cause these types of serious reactions does not mean that you should gorge on sweets or soft drinks just before exercising. Those of us who are not diabetic have a built-in insulin reaction that puts this hormone into the bloodstream to keep sugar levels under control. Exercise limits the release of insulin, which is to the exerciser's advantage since a small amount causes glucose to be used selectively by the working muscles and the brain.

Solid food may cause intestinal problems caused by a slow digestion process. Blood normally used for digestion is being shunted to muscular activity. The most easily digested sources are those in replacement drinks, which contain glucose. They empty from the stomach at a slower rate than plain water, but this is compensated for by the added energy provided. Most experts recommend drinking 5 to 8 ounces of liquids contaning about 10 percent glucose every 20 minutes and even more during humid, hot weather. Do not worry, though, about glucose intake except for distances more than 10 kilometers—water will suffice.

Fat for Energy

Fat has more calories per gram than carbohydrates and protein (9 versus 4). Some fat calories supply energy to the brain but only because fat can be used as a fuel in the presence of oxygen. Glucose, however, can be burned either with or without oxygen. Because endurance training greatly increases aerobic capacity, fat can be used more effectively by the muscles to do their work. Training also allows the muscles to store more glycogen. This increases exercise capacity and more work can be accomplished comfortably with less perceived effort. We should all be in training for life at whatever level is comfortable for each of us. See chapter 4 for nutritional information on ideal diets for energy production.

12 Environmental Considerations in Walking

"The existence of a cold acclimatization process in humans is an interesting phenomenon for physiologists. However, the advantage provided by these adaptations in terms of conservation of body heat is small, particularly in comparison with the protective effects available from increases in body fat and modern clothing."
—Michael Toner, Ph.D.

"Man is the only animal native to sea level who purposefully subjects himself to the rigors of hypoxic environments, such as those found in mountainous regions of the world for other reasons than pure survival."
—Allen Cymerman, Ph.D.

Coping with Heat

Exercisers often find themselves at the mercy of environmental conditions that they must learn to control if they wish to exercise safely and comfortably. Our bodies build up a large amount of heat during bouts of moderate to intense exercise, which can be dangerous when temperatures are high, especially humidity levels. The most important thing a person can do when coping with heat is to drink plenty of liquids, especially plain, cool water. There are four ways that the body can dissipate heat—convection, conduction, radiation and evaporation.

The Dangers of Heat Stress

The body goes to great lengths to maintain a core temperature of around 98.6° F through a complicated thermoregulatory system designed to dissipate the heat produced through normal activities. In cooler weather, an exerciser can diminish heat buildup through conduction, convection, radiation and the exchange of air through breathing if the exercise is moderate. Heat stress is not merely reflected by air temperature. Humidity, wind and thermal radiation also contribute to the total heat load on the body. When the exercise is intense the body's internal heat buildup can increase up to 10 to 15 times the resting, normal amount. If you engage in intensive exercise during hot weather, the body needs all the help it can get to avoid heat stress. When the ambient air temperature is greater than your skin temperature, sweating is the body's way of releasing heat. If the level of humidity is also high, even sweating is compromised and some rather nasty things can happen as excess heat builds up and raises the body's core temperature. There is a competition between active muscles and the skin for active blood supply—the muscles need the blood and oxygen to sustain activity and the skin needs it for cooling.

Sweat must evaporate to provide cooling—if it merely drips off, there is very little cooling effect. By sweating profusely, a walker may lose as much as 3 quarts of body fluid in just one hour. It has been noted that some endurance athletes have perspired as much as 10 to 15 quarts per day. When this amount of dehydration takes place, it causes severe heat stress. If sweating stops entirely because of this fluid loss, heat can no longer be dissipated and all exercise must cease or heat exhaustion or, even worse, heat stroke will result. You may need aid from others to get cooled down to a reasonable level. This can be serious business, but all of this stress can be avoided if you drink copious amounts of fluids and pour water over your head and body to aid the cooling process.

In hot weather it is a good idea to weigh yourself before and after exercise sessions to help gauge your water loss, which must be made up before another such session. Exercise where there is some shade and expose as much skin as modesty will allow. Saturated clothing does not allow for proper evaporation of moisture from the skin.

Acclimatization

Your body, in its infinite wisdom, can become acclimatized to heat to a certain degree by repeated exposure. Adaptation can occur by exercising in heat for an hour or more daily for a week or so. Cardiovascular changes may occur in 5 days but optimum changes in the sweating mechanism may take as long as 10 days. The sweating mechanism becomes more active as the body attempts to cope with the new environment.

The Sweating Mechanism

One of the most pervasive deterrents, and indeed misconceptions, to exercising at certain times is that of body odor, which is inherent in the sweating process. Sweat itself, however, is not the culprit in producing body odors. Rather, it is the interaction of sweat with bacteria found on the skin that produces the odor. There are three types of glands that produce normal and odorless secretions of sweat—eccrine, apocrine and sebaceous. Each has a different way of potentially producing a body odor when decomposed by bacteria on the skin.

The eccrine glands play very little part in odor formation because they have only trace amounts of organic material in their secretions on which bacteria can act. These glands are active during exercise, when the temperature of the body has built up heat that must be dissipated. In some areas of the body such as the underarms, palms of the hands and soles of the feet, these glands produce sweat at lower temperatures than in other parts of the body.

Apocrine glands produce sweat rich in organic material to react with the body's external bacteria. These are concentrated in the underarms, the nipple area of the breast and the genital area. The first and third areas are ideal sites for bacterial growth where moisture does not readily evaporate. They are stimulated by emotional stress such as pain, fear, anger and sexual urges, but their activity is little affected by hot weather or exercise.

Sebaceous glands lubricate the skin with an oily material called "sebum" and play only a minor role in producing body odor for exercisers who bathe at reasonable intervals. The only areas that should cause concern about not offending your fellow workers after your noontime workout are the underarms and the feet. The other areas of the body (except the genital area) allow for adequate evaporation and little cause for malodorous concern. Sponging off the underarms and the feet in a rest room should do quite nicely in avoiding unwanted odors during the workday afternoon.

Overweight and out-of-shape people have more concentrated sweat than lithe, trim athletes who are in excellent shape. Sometimes those who are not very fit will evidence salty deposits on the skin after exercising in the heat. The better shape you are in, the less bathing is needed to avoid offending others. Some people have a habit of bathing too often, which results in washing away too many of the skin's natural oils and causes excessive dryness of the skin.

Hydration Is Vital

Remember that only a few things can destroy a healthy athlete, and number one on this list is dehydration. If you reach a sufficiently dehydrated state, your body may react by taking water from the blood supply, which is trying to deliver fluids and oxygen to the working muscles. This may cause the body to go into a state of shock from decreased blood supply. Another problem that often occurs is muscle cramping from loss of salt and/or potassium. After exercising it is essential to replace these minerals as a way of alleviating muscle cramps. Certain commercial replacement drinks that provide the proper fluid-mineral balance can be very useful in the postexercise period. However, these replacement drinks do not assimilate into the body as fast as plain, cool water, which is the very best fluid to replace losses. It enters the system more quickly than other fluids except alcohol—the great dehydrator and definitely not a suitable hot weather drink. The body absorbs its fluids mostly from the intestines, so the idea is to drink those that can pass through the system as rapidly as possible. Those factors that affect gastric emptying are the fluid's temperature, volume and sugar content. Cool water not only speeds the gastric emptying but cools the body as well.

About a half hour before exercising in hot weather, drink up to a quart of cool water. Be sure not to ingest a lot of sugared drinks prior to exercise because they affect insulin and glucose levels, which can cause fatigue to set in prematurely. It is fine to have energy drinks during exercise though. If the walk is long, carry water to drink along the way. The best way to carry water is a Boda Belt or the Water Belt, which are similar to fluid-filled belts that hold about a liter with the weight distributed around the body. Another useful item is the Camelback, which goes on like a pack and distributes the weight on the back. This pack has an attached plastic water hose that allows drinking without even stopping. Drink a pint or so every 30 minutes. The body's thirst-sensing mechanism does not keep up with actual dehydration, so in hot weather always drink a little more than your thirst perception seems to dictate.

If there is sugar in the solution, gastric emptying slows because a digestion process takes place. Sports drinks should have no more than 2.5 grams of sugar per 100 cc. of liquid. Since many drinks exceed this amount, dilute them to conform to this standard.

The first specific runner's drink, ERG (Energy Replacement with Glucose), was developed by Bill Gookin of San Diego in the early 1970s. This solution was designed to imitate perspiration, which was then thought to be lost during exercise. It has since been found that electrolytes (e.g., sodium, potassium and calcium) are not depleted during hot weather exercise. In fact, as water is sweated out, electrolytes can become more concentrated, which means that more water intake is necessary to bring about a balance. Remember, if you eat a well-balanced diet, then electrolyte replacement may not be necessary at all.

A fairly recent development in fluid technology is a new generation of drinks called "glucose polymers." These drinks were scientifically formulated to be quickly absorbed in the gut and can replace both fluids and carbohydrates. However, they are of little use if the exercise does not last for more than 45 minutes.

There is no denying that cool water is the liquid of choice in most cases. Up to a certain point (about a quart at a time) the more water you drink, the faster it is absorbed and is made available to the system. Drink too much, however, and the volume of liquid can cause an uncomfortable feeling during exercise. Only drink as much as you can tolerate. Below is a list of popular exercise drinks and when to use them to replace fluids lost in hot weather:

1. The following drinks can be used safely before, during and after exercise: glucose polymer drinks, unsweetened iced tea, and tap or filter water.

2. The following drinks can be used in all three situations, but should be diluted before and during exercise: fruit juices, defizzed colas, carbohydrate replacement fluids and electrolyte replacement fluids.

3. The following drinks are best if used before and after exercise: carbonated mineral water and diet colas.

4. A cup of coffee before exercise may help give a jump start, but should not be used during and after.

5. A beer or two can be a pleasant drink after exercise, but should not be used before and during.

6. Wine, hard liquor or milk do not enhance exercise before, during or after exercise.

Coping with Cold

Many people who live in frigid, snowy climates during the winter months may worry about losing their hard-earned fitness because of the added darkness and cold. Many times our lazy natures tell us to wait for spring and then walk ourselves back into shape. By doing so we are doing our bodies a great disservice. A maintenance exercise program that lasts throughout the entire year is vital to keep our bodies moving through the winter and requires only a few modifications to make allowances for colder weather.

Avoid walking on slippery surfaces because of the danger of falling or straining something if you slip unexpectedly. When there is a layer of snow that seems to afford traction, you never know if there might be an icy spot underneath that can cause you to slip and fall hard to the ground. This danger can easily be underestimated. Even subtle imbalances caused by a slip may produce an injury of some sort. On days when it is hazardous to walk either get out the cross-country skis and head for the grassy snow-covered surface of the nearest park or find some indoor place to do some walking, such as a mall. Many dedicated exercisers have in their homes their own treadmills, bicycle ergometers or cross-country ski trainers such as Nordic Track. I find it invigorating to get out in almost any type of weather short of a blinding snowstorm, being careful to dress appropriately and to adapt to the conditions with safety in mind. Remember that it takes less effort to maintain fitness than it does to acquire it, but nonetheless, be persistent in its maintenance.

Some Precautions and Suggested Apparel

Here are some simple precautions to make your exercising in cold weather more comfortable and safe. Dress for the occasion by wearing clothing that is adjustable (i.e., dress in layers that can be taken off and put back on according to the conditions). Many people underestimate the amount of heat that a body produces when exercising briskly. You can be freezing as you start but 10 minutes into the walk you can be getting too warm for comfort. If you overdress and get sweaty, a great chill can occur when you slow down or stop. Have warmer clothes ready to put on after stopping.

A hooded sweatshirt that zips down the front is a very useful item. You should also have a windbreaker such as a nylon jacket to wear over your warm underclothing. If you can afford it, get a jacket that repels the windchill and yet breathes without trapping the moisture inside—Gore Tex, ProMAX IV and other similar modern fabrics work well in this regard. See chapter 16 for more information.

Even if the temperature is around zero, you should not have more than three layers of clothing, but all should be adjustable either to retain your body heat or let it escape. The legs don't need a lot of insulation. There is a great amount of blood circulation coursing through them that increases their metabolism, which in turn ensures their warmth. It might help to wear insulating socks to prevent cold toes. You can usually get by with a pair of tights in moderately cold conditions or sweatpants and/or thermal underwear in severe cold.

A point to remember is that the head can release a great amount of heat when uncovered in cold weather. A wool or spun polypropylene headband to cover the ears is a very useful item because it keeps you warm until you don't need it any more, and easily slips into your pocket until you start to get cold again. Use a good wool hat if it is very cold to help maintain body heat and keep the vulnerable ears from freezing. A good hat can conserve as much as 40 percent of the body's heat. The ears, fingers, groin and toes are the areas on the body most susceptible to cold, and as long as you protect them you can get by with surprisingly little clothing as long as vigorous exercise is undertaken. It is far better to wear mittens rather than gloves for protection of the fingers, because the fingers share heat. A heavy pair of wool socks can be used as mittens in case you don't have any mittens handy.

Generally, try to let the sweat evaporate before it builds up much. Sweat-soaked clothing can get you cold, by some estimates, 20 times more quickly than dry clothing. If you have the choice, you should head into the wind on the first part of your walk so that there will be a tailwind on the way back. As long as you keep moving briskly at first any discomfort should not last long and you will face the worst conditions while your clothing is dry.

Sometimes temperatures and weather conditions can fluctuate rapidly. Walking in direct sunlight and getting solar radiation is far different from walking when the sun is covered with clouds or when it is low on the horizon. Walking through a long, shady spot may dictate an adjustment in your protective clothing. It is crucial to be aware of the windchill factor. Even if it seems relatively mild when you start out, a stiff wind can come up suddenly, changing things drastically, especially if it becomes cloudy at the same time. If you walk in darkness, wear something reflective so you can be seen by motorists.

So don't let Old Man Winter deter you from your quest for health and fitness. One of the most delightful and invigorating times to walk is when the weather is very cold with the sun out in still air. If you take the necessary precautions, you can feel good and fit all winter long and head into spring with increased momentum.

Coping with Altitude

Going to an altitude higher than what our bodies are accustomed to is something we may need to cope with from time to time. When exercising at higher altitudes, aerobic power is diminished because of the lowered oxygen pressure in the air. "Hypoxia" is the name of this phenomenon. Those who travel from sea level to higher altitudes need to take precautions to respect the change in elevation. Altitude acclimatization, meaning the body's adaptation to altitude, must be accomplished gradually.

To prevent altitude sickness at higher elevations, heavy exertion must not happen in the first few days until the body has become used to decreased oxygen in the atmosphere. Symptoms of altitude sickness include dizziness, weakness, headache, nausea and vomiting. Those who are in excellent physical shape will not notice the change in environment as much as an unfit person. The blood lactate concentration rises at high workload more rapidly than it does at sea level and the result is that aerobic exercise changes to anaerobic much sooner.

It is interesting to note just how much altitude decreases a person's performance capabilities as they go to higher and higher elevations. Scientists have measured an average oxygen consumption decrease of around 3.5 percent for every 300 meters, or approximately 1,000 feet. But it has also been proven that cardiac output rises out of proportion to oxygen decrease in the atmosphere. When maximal work is done at 2,300 meters (7,550 feet) such as in places like Mexico City or many areas of Colorado, the body's oxygen transport capacity is reduced by about 15 percent and reduced by 30 percent at 4,000 meters (13,000 feet).

Those moving into a higher altitude should recognize the following precepts:

- Full acclimatization may take more than a month or even several months depending on an individual's physical fitness.
- The rate of acclimatization is not affected by brief visits to sea level.
- During the first days at higher altitude there will be a marked reduction in work capacity.
- Altitude training has a small beneficial affect on sea level performance, but acclimatized individuals have a marked advantage on those who are new to altitude.
- Dehydration occurs rapidly at altitude because of very dry air and increased water loss through the respiratory tract; there must be an increase in fluid intake.
- There is more intense solar ultraviolet radiation at high altitudes, which causes increased susceptibility to sunburn and snow blindness.
- The mean annual temperature is about 4 degrees lower for each 1,000-foot rise in altitude, depending on the latitude.
- Sprinting or other anaerobic activities that last for a minute or less are not affected by high altitude and may even be enhanced because of lowered air resistance.

A dramatic change in altitude requires a period of acclimatization if one wishes to avoid the miseries of altitude sickness or even death from pulmonary edema (fluid in the lungs). An average person, dropped on a mountain in the Himalayas at an altitude of 24,000 feet or more without acclimatization, would lose consciousness in about 10 minutes and possibly die in a half hour. A mountain climber, on the other hand, who has gradually ascended to that altitude might camp there for several days without harm. Be prepared for a rapid change in altitude if you wish to avoid problems associated with the new environment.

Coping with Air Pollution

If you live or walk in a major metropolitan city, you are undoubtedly faced with varying degrees of air pollution. Modern pollutants are definite threats to quality of life. While some harmful substances may not be troublesome by themselves, their combination with other pollutants can produce potent biological effects. Experts say that carbon monoxide and tobacco smoke cause the most harmful effects on the human body. Exercise increases the amount of pollutants taken into the lungs. On the worst days, difficult breathing, chest pains, nausea or vomiting might be experienced.

When certain metropolitan areas get into the season of temperature inversions and the resulting higher concentrations of pollutants, it is interesting to know what bad effects exercisers are experiencing, breathing less-than-clean air. The publication *Atmospheric Research* suggests that air pollution truly does adversely affect breathing capacity and performance during training and competition.

The content of air pollution absorbed by the lungs during exercise is much higher than that absorbed during periods of rest because of the more rapid and deeper breathing through both the mouth and nose. For example, sulfur dioxide, which is a highly water-soluble gas, is almost entirely absorbed in the upper respiratory tract during nasal breathing. With heavy oral breathing a significant decrease in upper airway absorption occurs, resulting in a significantly larger dose of this pollutant being delivered to the lower part of the airway system.

Several controlled human studies have shown that the combination of exercise and pollution exposure (sulfur dioxide or ozone) caused a marked bronchoconstriction and reduced passage of air when compared with breathing polluted air while at rest. If you are in excellent physical condition, then you are in a better position to overcome air pollution's harmful effects even though performance is being adversely affected. Because of pollution, the oxygen available to the exerciser becomes somewhat reduced. Exercising in these conditions can be likened to training at higher altitudes as far as effort is concerned, and endurance is reduced.

13 Walking and Pregnancy

"The risk of health to the fetus during pregnancy for women performing aerobic exercise appears to be very low, especially if established guidelines for exercising during pregnancy are followed."
—Jack H. Wilmore, Ph.D.
and David Costill, Ph.D.

Doctors have long been concerned about fetuses during exercise because the temperature of the body rises during exercise with an attendant increase in cell metabolism. They have theorized that the growing and dividing embryonic cells would be killed by increasing the metabolic load on the body and that the exercise would divert blood supply from the internal organs associated with the fetus to the working muscles and the skin. They wondered if this would restrict oxygen and nutrient supply to the fetus and inhibit removal of waste products. Doctors and the general population thought that jarring, heat-producing activities such as running could have very detrimental results. This is no longer true. For those women who become pregnant, rest assured that even vigorous activities such as racewalking will not harm your fetus.

In a 10-week study by Dr. James F. Clapp III, an obstetrician at Vermont University, it was found that exercise was safe even in the late stages of pregnancy with pregnant women who exercised from less than one hour to six and one-half hours per week. The study was conducted on 49 women runners, 38 aerobic dancers and 28 controls who did very little exercise at all. The subjects could raise their heart rates to a high level and produce significant body heat with no harm done. This should make women who are partaking in the nonjarring action of walking feel doubly safe as they keep their bodies in excellent shape.

Every woman should evaluate her own needs, athletic ability, medical history and her own "gut" feeling about her body. She should cease exercise if she experiences dizziness, shortness of breath, palpitations, pain or bleeding. These disturbing symptoms can occur if a woman exerts herself beyond what her body is conditioned for. The worst thing she could do for her fetus is to sit around and engage in no exercise at all. The condition of the fetus is tied directly to the condition of its mother. Dr. Clapp found that the incidence of problems such as miscarriage and placental abnormalities were very similar to those in the population at large. In addition, he proved that pregnant exercisers demonstrated better body efficiency and used less oxygen for specific tasks than nonpregnant exercisers.

Guidelines for Exercise during Pregnancy and Postpartum

The following guidelines, taken from the American College of Obstetricians and Gynecologists, are based on the unique physical and physiologic conditions that exist during pregnancy and the postpartum period. They outline general criteria for safety to provide direction to patients in the development of home exercise programs.

Pregnancy Only

1. Maternal heart rate should not exceed 140 bpm.
2. Strenuous activities should not exceed 15 minutes in duration.
3. No exercise should be performed in the supine position after the fourth month of gestation.
4. Exercises that employ the Valsalva maneuver (forceful holding of the breath causing excess pressure in the intra-abdominal cavity) should be avoided.
5. Caloric intake should be adequate to meet not only the extra energy needs of pregnancy but also of the exercise performed.
6. Maternal core temperature should not exceed 100.4° F.

Pregnancy and Postpartum

1. Regular exercise (at least three times per week) is preferable to intermittent activity. Strenuous competitive activities should be discouraged.
2. Vigorous exercise should not be performed in hot, humid weather or during a period of febrile (with fever) illness.
3. Ballistic movements (jerky, bouncy motions) should be avoided. Exercise should be done on a wooden floor or a tightly carpeted surface to reduce shock and provide a sure footing.
4. Deep extension of the joints should be avoided because of connective tissue laxity. Activities that require jumping, jarring motions or rapid changes in direction should be avoided because of joint instability.
5. Vigorous exercise should be preceded by a five-minute period of muscle warm-up. This can be accomplished by slow walking or stationary cycling with low resistance.
6. Vigorous exercise should be followed by a period of gradually declining activity that includes gentle stationary stretching. Because connective tissue laxity increases the risk of joint injury, stretches should not be taken to the point of maximum resistance.
7. Heart rate should be measured at times of peak activity. Target heart rates and limits established in consultation with the physician should not be exceeded.
8. Care should be taken to gradually rise from the floor to avoid orthostatic hypotension (lack of blood to the brain). Some form of activity involving the legs should be continued for a brief period.

9. Liquids should be taken liberally before and after exercise to prevent dehydration. If necessary, activity should be interrupted to replenish fluids.
10. Women who have led sedentary lifestyles should begin with physical activity of very low intensity and advance levels very gradually.
11. Activity should be stopped and a physician consulted if any unusual symptoms appear.

14 Fitness Motivations

"Desire is the key to motivation, but it's the determination and commitment to an unrelenting pursuit of your goal—a commitment to excellence—that will enable you to attain the success you seek."
—Mario Andretti

Although walking has the lowest dropout rate of any major exercise in the United States, no exercise program is likely to be maintained unless it is enjoyable. Strolling at very slow speeds can be enjoyable and good for mental health, but does little to benefit physical health—it is so easy to do that it doesn't qualify as aerobic exercise. Brisk walking is necessary to achieve the joys of fitness. It is inherently enjoyable once a person starts to get into reasonable shape, but there may be some fatigue, muscle soreness and weary feet at first. It doesn't take long to get to the point where it is pure joy to get out and stretch your legs and ventilate your lungs.

What should you do to keep your motivation up in the beginning stages of aerobic walking? You can find ways to make it more convenient and enjoyable. Pick out the most pleasant routes you can find, away from heavily traveled streets or roads. Most parks are excellent places, and trails through the woods can be fantastic. Determine the most logical time of day for your own particular situation and try to make it a habit to set aside 30 uninterrupted minutes or more for the activity.

Setting and Achieving Goals

Establish achievable goals in your walking program. Don't "bite off more than you can chew." Goal setting is an important motivational tool. Goals that are unreasonably tough to attain, however, can cause a stressful situation. Flexibility in establishing your own personal goals is important to success in obtaining real benefits. If you use a moderate approach, are patient and look only for gradual improvement, you are on the right track.

Seek the support of your family members or friends, or ask them to join you in the activity. Walking can be a very social and pleasant activity when shared with others. Learn to relax as you develop a rapid, fluid stride. Tight muscles tire easily so relaxing them is important. Allow your body to unwind and flow through the movements. If you get breathless or if you have difficulty talking to your walking partner it is time to slow down until you are more comfortable. Learn what your training heart rate range should be and try to stay within that range. You will soon notice the difference between your working and resting heart rates.

A great advantage to an aerobic walking program is that it eventually gets you in such good shape you will be able to participate in practically any other activity that you choose. In this way you can broaden your interests and make life more interesting. Experiencing a new area is much more interesting and intimate when experienced at an ambulatory 3 or 4 miles per hour than from a car or bus window. There is no better way to capture the essence and flavor of a new place visited than to amble through it. When possible, we have the opportunity to save money by walking to places instead of driving.

Remember that no one else but you can make the commitment to improve your health and well-being. You should realize that a workout is one-fourth perspiration (or physical exertion) and three-fourths determination (or self-discipline). In truth, the hardest part is just to start moving—after that it is easy. It is a personal triumph over laziness and procrastination—a sign that you have taken charge of your own destiny. It is an investment in excellence. You can release a vast untapped reservoir of energy that you never knew you had. The human body gets stronger as you use it more and more, which gives you an excellent return from your investment of time and energy. Most of all you will increase your self-esteem and feel much better about yourself.

Here are some ideas to consider so that you can better decide what your realistic goals for success should be:

1. List some barriers that might prevent you from reaching your goal and think about how can you counteract them.
2. Think of people who might assist you in reaching your goal and try to get their support.
3. Think of ways to personally assess your chances for success.
4. If you achieve your goal, what are the possible positive or negative outcomes?
5. Can you think of ways to combat the possible negative outcomes?
6. List ways and means that will help you start on your way toward your fitness goal and make an honest effort to carry them out.

Following these suggestions will not guarantee that you will remain motivated to be a fit and active walker the rest of your life, but they should help. Intelligent management of mind and body will allow you to take charge of your own destiny, and through your walking program you will exercise yourself into excellent fitness.

15 Learning Efficient Walking

"Nothing ever becomes real until it is experienced—even a proverb is no proverb till your life has illustrated it."
—John Keats

In teaching people to walk efficiently, the biggest hurdle to overcome seems to be faulty habits that have become automatic motor patterns over many years. Certain unconscious movements become so ingrained that a great deal of concentration is needed to change them and make walking form and style more efficient. Children are the easiest to teach because lack of inhibitions, self-consciousness and tightness in the body and joints allow them to be great imitators. All you need to do with youngsters is let them walk behind you and tell them to imitate. This does not work well with adults, especially in their first walking session. Adults, except for the most coordinated, must concentrate on one movement at a time until that motion is learned correctly and they can move on to the next movement. In most cases it takes three sessions with a week of practicing in between sessions to get adults "into the groove" with reasonable coordination.

Established modalities related to body movement may aid people wishing to racewalk or fitness walk more efficiently and to speed up the learning process. The Feldenkrais technique, developed by Moshe Feldenkrais in the mid-twentieth century, teaches the conscious control of nerve and muscle. Throughout life many people suffer increasingly from sensory motor amnesia, in which specific motor responses are characterized by a restricted range of movement, a tightness caused by muscle contractions that we don't voluntarily release by relaxing them. We don't give a second thought to this tightness and we forget the motor patterns that allow us to move about with flexibility, looseness and freedom from stiffness. Our muscles do not flow through their normal range of motion as freely as in the past.

The Feldenkrais technique could be just the ticket to let our bodies and minds work together to alleviate tension and lack of mobility. This method was developed from a lifelong study of the mechanics of human movement and how they relate to behavior and learning. It has to do mainly with unlearning habits that cause poor posture and tightness in the body. This is accomplished by learning motor awareness and adopting unconventional muscle movement through the mind—that is, by making unconscious movements conscious.

Feldenkrais once explained that, "To begin with the lessons take place in the lying position, prone or supine, to facilitate the breakdown of muscular patterns so that gravity does not exert the same pressures on the soles of the feet and the joints." A series of exercises follow, done as slowly and as pleasantly as possible with no strain or pain. The exercises help the person come to terms with his or her body until by the end of the lessons the individual feels as if their body is hanging lightly from the head, gliding with every movement. Feldenkrais calls this "Awareness Through Movement," which is also the title of his book on the subject.

All personal actions are composed of four components: movement, sensation, feeling and thought. A melding of all four is the optimal condition. Unfortunately, as we grow older, it seems that our movements are to a great extent governed by societal pressures and accepted images. Our coordination and exercise potentials can become severely limited because we have no idea what is happening, and the longer these conditions exist, the worse they become. Many are doomed to wind up walking with an old-age shuffle caused by restricted range of movement of the necessary muscles, tendons and joints. Feldenkrais realized that awareness of our own movements—that conscious unorthodox movements—are the key to changes in the motor cortex to give us better control of ourselves. We can then learn to freely choose motor patterns more appropriate to certain new movements and thus learn to walk more efficiently.

In his book *Somatics*, Thomas Hanna wrote the following regarding improving walking:

> If the muscles in the center of the body gradually become stiff, the ability to walk is gradually diminished. The pelvis does not rotate horizontally as you step forward; nor does it move upward and downward as the weight comes off and onto the leg; nor does the leg twist, so that the right arm and shoulder come forward as the left hip and leg come forward ... . As this stiffness in the center of the body increases, and as a person becomes accustomed to this diminished ability in moving the pelvis and trunk, the art of walking is forgotten. Sensory motor amnesia occurs, and one cannot help walking like an "old person." Humans are the only creatures on earth that walk on two legs with the arms swinging freely in counterbalance. That is why you will find it so deeply satisfying to experience the wonderful circular movement of the hip that occurs in smooth, effortless walking.

Mr. Hanna has developed some excellent walking awareness exercises that can be done at home in a relaxing and nonthreatening atmosphere (without some instructor barking at you). The torso has our most powerful muscles, and is the main driving force in walking rapidly. Mr. Hanna's training exercises are excellent for racewalkers and fitness walkers alike in loosening up this part of the body. Even though he is not a racewalker, his principles fit them extremely well.

PART 3

Walking for Sport

16 Getting Started in Racewalking

"All glory comes from daring to begin."
—Ancient Proverb

The technique of racewalking is generally misunderstood by most of the American public. Inflexible and inefficient walking looks perfectly normal because people are not used to seeing others using their bodies to maximum efficiency and flexibility as they walk. People who walk in a relaxed manner move in the same way that racewalkers do except that their movements are far more subtle. Most children walk relaxed because they have no preconceived notions on how to walk "properly." When admonished by lifeguards not to run around the pool, they often unconsciously change from running to good racewalking form.

Racewalkers utilize the natural biomechanics of the body at the highest level for maximum performance. Simply stated, biomechanics is the way parts of the body work together for various movements as nature intended. When relaxed techniques are used properly, the body utilizes its biomechanics extremely well.

The best way to get started is to find someone knowledgeable in racewalking instruction to teach you the basics and offer constructive criticism (see appendix 8 for the addresses of contacts in each of the 50 states who can supply you with pertinent information on how to get started in racewalking). In many of the areas of the country there are classes in efficient walking put on by various organizations such as the YMCA, adult education programs, community colleges, corporations (for employees) and school districts. Olympic competitors and racewalking champions often use their valuable time to teach rank beginners how to get going. One such athlete is Carl Schueler of Colorado Springs, Colorado—known as the "Olympic God" because he made four consecutive Olympic racewalking teams in the period of 1980 to 1992. Ask around to find the best instructor for you. He or she can speed up the learning process tremendously. With proper initial instruction, the basics can be easily mastered.

The Growing Popularity of Racewalking

The United States is now experiencing an unprecedented rise in the popularity of the once obscure sport of racewalking. To the general public, the term "racewalking" formerly had a certain amount of stigma attached to it. Some sports commentators did not realize that the technique of racewalking, which has been developing for almost the entire century, was created to make fast walking as efficient as humanly possible. At this time, we can readily see a new breed of fitness walkers, health walkers and racewalkers flooding the pathways of America as health professionals everywhere are prescribing walking as the best and most convenient form of aerobic exercise. The media and shoe companies also are hyping fitness walking and racewalking as a valid and injury-free method to get into and stay in shape.

Why Racewalk?

Most people fall in love with this sport once they get involved. They enjoy its extremely low injury potential while getting great aerobic benefits. Perhaps there is no other sport in which participants have such an affinity and camaraderie. Many find it fun and others say it motivates them to keep in excellent shape with an incentive to "do better the next time." Others enjoy the carnival-like atmosphere at racewalking events. Racewalkers' energy levels mirror those of people decades younger. It seems to add more years to their life. It is a sport for all generations. There seems to be less jealousy of other walkers' ability than in runners, for example. Walkers often offer helpful advice to their competition. The constant dedication that is necessary to master excellent technique may have something that causes an indefinable common bond between those striving for the same goals. In addition, walkers, proud of their sport, have often been ridiculed for engaging in a "wimp" sport to which only those who cannot run well are relegated—a perception that walkers are glad to dispel. Other endurance athletes, especially elite ones, respect and admire the sport of racewalking.

Is Fast Walking Really Good for You?

Do you wonder why or how the sport is going to be good for you? Let's take a look at some of the specifics. Do not be misled by the perception that racewalking involves a highly complicated technique. In reality, it is just an extended version—an exaggeration, if you will—of ordinary walking movements. I have discovered that when I consciously relax every muscle in my body and start walking fast that the result is a "rag doll–looking" version of the accepted racewalking technique. Just because the speed of walking is increased, there is no change in the natural biomechanics of the body that converts a fitness or health walker into a racewalker.

Exercise Clothing

Deciding what to wear when exercising is mostly a matter of common sense. Comfort is very important, and weather has a great deal to do with what you wear. On warm days wear whatever you wish, but on cold and windy days avoid heavy clothing and instead use a light, layered approach. A good wind-breaker is essential if you live in cooler climes and should be used as the outer layer. There is a new generation of materials that are both waterproof and breathable. Unfortunately, all are somewhat expensive. Such fabrics include:

- ProMAX IV is a fairly new product that combines the warmth of spun polypropylene and the body-hugging fit, stretch and recovery of Lycra. The tight weave blocks out cold and wind.
- Gore-Tex, the original miracle fabric, is a thin microporous membrane of Teflon laminated to an outer layer of nylon.
- Action-Tek is a tightly knit fabric of polyester fibers that have been treated with a Teflon-like substance.
- Bion II is a thin, solid coating of polyurethane deposited on a breathable base fabric.
- Entrant is a microporous coating of polyurethane applied over a base fabric.
- Gamex is a high-density polyester knit in which the fibers are treated with a fluorocarbon.
- Helly-Tech is a microporous coating of polyurethane on Tactel, which is a nylon that looks and feels like cotton.
- Permia is a microporous abrasion-resistant coating on a base fabric.
- Savina DP is a polyester and nylon fabric that is shrunk then treated with a water repellent.
- Versa-Tech is a soft, lightweight, densely woven fabric of fine polyester fibers.

If you can afford it, these state-of-the-art, all-weather fabrics are excellent. If you can't, there are low-priced suits of nylon, lycra and polyesters available. However, an old-fashioned sweat suit or anything else that is not too heavy and will protect you from the elements is just fine. Cotton undergarments are good, and Norwegian net underwear is great for cold weather. Nylon or polypropylene running shorts are a good investment as they are durable and light. Lycra tights are excellent for cool days.

The Rules

The two essential rules in the racewalking technique are: 1) one foot must be on the ground at all times, and 2) the supporting leg must straighten as the heel strikes the ground and then remain straight until in the vertical upright position. People who walk with their knees and quadriceps relaxed straighten their knees when walking because as the heel lands and the leg pulls the body forward, the result is a straight leg. Lifting the toes at heel strike is an important factor in aiding the leg to straighten naturally. Perhaps you will discover that you have been walking with tight knees without realizing it ever since childhood. Most people don't have much trouble with the lifting rule (not staying on the ground) unless they adopt a jogging mode of progression or they try to go too fast for their ability. See chapter 17 for a detailed description of correct technique.

There are plenty of advantages for using fast walking as your exercise mode. The late, great running philosopher Dr. George Sheehan wrote: "Racewalkers are part of a ground swell that may become the wave of the future. The racewalker, for one thing, can make do with very ordinary feet. He can put miles and miles on feet that would break down in any other sport. ... Racewalking is virtually injury free."

The Five Training Basics

There are five training techniques for racewalking listed below in order of importance and sequence: training for technique, training for flexibility (massage, stretching, etc.), training for endurance, training for speed (sharpening), and training for strength. Training for flexibility and training for endurance can be worked on concurrently.

Understanding Training— The Training Effect Defined

The athletic training effect on the human body is almost never thought of except by coaches and athletes. But anyone who wishes to live life at its fullest should consider him- or herself an athlete at some level, whether that level is extremely high or extremely low. It all depends on the individual and their unique innate abilities.

When you get into racewalking and wish to increase your performance capabilities, you should become interested in the physiological changes that occur as a result of your program, such as increasing your aerobic capacity and lowering your body fat percentage. Training can help you attain better performances by paying systematic attention to how much, how often and how hard you exercise.

One principle of the training effect is that it must overload your present training capacity to some extent. This overload must be customized to the individual, which is why a competent instructor is so important in gaining steady improvement. If you start out completely untrained, large improvements in performance can be attained in a short time. In contrast, world-class athletes must train very hard to gain minimal increases because they are already approaching their ultimate capacity for work.

A person who undertakes a training program will inevitably experience "plateaus" where improvements seem to be on hold. Periodically they experience breakthroughs, providing they are consistent with a sensible training regimen. Reaching plateaus often discourages potential athletes because they think that they have leveled off at their best performance capacity, not realizing that improvements will come later. In reality, when you become comfortable on a particular plateau, it is time to increase intensity to pursue a higher level of fitness, endurance and speed.

Specificity of Exercise

In addition to this gradual increase in workload, you must remember that specificity of exercise is very important. For instance, sitting inside and working hard on your exercycle during the winter months may increase your aerobic capacity but not much in your walking ability. You must walk to be a good walker. That is the rule of specificity of exercise for the training effect. In addition to an increase in cardiovascular capacity, muscles directly involved in the exercise must undergo changes that increase their ability to utilize blood and oxygen more efficiently and to make them work harder than before. This is vital to improvement in performance. You may be a good marathon runner with superb conditioning for running long distances, but until you have trained the muscles that are specific to the racewalking movement, you cannot walk with the best walkers. Lack of specific walking training will cause you to become exhausted quickly if you try to comply with the rules of racewalking. Therefore, keep your training mostly oriented toward walking. Cross training is good to keep you from getting bored. Running is not too bad as a cross-training mode because its movements are more similar to walking than swimming, for example, but don't overdo it (see chapter 26 for advice on cross training).

Most people who take up walking and learn the technique don't care much for the pounding on the legs that running causes. By providing small overloads to the walking muscles systematically, you will find your times decreasing rather consistently until you start approaching your physiological limits.

Athletic Shoes for Fast Walking

Foot comfort is all-important to your walking program. Because shoes are the only major expense required in your walking program, and aching feet are the biggest disincentive to discourage you from continuing it, it is important not to skimp on good footwear. Most running shoes have the wrong heels, flexibility and cushioning for walking. There are, however, some running shoes that are better for walkers than others. Addidas and Reebok make shoes specifically for racewalking competition. These shoes are too lightweight and of too low durability to be used extensively in training. They do feel good, though, when you are trying to go fast in races.

The following brands and models are well made and therefore are not among the cheapest brands: Addidas (Race Walk or Advance Challenge), Avia, Asics (Gel Racer), Brooks (Chariot), Etonic, Mizuno (Phantom or Spider Racer), New Balance (640, 999 or MW600WB), Nike (Streak Lite), Reebok (Athletic Racewalker or Racer X) and Saucony (AYA, Instep RW or Speedwalker). Remember that shoe models inevitably change over time and some may be discontinued upon this reading, but if you know the characteristics that promote fast, efficient walking, you will usually find some models that will work for you whether they are running racing flats or specifically designed racewalking shoes. Remember, though, that most ordinary running shoes do not have the desirable characteristics required for efficient fast walking.

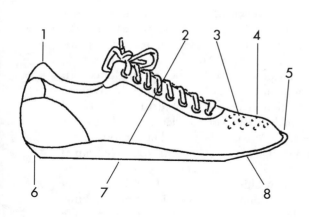

Many shoes labeled as walking shoes are heavy and durable with thick soles, which is fine for strolling around but not very amendable for going fast.

If you're having trouble finding the ideal shoe to conform to the sole of your foot, there are products now on the market that provide, for about $50, insoles that can be chemically activated to form exactly to the bottom of your foot. These are far less expensive than the normal, more rigid orthotics designed by podiatrists. One such insole, called Magifit, allows more of a natural foot action because of its flexibility combined with the custom fit. It is excellent in controlling overpronation (excessive rolling inward of the foot after the heel strike). These insoles can be placed in other shoes or hiking boots of the same size, provided that they are not too tight to begin with.

The numbers with explanations below relate to Art O-1 of the profile of a good racing shoe. One point to remember is that you don't need nearly the amount of padding in your shoe that the average runner needs. The bottom of the sole should be fairly smooth since knobs or other projections tend to trip you up when swinging the feet close to the walking surface. Look for a hard rubber durable sole. Shoes should be firm until just ahead of point 7, but should bend very easily ahead of that point. Conduct a torsion test by bending the toe clockwise and the heel counterclockwise. Torsional flexibility allows heel and toe to act independently, allowing for a more natural, smooth-flowing foot action and a smooth roll from outside of the heel at foot strike to a big toe push-off at the rear of the stride (7).

Avoid shoes that press into your Achilles tendon—this is a trait in many running shoes and causes discomfort when walking. Heels must be held firmly with no slipping while walking (1). Look for shoes that are rounded at the rear of the heel because the walking motion starts by landing on the heel and rolling off it (6). There should be a good, firm arch support.

The toe box should allow adequate room so that the toes are not pinched together. Test to see that there is about half an inch ahead of the toes when standing in the shoe (4, 5). There should be some type of ventilation such as perforation holes above the instep to keep the feet from getting sweaty (3).

Find shoes that are flexible at the midsole—if they are too rigid they will adversely affect the toe push-off of efficient walking (7, 8). Take out the innersole and look at the stitching on the sole (2). The best shoes are combination-lasted, which means that the heel is board-lasted (no stitching visible) and the forefoot has a stitch down the middle, making it more flexible for better toe push-off. Go for perfect foot comfort if you can find it—not just for style. If you can find both you are lucky. Having more than one brand or style of shoe can be helpful; if, for some reason, you develop a sore spot, you can switch to the other pair.

Additional Considerations

When purchasing shoes it is best to buy them from established athletic shoe stores. It is risky to order by mail, but that may be your only alternative. Ideally, you must be able to try the shoes by walking around a store to see if the particular shoe you are trying is comfortable right from the start. Check to find out if there are outlets in your area who deal with walkers regularly and who have an interest in fitting individuals with good shoes. Some stores even have treadmills for the customers to use. If you live in an area remote from shoe experts, you may be forced to do some research in magazines or other places to find what experts recommend for recreational walking shoes or performance shoes for racing. There are also web sites now on the Internet with good shoe information.

Shoe Lacing Techniques

Here are some shoe lacing techniques suggested by the Nike Shoe Company to accommodate different types of feet that can be implemented to increase comfort and walking efficiency.

If you need extra support.

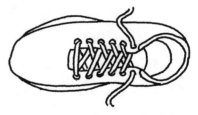

If your heel tends to slip up and down.

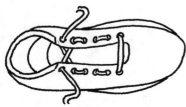

If you have a high instep.

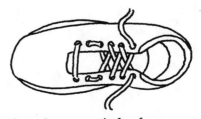

If you have a wide forefoot.

Discard Worn Shoes

It is advisable to discard shoes when they become badly worn, but often the soles wear faster than the uppers and can be restored satisfactorily with sole patching compounds or new soles. Don't let your heels wear down on the edge because it may throw your stride out of kilter, which could cause an accumulative injury-producing effect.

Custom Shoes

For those who don't mind spending more (around $120–$150) there is a custom-made racewalking shoe manufacturer in Wilton, Maine, named Hersey Custom Shoes. When the soles get a bit worn they can be sent in for resoling and made as good as new for around $25. Some of the good racewalkers are delighted with a custom-fitted shoe—they find the comfort and performance outstanding. This can be a good alternative for those who have abnormally big, small, narrow or wide feet. For more information, call Hersey at (207) 778-3103.

17 Technique Training

"Although a competitive racewalker may actually spend more time training for endurance, strength and speed, 'good technique' must be the primary goal of a racewalking training program, and all else must be secondary to that goal."

—Martin Rudow, former Olympic racewalking coach

Technique is by far the most important aspect of the sport of racewalking. If sound technique is not practiced from the beginning, faults in form will delay progress as the walker tries to walk at faster speeds. In order to do well, all competitors must use the same fundamental technique but still comply with the two essential racewalking rules mentioned in chapter 16—one foot must be on the ground at all times and the weight-bearing supporting leg must be straightened at heel strike until in the vertical position. The walker's "style" is an individual matter—it is the combination of body movements and attitudes that distinguish him or her from others. We are all different in body type, length of limbs, joint mobility, etc., which adds up to an individual style. In other words, your style is your own particular version of legal walking technique.

The Physical Benefits of Efficient Racewalking

Racewalking has had constant development since the early twentieth century in increasing the efficiency of technique in walking faster with less effort. Efficiencies are just as important for fitness walkers as for competitive walkers because, as champion walkers well know, even minor form faults when repeated thousands of times can be quite detrimental to technique and can jeopardize speed and efficiency of movement.

The physical benefits of racewalking are quite similar to long-distance running. Good walkers have an abundance of endurance and speed. Walking at higher speeds strengthens the leg muscles, stomach muscles, the flexor muscles of the hip and the muscles of the arms and lower back. In addition, rapid walking produces a considerable mobility in the shoulders, trunk, hips and ankles. Runners must, on the other hand, commonly do supplementary exercises to develop muscles in the upper body.

Racewalking is an extension of relaxed health and fitness walking—just done at a faster pace. The biomechanics of walking are the same regardless of pace. The slower you go, the less muscle movement results, but as you speed up, the muscular movements are extended. Correct racewalking form utilizes, strengthens and tones more of the body's muscular system than practically any other exercise. It is as aerobically beneficial as running and jogging, and even more so at higher speeds.

The Characteristics of the Movement

The technique of racewalking allows exercisers to get the maximum ambulatory speed possible, short of running. There is a feeling of pulling the ground surface beneath you (like a treadmill) as you move along. Maximum efficiency is gained if the leg is straight, providing a firm, level stride, but the rules allow the leg to bend after it has passed the vertical upright position. If the striding leg is allowed to bend under the body, the exercise mimics running in which the bent knee prevents efficient hip action and may cause the quadriceps to aid in a push-off similar to running. This is referred to as "creeping" or "bent knee."

If you want to walk fast efficiently, then it is essential that you learn and practice form correctly from the beginning. Do not attempt to walk too fast initially—the ability to walk with the best efficiency will not happen immediately. Technique is the first priority, endurance second and then speed. At first, you may find that the correct form is slower than a natural, rapid hiking pace, but as technique improves, so will speed and efficiency.

Body Posture Is Important

Be aware of a posture that will constantly maintain or improve forward progression and proper body balance whether you are walking uphill, downhill or on a flat, level surface. Maintain an upright body position with your hips directly under the upper body. Try to get the feeling of sitting on the hips. The pelvis must not be tilted. A tilted pelvis will cause a tense swayback position, decrease power and put strain on the lower back.

A slight lean of about 5 percent forward from the ankles at the time the toes are pushing off is good for purposes of maintaining momentum, but leaning too far forward will shorten the stride, put strain on the hamstring muscle and cause a flat-footed plant. Stand erect with no bending at the waist, keeping the chin up at all times and the eyes looking about 20 meters ahead. Don't let the head sway from side to side. The head makes up about 10 percent of the total body weight and can have a significant affect on technique. Incorrect head position can cause tension in the shoulder area, which can transfer to other parts of the body. Good posture means keeping the body straight in alignment and letting the body rotate around your central axis—your spine.

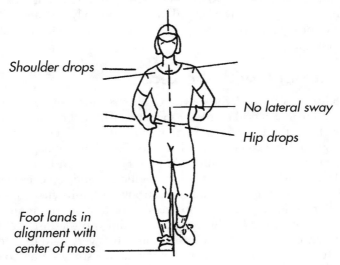

Vertical alignment perfectly straight

Shoulder drops

No lateral sway

Hip drops

Foot lands in alignment with center of mass

Get Hip to the Hips

Flexibility and relaxation of the hips is all-important since it allows the necessary rolling, dropping and twisting movements for the legs to move quickly and efficiently. The more the hip movement, the less strain on the legs. Good stride length will be achieved with the correct hip rolling and leg straightening style, which is the only way to maintain efficient and rapid leg movement. Only two things govern speed: stride length, which increases up to 8 inches through hip mobility, and stride frequency, which is often referred to as "turnover."

Rapid turnover of the legs is the biggest key to fast walking, and the stride length increases as a natural by-product of speed. Roll the hips and keep them pushing forward with a minimum of side movement. Exaggerated side movement of the hips is inefficient and looks ridiculous. In addition, body balance will be compromised by excessive side movements.

Place the leading foot down quickly in front of the trailing one so that the inner edges of the foot land on the same straight line. Increased flexibility in the hips and midsection will increase stride length. Strong driving action of the stomach, hips, lower back and waist allows faster movement with less effort and strain on the legs. Swing the front leg in landing on the heel with the toes pointed up and relax the knee, allowing it to straighten. If you overstride and put the heel too far in front, there will be a braking action until you pull your center of gravity over the weight-bearing leg. The leg can push much harder than it can pull. Research has shown that the most efficient stride at speed is about 30 percent to the front and 70 percent to the rear for most good walkers, but only 18 to 28 percent in front for national and world-class walkers—not an equilateral triangle at the instant of double contact. Riding over a straight leg aids in the hip rotating and twisting action and adds speed and smoothness to forward progress. Proper hip rolling eliminates all rising and falling of the upper body by absorbing it. If the body rises and falls during each stride through faulty technique such as a hiking style, a great deal of energy is wasted.

Drive Through with the Legs

As the body moves forward, the weight rolls across the outside edge of the foot to the toes. The foot acts like a rocker so that no part of the structure takes the entire weight of the body for more than an instant. When the trailing leg leaves the ground and swings forward, the knee bends just enough to allow the foot to skim just above the ground as it passes beneath the body. As the heel lands, splaying the toes in or out is very inefficient and can cause leg strain. The easiest way to get the feeling of a strong toe push-off is to walk up a significant grade and concentrate on keeping the foot on the ground on each stride until it forces itself to lift off. Avoid rolling on the inside of the foot since this may cause pain and eventual injury. It is very hard to land on the inside of the foot if the feet land on the ground in a straight line, so concentrate on the straight line and a lot of good things will happen automatically. Do not walk with the feet apart or strain in the groin will result. The swing phase allows the leg to relax before pressure on the ground is applied in the next stride. The quadriceps (front thigh muscles) should be very relaxed during the swing phase and then tighten slightly after heel strike to aid in knee straightening. In walking, the striding foot is on the ground for over two-thirds of the stride time, while in running it is on the ground one-third or less of the time, depending on speed and stride length.

Use Arms for Efficiency and Balance

Strive for consistent, relaxed and balanced arm action at all times. Balanced means that the actions of both arms are identical and that the range of the rear swing is equal to the front swing. The arms are moved as in normal walking, swinging counter to the legs but bent at about a 90-degree angle to allow a shorter and faster pendulum with the elbows close to the body. By using the word pendulum I mean that the fulcrum at the shoulder is completely relaxed, allowing the arm to swing free of any interference. The upper arms dangle straight from the shoulder socket in a fully relaxed fashion. Partially or totally straightening the arms puts the hands too far down at the sides, which causes blood to pool in the fingers and creates annoying swelling. The bend in the arms is a function of speed. At very slow speeds they dangle low at the sides, but as speed increases they naturally change the angle more and more until the 90-degree angle at the elbow occurs, which is seen in fast racewalking. In extremely fast walking, racers often close that angle down to 45 degrees or less to make the pendular action even faster.

Good arm action is necessary to counter the actions of the legs when walking at higher speeds. The action of the drive of the propelling leg acts up through the hip instead of through the center of the body. As one leg drives the body forward there is a twisting action of the trunk. The trunk is too heavy to twist unaided rapidly enough to keep up with a fast stride rate, and the resultant rotation is instead taken up with the arms. The arms, being lighter than the trunk, can move much more swiftly, and since they are moving counter to each other, they create a balancing effect on the motions. A good pendular action of the arms reacting with the hips can extend the hips' range of motion, which can have a positive effect on stride length. Avoid swaying the shoulders from front to back, a common fault in beginners. They should remain relatively stationary as the arms swing back and forth.

Keep in mind that while the leading arm is still going forward, the opposite leg will also be driving forward. The leading leg will not make contact with the ground until the arm drive stops. For this reason it is very hard on legal technique if you drive the arms too far ahead of the torso. Similarly, as long as the rear arm is being driven backward, the rear foot will remain in contact with the ground, thus allowing more time for the leading foot to make contact. For this reason it is better to concentrate on pulling the arm backward rather than forcing it to the front. Pulling it too far back, however, will lift the shoulder and cause tension.

Do *not* let the elbows "chicken wing" out to the side because the arms will then swing from side to side rather than from front to back. Vectors of force to the side are useless in propelling you forward. The hands should never swing past the centerline of the body in front. Let the hands move naturally to the front but no higher than the breastbone, since driving them any higher expends extra energy and may lift you off the ground, which is illegal in races anyway. An oval movement of the elbow caused by relaxing over a straight leg will cause the shoulders to roll and get the side muscles into the action. This movement can be exaggerated at first as a training aid, but should become more subtle as technique improves. Be careful not to hunch the shoulders or lift them above their normal position since this tightens the neck and shoulder muscles, wastes energy and causes fatigue sooner. A rigid upper body limits the motions of the arms and may reduce effective hip motion. The muscles that are responsible for the arm extension and retraction of the arms in their pendulums need to be loose and efficient for good walking form. Without their use, or if they are too tight and rigid, much extension and power is lost.

The hands should be held with the thumbs up and a loosely clenched fist. This seems to be the most effective position for generating power and maintaining a relaxed position. Don't walk with the palms facing up or down, and don't let the wrists and hands flap loosely. This angles the force in the wrong direction, lengthens the arm pendulum and results in a loss of efficient power in the arm swing.

You Must Remain Relaxed

The most important point to remember is that the more relaxed you are in doing any of these described movements—whether in the legs, upper body or arms—the faster and more efficient you will be as a walker. All of this advice

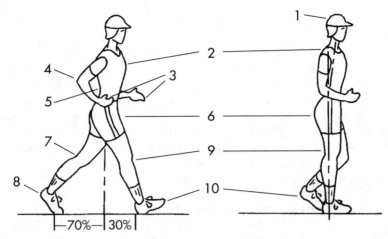

Front and back stride percentage for nonelite athletes.

Forward lean varies throughout stride and averages about 5 percent.

is not as complicated as it sounds, because these movements are merely extensions of natural movements and will become automatic as soon as speed increases—that is, if you truly relax. Relaxed form will allow the firing muscles to act without any interference from other muscles. Many high-level competitors constantly remind themselves to relax to go faster. The above diagram shows the correct racewalking form.

Now let's review the elements in correct racewalking form:

1. Head aligned with body, neck relaxed, no side movement, eyes focused at least 20 meters ahead; do not bob the head up and down.
2. Shoulders relaxed, minimal rotation in opposition to hips, small drop at midstride over weight-bearing leg.
3. Hands relaxed in comfortable position with thumbs pointed up. Swing arms forward along waistband. Never cross body centerline in front; never let arms rise above sternum; pull arms back until hand is near rear of buttocks; do not drive forward vigorously.
4. Elbows bent at 90 degrees or less depending on speed. The higher the speed the sharper the angle.
5. Back must neither be flat nor arched, since it will interfere with hip rotation and cause strain.
6. Hip rises slightly over weight-bearing leg, rotate front to back with no side sway; must be very relaxed to allow maximum rotation; upper body does not rise or fall since hips absorb vertical movements.
7. Leg nearly straight until time of toe push-off; push-off power comes from rear of leg and ankle muscles, not the quads.
8. Foot rolls to nearly vertical at push-off; toe pushes directly to rear aided by ankle and calf muscles.
9. Knee remains straight from time of heel strike until in vertical position; knees must be relaxed to allow straightening.

10. Heel strikes ground with toes pointed forward between 20 and 40 degrees; land with toes pointed straight ahead; feet should always be very close to walking surface.

Common Faults and How to Correct Them

It might be advantageous to address some common faults in walking and racewalking and the various solutions in how to correct them.

FAULT: Walking with the head leaning forward.
CAUSE: This is a common fault of beginners and is caused mainly by fatigue or lack of concentration on good form. This fault can affect balance and breathing.
SOLUTION: It is easily corrected by just straightening up and concentrating on holding the head erect.

FAULT: Bending forward at the waist instead of leaning from the ankles.
CAUSE: This is a very common fault. When a reduction in stride length results, it makes it difficult to straighten the leading leg. Usually caused by fatigue from underdeveloped back and stomach muscles, this fault can strain the lower back.
SOLUTION: Concentrate on walking tall so that the body is straight from the feet to the shoulders with a slight forward lean only from the ankles.

FAULT: Overstriding.
CAUSE: Swinging leg is forced too far in front of the body's center of gravity. This can also be caused by incomplete straightening of the striding leg, bending it too soon or lifting the forward-moving leg too high off the ground.
SOLUTION: To correct this, work on a faster stride rate, keeping the striding leg braced as long as possible and moving the other foot close to the ground as it goes forward.

FAULT: Feet not landing in a straight line.
CAUSE: This may be from lack of balance, walking too slowly or swinging the hips laterally.
SOLUTION: This fault can be corrected by walking with the heels landing on either side of a marked straight line. Experiment with your arm action to see if it is causing lack of balance.

FAULT: Feet splayed to outside.
CAUSE: This often happens when you walk with the feet too far apart or have problems balancing. This causes diminished lack of drive off the toes and a tendency for the rear leg to flex too soon. It is a common fault for people who have flat feet or a tendency to walk that way normally.
SOLUTION: Exercises to strengthen the feet often will help here. Practice walking with the feet in a straight line with the toes pointed directly

ahead. If you cannot correct this by concentrating on it, a podiatrist may need to be consulted.

FAULT: Lateral swinging of the hips.

CAUSE: This fault may occur from too forced a hip action instead of using a more relaxed, natural rolling action or from a lateral swinging of the arms caused by "chicken winging" the elbows out away from the body. This can cause tension in the trunk, loss of balance and a waste of energy.

SOLUTION: The arms should dangle off a loose shoulder socket. It may be necessary to slow down to work on smooth striding and to move the arms to the front and back instead of side to side.

FAULT: Stride length too short.

CAUSE: The main cause is insufficient hip mobility and movement.

SOLUTION: The best solution is to work on hip stretching and mobility exercises. See chapter 19 on flexibility training.

FAULT: Lack of straightening the striding leg.

CAUSE: This fault is very important to be aware of because it results in disqualification in judged events. It can be caused by a walker trying to go too fast, bringing the trailing foot forward too high and not landing the foot with the toes pointed up at an angle to the ground. It may also be caused by weak quadriceps (front of thigh) or inflexible muscles in the back of the leg.

SOLUTION: The way to correct this fault is to slow down by concentrating on pushing back with the supporting leg throughout the complete stride. Always land on the heel with the toes pointed up. Work on strengthening the quads and stretching out the hamstrings and calf muscles.

FAULT: Backward lean of body.

CAUSE: This fault is caused by weak back and stomach muscles and results in a jarring of the back and a shortened stride length. Often there is a "bouncy" look caused by this fault.

SOLUTION: Usually it can be corrected by concentrating on leaning forward from the ankles and strengthening the back and stomach muscles.

FAULT: Tilting of the pelvis and resultant swayback.

CAUSE: One of the most common and troublesome faults, it is caused by lack of abdominal muscle strength and lack of flexibility in the lower back muscles. This poor posture causes weak, ineffective hip action and lack of power. In this posture it is almost impossible to attain proper vertical and horizontal hip action.

SOLUTION: Correction consists of doing hip and lower back flexibility and stretching exercises. Do curl-up exercises and curl-ups with rotation to strengthen the abdominals. Make a special effort to stand tall with the upper body directly over the hips while walking. Consciously rotate the pelvis forward over the striding leg.

FAULT: "Bouncy" trunk action.
CAUSE: Caused either by lifting the supporting leg off the ground before foot has rolled past the ball of the foot onto the toes or because the hips are not rolling properly. This may cause lifting off the ground or a shortened stride length and results in disqualification from judged events.
SOLUTION: Correction is to slow down by concentrating on full range of motion of the driving foot. Work on increased mobility of the ankle and hips.

FAULT: Uncoordinated and excessive arm action.
CAUSE: This comes from lack of knowledge of proper arm action or attempting to walk too fast for current ability. When the arms swing too far in front, it creates an unequal pendular action and lack of balance and can cause tension in the upper body.
SOLUTION: This fault can be corrected by stationary walking in front of a mirror, concentrating on correct compact front and back arm action and walking at slower speeds until corrected.

FAULT: Leading foot appears to fall upon landing.
CAUSE: This is caused by swinging foot through too high because of lack of vertical hip movement, weak ankle and shin muscles or not landing on outside edge of foot.
SOLUTION: The fault can be corrected by improving hip flexibility and attempting to keep the foot skimming as close to the ground as possible during its swing phase. Sometimes it helps to pretend you are kicking a pebble with the bottom of your heel as the foot swings forward.

One of the best ways to correct faults is to have videotapes made of your form and then have them analyzed by a knowledgeable instructor. Even better is to have videotapes made on the spot and played back directly afterward for analyzation. It is best to get faults corrected as soon as they are detected. The longer they have been present the harder they are to correct.

Walking Up or Down Gradients

When walking uphill, try to keep your normal cadence but with a shortened stride length. A little extra forward lean is fine as you drive with the toes up the hill. However, if the forward lean is exaggerated, it becomes very difficult to bring the swinging leg through properly. It can be helpful to bend the elbows to an angle sharper than 90 degrees.

When walking downhill, there is a great danger of losing contact with the ground. If the body's center of gravity moves too far forward and excessive forward rotation occurs, it becomes very difficult to maintain double contact, especially if overstriding occurs. Many walkers adopt a slight backward lean when encountering a down gradient, which causes jarring of the back and legs when landing on the heel. That makes it hard to get the heel down before the rear foot leaves the ground. It is vital that the upper body remain as relaxed as possible, especially when walking down a gradient. Good walkers with proper technique can walk with their bodies perpendicular to the slope. Frequency of stride can be increased since gravity aids in pulling you along.

Efficient Technique Is Good for All

It is mentally stimulating and fun to practice the components of a good style by working on one thing at a time until perfected. You will naturally feel when things fall into place and efficiency and speed improves. You get a sense of accomplishment as you conquer the elements of good form. The techniques of good posture, hip rotating, riding over a straight leg, proper foot rolling and arm pumping apply to everyone regardless of age, body conditioning or body type. Everyone can take advantage of the beneficial effects on the total body.

Our best American walker of the late 1960s and early 1970s was Larry Young of Missouri, who won two Olympic bronze medals. He likened racewalking to a combination of the agility and strength of gymnastics, the grace of dancing and the endurance of distance running. As flexibility and strength are gained in the motions and positions of this healthful exercise, a smooth style will develop that is naturally suited to your unique body build and current level of fitness. You will begin to feel rhythm and ease as the ground flows below you, moving with the same sense of confidence and grace that a champion racewalker has. The best racewalkers do better than seven minutes per mile in races by using an efficient technique.

However, do not expect good technique to happen immediately. It often takes a fair amount of time to learn to roll the hips effectively. In a few weeks almost anyone who gets a little instruction from an experienced racewalking teacher can learn reasonably efficient form. It can take years, though, to develop a flawless form such as those that some champions have. This fact may be more of an advantage than a disadvantage since it challenges a person to improve efficiency little by little during each practice session.

18 | Endurance Training

"Once one has the strength to perform a repetitive task, additional improvement in performance will depend on muscular endurance."
—Brian J. Sharkey, Ph.D.

Walkers must develop a base endurance to work from. Base endurance, as it is enhanced, is the capacity to walk at moderate speeds for longer and longer periods of time. This is the very next priority after technique training. A trainee gains endurance by taking long walks at cruising speed. This is true for both fitness walkers and racewalkers, but is more vital for racers. All the technique and speed in the world does little good unless there is proper endurance to keep it going for an adequate amount of time. To be successful in endurance walks, the walker needs to develop some of the following attributes:

1. A reasonably high maximum oxygen uptake value (VO_2 max) developed with training.
2. A high lactate threshold (becoming more resistant to buildup of lactic acid in the muscles through training).
3. A high economy of effort (the ability to do more work for the same oxygen uptake).
4. Development of slow twitch muscle fibers (the percentage of these is largely determined early in life but can increase with training and age).

Progressive Stress Adaptation

Base conditioning must be developed over time—strength and endurance will not happen overnight. The body gradually adapts to higher and higher levels of stress through a process called progressive stress adaptation, which was first promulgated in the 1950s book *The Stress of Life*, by Dr. Hans Selye, the world's foremost researcher on stress. Progressive stress adaptation base training develops the circulatory system and capillary buildup in those areas that are stressed by exercise. Stress adaptation can be improved gradually over many years, and only at a slow rate. There is no way to speed up the process. Sometimes short bursts of faster walking can be done early in a training program, but they do no good unless there is a base of endurance to support them for longer distances. Too much speed before adequate technique is attained can cause bad habits such as pushing off a flat foot and lifting off the ground, which causes a modified "jogging mode." It has been found by coaches that athletes can adapt to stress more easily, both physically and mentally, if they use a variety of distances and routes in their training. Changes can help avoid boredom and keep enthusiasm alive.

Build Up Endurance Slowly

Although endurance base training is built up slowly, its effects are long lasting and not easily lost. This good base, built up from a large amount of training at a moderate pace, fortunately allows competitors to reduce their training and essentially race at the same pace for long periods of time. Endurance comes from the conditioning and buildup of the cardiorespiratory system and the metabolic processes of the body to delay fatigue. Unless the walker gets in shape by putting in the miles, progress will be painfully slow regardless of technique and the walker will be far more susceptible to breakdown. Base training, because of its nonstraining nature, tends to keep the walker fresh and resistant to strain and possible illness. Walks of an hour or more at a moderate pace several times per week can build up a very good base if done persistently over a long period of time, such as a year or more.

The Aerobic-Anaerobic Threshold

People serious about enhancing their endurance should work within their aerobic-anaerobic threshold area. Experience indicates that for most people, the aerobic state, in which a steady oxygen supply to the heart and muscles is maintained, lies below 130 bpm during exercise. The anaerobic (oxygen depletion) state normally occurs above 150 bpm. At this rate one tires rapidly and the waste by-product of insufficient oxygen to the muscles—lactic acid—builds up, diminishing the muscles' ability to perform work. Between heart rates of 130 to 150 bpm, the system is being stressed enough to get the optimum effects of progressive stress adaptation. Oxygen is carried through the system in the red blood cells, but many of these cells are destroyed in hard training. Racewalking is an exercise in which the feet are constantly hitting the ground and the muscles are continuously taxed enough to cause red cell depletion. This is especially true when training increases in intensity and can become a problem if there is not enough rest between hard training sessions and the principles of good nutrition are neglected. Progressive stress adaptation comes to the rescue in this case and the body begins to manufacture more red blood cells to overcome the deficiency.

The capillary network is instrumental in getting the oxygen and energy fuel (glucose) in the blood from the heart to the muscle tissues. A lot of racewalking must be done in order to increase the specific supply routes to the muscles needed for the sport. As the exercise progresses and muscles and joints are worked longer, the surrounding capillary network compensates and expands so that the red blood cell supplies are increased where needed. Endurance training is the way to get this beneficial effect on the circulatory system as an aid to progressive adaptation to rapid walking.

As the walker gets into better shape, the fuel supply—glucose that is stored in the muscles as glycogen—to the muscles and liver is increased, providing needed energy to the body. We know that the best source for this glycogen comes from ingesting complex carbohydrates. When training commences, the first glucose to be used is the small amount in the bloodstream. When that is used up, stored glucose in the muscles and liver is converted back into glucose for energy release. If the training is overly strenuous, the dreaded lactic acid builds up rapidly as a waste by-product and causes a deterioration in the efficiency of movement of the muscles affected. This happens when anaerobic work is done—it cannot proceed for a long time. If the work is aerobic in nature, the amount of stored glycogen may be good for 16 or 18 miles and even more in highly trained individuals.

Increasing the anaerobic threshold through endurance training also increases the amount of work a walker can do in the aerobic state, and less effort will be used to move at a certain pace. He or she can do this by training periodically at 5 kilometers or longer at near race pace, but if it is done more than once or twice a week there is danger of getting overstressed. In recent developments, researchers are questioning the need for long daily workouts. Many feel that some endurance athletes have developed a "mileage mania" to such an extent that it becomes counterproductive and risky to the hazards of overtraining. Training programs must use rest and changes of volume and intensity to avoid excess stress on the body.

The wise trainer will always take care to build up both the intensity and distance aspects of training gradually, building up aerobic capacity and always thinking of gradual progressive stress adaptation to avoid problems that may be brought on by overstressing the system. The walker will gradually build up strength and endurance in little plateaus, gaining more and more with time.

19 Flexibility Training

"We can learn a lot by observing animals. Watch a cat or dog. They instinctively know how to stretch. They do so spontaneously, never overstretching, continually and naturally tuning up muscles they will have to use."

—Bob Anderson, from his book
Stretching

Stretching comes high on the list of activities for keeping the body toned and resistant to injury. Everyone can benefit from a sensible stretching program no matter what age or physical condition. Tight muscles, ligaments and tendons create the potential for injury when they are extended too rapidly beyond their normal range of motion. If stretching is not done correctly, the body can suffer from harmful side effects. One harmful technique is called "ballistic stretching," which is a bouncing type of stretch that forces the muscles to stretch too rapidly. When this happens the body has a natural reflex to protect the muscles wherein they become even tighter and susceptible to tearing. Stretching should not be stressful but rather a peaceful, gradual and relaxing form of flexibility training. It must be tailored to your own body and the present condition of structure, flexibility and tension level. A gradual stretch should feel good with no pain at all. It can put you in touch with individual muscles and tendons.

Bob Anderson's book *Stretching* illustrates specific stretching principles that are useful for almost every sport or activity and is considered by many prominent exercise authorities as the "bible of stretching."

Light stretching can be done before walking, or, if you prefer, just start out walking slowly and build up to medium speed until the muscles have been warmed up. Serious stretching should be done after exercise when the muscles are infused with blood, warm and flexible. You may also find time to stretch while watching TV, reading, listening to music or hanging out with family or friends. Those who have stressful jobs may find that a good stretching session reduces tensions during the workday. If you feel stiff for any reason, some light stretching can work wonders. Bob Anderson recommends stretching on a regular basis to achieve the following results:

- reduce muscle tension and make the body feel more relaxed;
- help coordination by allowing for freer and easier movement;

- increase range of motion;
- prevent injuries such as muscle strains (a strong, prestretched muscle resists stress better than a strong, unstretched muscle);
- make strenuous activities such as running, racewalking, skiing, tennis, swimming and cycling easier because it prepares you for activity—it's a way of signaling the muscles that they are about to be used;
- develop body awareness (stretching helps to focus on various parts of your body and get in touch with them);
- help loosen the mind's control of the body so that the body moves for "its own sake" rather than for competition or ego;
- promote circulation;
- feels good.

Remember that learning to stretch is an easy process as long as you use some precautions and don't overdo it. Never force a stretch—allow the muscles to lengthen gradually with absolutely no bouncing. Bouncing, or ballistic stretching, as previously mentioned, actually tightens the muscles into a contraction phase to protect them at the very same time that you are trying to lengthen them. There might even be a microscopic tearing of the muscle fibers, which leads to the formation of scar tissue and reduces the fibers' elasticity. Start out with easy stretches and hold them for 10 to 30 seconds at a point of mild tension. If the tension subsides you can then go into further stretching. If you keep repeating the process, your muscles will gradually lengthen more and more. Your breathing should be natural and the breath should not be held. If you find yourself not breathing normally, perhaps you are trying too hard and not relaxing enough. Ease off on the stretch if you find this happening. The key is not to get impatient and try to lengthen the muscles gradually.

Massage Therapy

In the past the art of massage has received an unsavory and undeserved reputation from many unskilled practitioners and brothels using the name "massage parlor." Today, skilled massage therapists have largely overcome these negative connotations, and the benefits of massage are recognized by all sorts of athletes and their trainers. It is now considered a valid means of promoting well-being, muscle damage prevention and flexibility of the muscles, tendons and ligaments. The techniques of massaging the soft tissues of the body have been used since ancient times to relieve muscle soreness and to make people feel better and more relaxed. Massage produces wonderful therapeutic effects on the nervous, muscular and respiratory systems of the body and promotes excellent blood circulation.

A combination of massage and stretching can keep an active athlete's body in top shape as far as flexibility aspects are concerned. Licensed massage therapists, with their knowledge and skill, can affect such benefits as deep relaxation, body tone, improved circulation and drugless therapy. Four main types of massage are presently recognized on a worldwide basis:

1. Swedish, which uses vigorous, bracing movements to manipulate muscles in a specific part of the body.
2. German, which combines various Swedish movements in conjunction with submersion in water.
3. French, which uses soothing and subtle manipulations of the face, neck and arms.
4. Shiatsu (classified as eastern massage), which is directed toward stimulation of the body with hands and fingers.

The Beneficial Effects of Massage in Prevention and Therapy

- Massage dilates, or opens, blood vessels, improving circulation and relieving congestion.
- Massage increases the number of red blood cells, especially in cases of anemia.
- Massage acts as a "mechanical cleanser," hastening the elimination of wastes and toxic substances.
- Massage relaxes muscle spasms and relieves tension.
- Massage increases the blood supply and nutrition to muscles without adding to their load of toxic lactic acid, produced through voluntary muscle contraction.
- Massage helps to overcome harmful "fatigue" products resulting from strenuous exercise or injury of the muscles.
- Massage improves muscle tone and helps prevent or delay muscular atrophy resulting from forced inactivity.
- Massage can compensate, in part, for lack of exercise and muscular contraction in persons, who because of injury, illness or age, are forced to remain inactive.
- Massage helps return venous blood to the heart and eases strain on this vital organ.
- Transverse massage separates muscle fibers, preventing or healing the formation of adhesions.
- Massage may have a sedative, stimulating or exhausting effect on the nervous system depending on the type and length of the massage treatment.
- Massage may burst the fat capsule in the subcutaneous tissue so that the fat exudes and becomes absorbed.
- Massage combined with a nutritious diet and exercise may be an aid to weight reduction.
- Massage increases the excretion (via the kidneys) of fluids and nitrogen, inorganic phosphorous and salt in healthy individuals.
- Massage encourages the retention of nitrogen, phosphorous and sulfur that is necessary for tissue repair in persons who are convalescing from bone fractures.
- Massage stretches connective tissue, improves general circulation and provides nutrition to the body.

- Massage breaks down or prevents the formation of adhesions and reduces the danger of fibrosis and fibrositis.
- Massage improves the circulation and nutrition of joints and hastens the elimination of harmful particles. It helps to lessen inflammation and swelling in joints and alleviates pain, as in the case of arthritis.
- Massage increases glandular secretions and excretions that enhance the condition of the skin and increases the body's metabolic rate.
- Massage is an effective and inexpensive antistress therapy.
- Massage is used in the prevention and treatment of athletic injuries. It prepares the body for strengthening exercises and removes waste materials in the muscles and connective tissue that could limit performance.
- Massage promotes the excitation of sensory receptors in the skin that send reflex stimuli through the nervous system, exerting a profoundly healthy effect on deeper tissues, muscles and organs.
- Massage facilitates the transfer of healing energy between the therapist and client and can recharge the body and promote a general feeling of well-being.
- Massage brings people into harmony with their bodies, minds and spirits.
- Massage can help those muscles so important to walkers—those of the lower and upper back, hips, shoulders and lower legs.

If you keep your body flexible and toned through a fine balance of stretching and massage you will avoid that old-age shuffle so common to older people who do not stay active and flexible throughout life. See appendix 2 for illustrated loosening and flexibility exercises.

20 | Strength Training

"Once it was feared that engaging in resisted exercise would reduce the response to aerobic training. However, in practice, it is possible to combine aerobic conditioning with regular muscle strengthening exercises, so that the subject's strength is not only maintained but enhanced."
—Roy J. Shephard, M.D., Ph.D., D.P.E.

Strength is the ability of a muscle to apply pressure and overcome a resistance. A walker does not need to have extremely powerful muscles like a weight lifter or football defensive lineman. Such great power is of little use and may even make things worse by decreasing flexibility. Walkers seek to improve strength and endurance of the muscles used for propulsion through what is called "dynamic strength," or the ability to do many repetitions of required movements in a powerful manner. Strength training has a definite benefit to walkers. Any strength training done, however, should not cut into time and effort that could be better utilized to train for the big four: technique, endurance, flexibility and speed.

The Best Methods of Increasing Strength

The best way to increase specific muscle strength is with free weights or Nautilus machines. The best idea is to work on many routines with light weights rather than fewer repetitions with heavier ones. This way you lengthen the muscles rather than trying to "bulk up." For this reason emphasize wide ranges of motion in doing routines. As in all the other training techniques, build up gradually and don't increase the intensity of the workouts too rapidly. Remember that repetitions should be progressively increased if you wish to keep gaining more strength. Carrying weights while walking rapidly is discouraged because it changes the natural balance of the body and can cause muscle and joint strains.

Muscles that Deserve Attention

Certain muscle groups have the most affect on the movements necessary for efficient racewalking. Attention should be paid to increasing the strength and endurance of the following muscle groups:

1. The muscles on the top of the shoulder joint called the *deltoids*, which are used to move the arms to the front and back in their pendular motion.
2. The muscles over the front of the chest called the *pectorals*, which also aid in the arm swing.
3. The muscles of the lower back, which aid in maintaining the correct posture of the body sitting on the hips.
4. The muscles of the stomach called the *obliques*, which help in maintaining posture and pull the hip of the swinging leg forward to get the trunk over the striding leg rapidly.
5. The flexor muscles of the hip, which help pull the swinging leg through toward heel strike.
6. The calf muscles, which give impetus to the final part of the leg drive at the rear of the stride.
7. The rear thigh muscles called the *hamstrings* group, which are instrumental in flexing the knee as it swings forward and assisting in hip extension.
8. The front thigh muscles called the *quadriceps*, which can aid in straightening the knee at heel strike.
9. The *tibialis anterior* muscle, which is used to lift the toes at heel strike, and its opposing muscles *tibialis posterior* and *peroneus*, which are instrumental in push-off.

If you are interested in pursuing a weight training program, talk to a professional weight trainer who can advise you about progressive resistance exercises for the muscles listed above. See chapter 22 for more information on the roles of muscles in walking.

Home Strength Training for Racewalkers

The primary muscles involved in designing a specific resistance training program for racewalkers are the gluteals, hamstrings, hip flexors, extensors, abductors, adductors, calves and the tibialis anterior. The following exercises are recommended by biomechanist and coach Leonard Jansen and are designed for trained athletes. Although a suitable strength program involving weight training equipment will improve your walking, some aerobically trained athletes do not have access to such equipment. The exercises below can be performed almost anywhere and may be scaled down to suit your own personal needs or ability. Always remember to warm up with 5 to 10 minutes of slow walking or jumping rope and then some static stretching exercises prior to each training session.

Total Body

Squat jump—Stand with your hands on your hips and with one foot a step ahead of the other. Jump into a squat position so that your knees are at a 90-degree angle, and then jump again as high as possible, extending your knees. Change the position of your feet on the way down so that you land with the foot that was originally ahead behind, and jump again. Start with a few repetitions and build up each week until 15 repetitions per set is achieved.

Legs

One legged squats—Use a chair or block to aid your balance. Make sure the chair does not slide out from under you and will support your weight.

Step-ups—Use a bench, chair or block.

Lunge—Lunge forward over one leg and progress to where you are holding an object in your hands such as a book.

Calf raise—Balance on a step so that the ball of your foot contacts the edge of the step and the heel drops below the toes. Center your body weight over that foot. Raise up as high as possible on the ball of the foot and then lower the heel as far as possible. Repeat this motion 15 times and then alternate the legs.

Chest, Upper Back and Arms

Push-up—With your hands slightly wider than shoulder width and your back straight, bend your arms slowly and lower your body until your chest just touches the ground. Return to the original starting position and repeat.

Pull-ups—Some type of anchored chinning bar is needed. Take an overhand grip when doing pull-ups. A chair can be used for assistance. To begin with it may be necessary to start from the chair. Jump up to the point where your chin is over the bar, slowly lower yourself back to the chair and repeat.

Abdominals

Leg raises—Lie on your back with your hands under the curve of your lumbar area. Raise your legs until your heels are 4 to 6 inches off the ground. Hold this position momentarily, lowering your legs in a controlled manner, and repeat.

Crunches—Place the lower legs up onto a chair or bench so that the hips are 90 degrees in flexion and perform a sit-up with your hands behind your head. Raise shoulders as high as possible and repeat.

Bent knee sit-up with a twist—Lie on your back with knees bent and hands across chest and perform a sit-up. The exercise can be made more difficult by clasping the hands behind the head or by holding a weight on the chest or behind the head.

Lower Back

Hyperextensions—Lie on the abdomen with hands clasped behind the head. Legs and arms are simultaneously raised as far as possible off the ground; hold for a 5 to 10 count. Return to initial position and repeat.

General

Well-trained abdominals are a must. Well-developed trunk and abdominal muscles play a significant role in sparing the spine from strain and damage. The spine is under a lot of stress as your feet hit the ground several thousand times in every training session. Perform the prescribed exercises for three sets of ten repetitions three times a week with one day of rest between sessions. Gradually increase the number of repetitions to complete a goal of three sets of 20 to 25 repetitions. It is not necessary to complete all the above in the same training session.

Choose two exercises from both legs and abdominals sections and one exercise from each of the other sections for your training session. Taper your training sessions prior to competition in the same manner that you would in your other training. Always remember that people who are not yet well trained in racewalking can scale the number of repetitions down to suit their own levels of conditioning and then build up slowly to higher levels of strength training.

21 Speed Training

"But even at the end there is strategy. It is not enough to have the speed. Not enough to give your all. That sprint, that giving, must be done at the right time, at the precise moment that allows no adequate response. It must be checkmate."

—George Sheehan, M.D.

Speed training can be done by doing intervals and what is known as fartlek repeats, which is moving fast for short bursts of speed to train the muscles and increase neurological efficiency for handling that speed. Your body is taught to tolerate speed. Speed can be kept up for longer and longer periods by using the endurance of your previous base training. The effects of speed training are much more short-lived than base training and the results may be erratic if it is attempted for over three months at a time. If done properly, great improvement can be experienced in about six weeks. Power—the application of strength and speed—is of utmost importance for racewalking performance. Speed work teaches you to relax and learn efficient coordination at faster paces. It also develops cardiovascular capacity and strength at a rapid pace.

However, be careful. Overdoing it can rapidly cause soreness, staleness and possible illness or injury. Energy stores or reserves of adaptational energy can be depleted if too much is done too soon. Too much speed work can put a lot of strain on tendons and muscles, especially if a proper warm-up is not done beforehand. Back off from speed training when you feel stressed, washed out or apathetic about training. Overtraining can depress the immune system and expose you to increased infection risk.

The following symptoms of exercise overstress have been identified by that eminent researcher Dr. Hans Selye:

- nagging fatigue and general sluggishness that lingers from day to day;
- disinterest in normally exciting activities;
- low level and persistent soreness and stiffness in muscles, joints and tendons;
- diarrhea or constipation;
- drop in performance level that is unexplained;
- frequent mild colds and sore throats;

- unexplained skin eruptions;
- aching stomach possibly accompanied by loss of appetite and weight;
- swelling and aching in the lymph glands, particularly in the neck, underarm and groin areas;
- excessive nervousness, depression, irritability, headaches and inability to relax or sleep.

Injury or illness will likely result if the signs of overstress are ignored. Listen to your body and respect the message it is trying to tell you.

Fast and Slow Twitch Muscles

We are born with a preponderance of fast twitch and slow twitch muscle fibers. Energy is supplied to fast twitch fibers in a different metabolic route than slow twitch fibers, and they can be used for activities requiring quick action. Slow twitch fibers, on the other hand, receive energy more slowly and have high aerobic endurance for long-term exercise. Walking gradually uses only slow twitch fibers, but as speed increases toward a maximum level, more and more fast twitch fibers are recruited into action. Those with the fast twitch variety are better adapted to rapid movements such as sprinting and movements that require sudden, explosive action. Those with a high percentage of slow twitch fibers are generally better suited for events that require endurance. Many endurance athletes, such as marathon runners and long-distance walkers, have been shown to have 90 percent or more slow twitch fibers. Conversely, world-class sprinters often only have approximately 25 percent of this type of fiber.

Extremely fast walking requires very fast leg movements since the walkers must take about three and one-half strides per second to walk at seven minutes per mile or less. Great endurance is required to keep up this pace for 20 to 50 kilometers (the standard distances for men's world championships) and 10 kilometers (the standard distance for women's world championships).* Athletes who have half slow twitch and half fast twitch muscle fibers are the best off—both speed and endurance are necessary to legally race those long distances. In short races, such as a 3K or 5K, the fast twitch muscle fibers would bestow the athlete with a definite advantage. The difference in development of slow and fast twitch fibers is caused by the number of muscle fibers per motor unit, not the force generated by each fiber. A motor unit is defined as the motor nerve and all the muscle fibers it enervates into action.

Speed Should Be Developed Gradually

When a walker tries to go too fast for his or her present technique or conditioning, several bad things are likely to happen: the upper body may become tense, which would be very tiring; the arms may increase their range of motion

---

*They are possibly planning to change the women's championship 10K to 20K and the men's 20K to 30K in 1999 before the next Olympiad.

and the stride may shorten—all of which may lead to lifting off the ground in violation of the rules. The danger of this happening can be diminished, if when walking fast, the walker will keep the arms low close to the hips in a compact swing, not raising them up too high in either the front or back arm swings. If the walker will also concentrate on the forward thrust of the driving leg and pushing off very hard with the toes, then the stride length will be lengthened to the rear so that the swinging heel has a better chance to strike the ground in time to avoid lifting.

Interval Training

Using bursts of speed for training the body to move fast has been used as a training technique for many years and is effective if used properly and not overdone. The maximum oxygen uptake can be improved by working at speeds near the walker's maximum for short distances. The hard efforts should not exceed four to seven minutes in duration with slightly shorter rest periods in between. When the body is worked at speeds above present technique and conditioning, the body learns to adapt to the extra stress on a gradual basis. It is important to work as hard as possible on correct technique when doing speed training so bad habits are not picked up in the process. It should be noted here that even though a walker may have a very high oxygen uptake, he or she may be outwalked by others with a lower capacity in this regard if the others' training and technique work is superior. In 1972, when runner Frank Shorter obliterated the field in the Olympic marathon, he had a much lower oxygen uptake compared to most of his adversaries. His maximum oxygen uptake number was just over 70, while many of the others had an uptake over 80. Yet because he was so efficient, well trained and conditioned, he could run at nearly 90 percent of his maximum capacity for 26 miles, while the other competitors could not.

Ways to Increase Speed

Concentrate on developing a stronger toe push as it leaves the ground. This may be the best thing you can do to increase your speed. Another suggestion is to start jogging and lifting the toes so that you land on your heel. You will find that your leg straightens if the toe is lifted sufficiently and that you will be doing very fast racewalking steps. Walk a downgrade at faster than racing speeds, which will teach the legs how to accommodate a fast stride rate. Pay special attention to flexibility routines to compensate for the tightness that fast walking causes. Work at high speeds on a motorized treadmill where you can work in a controlled and relaxed environment. Follow someone who is faster and keep up as long as possible. Using the fast walker's tempo may pull you along faster than you could normally go on your own. Always warm up adequately before attempting speed work. Many muscles have been pulled by not paying attention to this detail.

Finally, prior to competitions, if you wish to perform at your best, you should ease up on your training regimen for a few days ahead. Hard training causes damage to the body, which can repair itself only if intensity and volume of training are reduced and rest is increased. Your body needs some relief prior to competition to build up stored energy reserves. So use slower training walks in preparation.

Speed work only comes after the proper technique, endurance, flexibility and strength are attained. Don't worry about stride length initially because stride lengthens as speed rises. Certainly, for those working on going faster in races and workouts, fast walking should not be attempted until proper technique is mastered.

22 The Roles of Muscles in Walking

> "The muscular system provides the force that causes movement of the skeletal system. The nervous system acts to initiate this movement. Just as the skeleton is motionless without the force production of the supporting muscles, the muscle is unable to move without activation by the nervous system."
> —Jack H. Wilmore, Ph.D.
> and David L. Costill, Ph.D.

Perhaps your first efforts when learning the racewalking technique will cause you to feel somewhat awkward. Unless you have studied kinesiology or physiology you might wonder why. The reason is that new motor skills, even relatively simple ones, require a great deal of coordination between voluntary muscles. The voluntary muscles move the joints of the skeletal system while the involuntary muscles are automatically controlled, such as those of the breathing mechanism, small intestine and heart. Slow, relaxed movements are often necessary to train muscles to accomplish new motor skills. Conscious thought seems to slow the process and beginners tend to move along somewhat awkwardly. With practice, these movements become fluid through familiarity. If you can learn to relax and work on one new movement at a time, the learning process will become much simpler.

All your voluntary muscles have the ability to contract upon demand when stimulated by a nerve impulse and to relax when the nerve impulse is removed. They can contract either singly or in groups in two ways—isometrically (tightening without shortening) or isotonically (when the muscles change length and produce a variety of movements). As your legs move in a walking movement, there needs to be a cooperative action of all the bones and muscles of the leg. For instance, the gastrocnemius (calf muscle) extends all the way from the heel to above the knee and is a strong extensor of the ankle and a weak flexor of the knee when it is contracted. When it contracts, its opposing muscles relax to allow movement.

There are many sets of opposing muscle groups in the human body. Depending upon the movement a muscle needs to make, it can assume a variety of roles. It can be an "agonist," which works against gravitational forces and acts as the prime mover as it contracts on demand. Or, it can assume the role of "antagonist," working with gravity in opposition to the agonist. Antagonist muscles must relax to allow a desired movement to occur efficiently. Scientists say that muscles working against gravity produce about 40 percent more tension than the opposing muscles. That being so, walkers should pay attention to weak muscles that are antagonists and strengthen them. An easy example to understand is the relationship of the triceps and the biceps. Each extends from below the elbow up across the shoulder joint. When you flex the biceps on the front of the arm, the triceps on the rear relaxes, and vice versa when the arm is extended. All the muscles that are used in the walking movement must be made strong and flexible if maximum efficiency is to be obtained. Muscle imbalances, where the agonist or antagonist is very weak compared to each other, can cause serious problems if the condition is not corrected with proper exercises.

Muscles are also needed as "stabilizers." If the gastrocnemius muscle is flexed it can cause movement both in the ankle joint and the knee joint simultaneously. If only one or the other is desired to be moved, there must be stabilizing muscle action in the joint to hold that joint firmly in place.

The last way muscles can act is as "synergists," or in combination with other muscles to produce movements that no single muscle could do. A good example of this are the external oblique muscles (a large sheet of muscle fibers covering the front and side of the abdomen). In contracting the left external oblique muscle the trunk will bend to the left and rotate to the right. This is an aid for efficient walking. However, if you contract both the left and right obliques simultaneously, there will be forward bending at the waist with no rotation, something we do not want happening in racewalking.

Specific Muscle Use

The tibialis anterior, the muscle that supplies the ability to lift the toes at heel strike, may be little used until the technique of race- walking is employed. This is why shin soreness may occur with beginners. Its opposing muscles, the posterior tibialis and peroneus—the agonists in this case—pull the toes down and aid in the powerful toe push-off so vital for powerful and speedy walking.

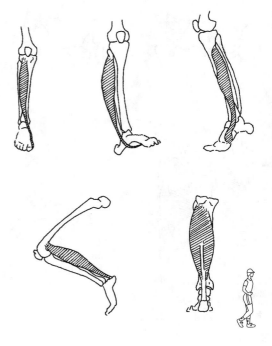

The gastrocnemius and soleus, which are the calf muscles, also plantar flex the ankle (forcing the toe down), giving the walker a more forceful pushing action. If you feel the calves working strongly during push-off, it is a sign that you are doing that part of the racewalk form correctly.

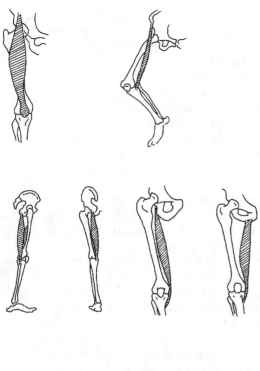

The quadriceps (front of thigh including the rectus femoris and sartorius) extend the knee and are an aid to hip flexion. The quads must be relaxed (flaccid), however, after the straightening takes place.

The opposing hamstrings group at the rear of the thigh, including biceps femoris, semi-membranosis and semi-tendonosis, assist in flexing the knee during its forward swing as well as hip extension and rotation. The adductor gracilis along the inside of the thigh pulls the thigh inward so the feet will land in a straight line at heel strike.

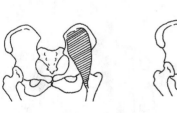
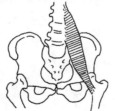

Heading up into the midsection, the iiliopsoas (actually two muscles—the iliacus and the psoas) are responsible for flexing the trunk and thigh as well as a slight outward rotation of the femur bone.

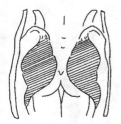
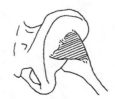

The large butt muscle, glutaeus maximus, extends and laterally rotates the hip joint. The smaller glutaeus medius and glutaeus minimus are hip muscles that abduct (pull outward) the thigh as the hips swing forward and the legs pass each other.

The abdominal muscles, which are neglected badly by so many exercisers, include: the rectus abdominis, which flattens the abdominal wall, depresses the ribs and flexes the spine; the internal oblique and external oblique, each of which flex the spine and rotate the trunk; and the erector spinae, which is a large muscle on each side of the spine on the back extending from the buttocks to the base of the skull. This muscle is important in keeping the spine and head erect.

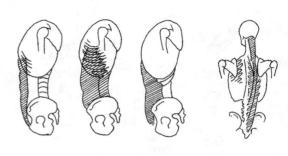

In the neck, shoulders and arms we find the pectoralis major covering the front of the upper chest. It adducts and medially rotates the upper arms as well as aiding in deep breathing. The rhomboid on the back between the shoulder blades adducts the scapula and helps in the downward motion of the arms.

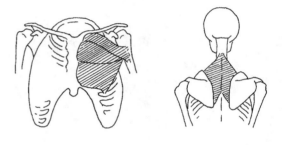

The latissimus dorsi is a large muscle extending from the tailbone up to the upper arm bone. It helps in operating the shoulder joint, rotating the arm inward and flexion of the trunk. The teres major and coracobrachialis are also major contributors to the movement of the arm in the shoulder joint.

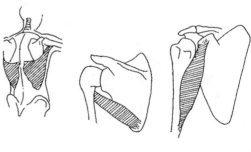

The trapezius, in the upper back and divided into four parts, extends the head and neck, and adducts, depresses and stabilizes the scapula. The deltoid covers the shoulder joint and raises the arm forward, sideward and backward.

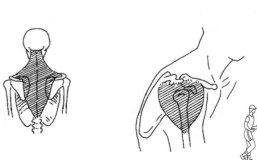

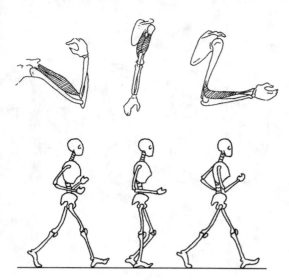

The biceps flexes the arm at the elbow. Its opposing muscle, the triceps, extends the arm at the elbow. The brachio-radialis helps hold the arm in a right-angle position.

The muscle groups just described are the main ones that are active in racewalking. A good trainer can recommend exercises to work and strengthen these muscle groups, or you might read a good book on exercise physiology such as those recommended in appendix 13.

23 Some Aspects of Competition

"We want not only to live but to have something to live for. For some people this means to pursue excellence through sport."
—Terry Orlick, Ph.D.

As many walkers get into better shape they wish to test themselves against others. Fortunately, now there are increasing opportunities for everyone to be involved in racewalking from junior and veteran competitions to open championship classes. To find out how to get involved in friendly competition, contact any of the clubs and promoters listed in appendix 8. Remember that you do not need to be a good athlete to enjoy racewalking—it feels good at whatever level you participate.

Road racing, which has been popular in the United States for the past 20 or so years, now includes racewalking divisions into their award structures. Everyone, regardless of ability, is invited to take part in these races. Huge races like the New York Marathon, Los Angeles Marathon and the Honolulu Marathon have special divisions for walkers with awards for the top finishers. These races are 26.2 miles and a bit too long for most walkers who usually like the popular and more moderate distance of a 5K race.

The overwhelming number of new racewalkers comes in the masters division, which is for people 40 years of age and older. The Masters Track and Field Committee of USA Track & Field has jurisdiction over the masters division and is responsible for scheduling the national championship events. These large events usually accept people of all abilities and are an excellent opportunity to make friends with other walkers. There is a National Senior Games and regionals all over the country for people 50 years and older who don't like to race against those 40-year-old "kids." For those striving for the very top, the World Veteran Games are held every two years. These events draw master athletes from all over the world as well as the most participants of any of the track events. For most of us who are less competitive, association and regional championships are held in most regions in the United States, and there are plenty of low-key races held throughout the year (mostly 5K) that everyone can enter and enjoy the fellowship of others.

Handicapping of Races

Being slow is no longer an obstacle to winning a race, as long as the race is based on a handicapping system. The Denver, Colorado, area has a series of races each year in which the walkers race against their own ability in an effort to improve. The races are held eight times a year at various parks and at distances ranging from 2 miles to 6.2 miles (10K). At these events you can work on your speed and form as well as meet some of the better walkers. The races are free to members who pay the membership fee to join the Road Runners and a nominal fee per race to nonmembers. The system is based on the premise that in time most people become faster walkers or at least keep from getting slower. You set yourself a handicap based on what time you have for the particular distance walked in the first race. Based upon that time, the computer figures how fast you should be able to go in the next race. Times are adjusted according to distance—the longer the distance the slower the pace. You are issued a "predict time," which is the time you try to beat if you do well in that race. If you beat the predicted time by a good amount, you'll likely win a ribbon for that race.

Warming Up and Cooling Down

Time after time, I have noticed that few racewalkers do a correct warm-up before races. Some stroll around for a few minutes and then stand in a big herd of racers for 15 minutes or so before the gun goes off. Others do a good job of getting their heart rates up and have a nice sweat going, but they also quit too far ahead of the starting time. This is a big mistake! While standing around, a competitor's heart rate and blood flow decreases to a remarkable degree and the muscles cool off. All of these functions are not ready for intense action required for effective racing. If you take off too fast under these conditions the body will rebel and you will go into oxygen deprivation, making your first mile a very uncomfortable one.

Some studies have shown that standing still for more than a minute before the start cancels much of the benefits bestowed by an adequate warm-up. It seems that you only see the well-experienced racers moving around until almost the start. One study showed that those who stood still for 60 seconds or less did the best during the first part of a race. If they rested two minutes their heart rates dipped to almost a resting rate—it made the body less ready to exert itself.

Ending your warm-up prematurely can cause a buildup of lactic acid in the muscles, something that shouldn't occur until near the end of the race. It can also cause insufficient oxygen to be supplied to the heart muscle during exertion, termed medically as coronary ischemia. Kinesiologist Don Franks of Louisiana State University has studied the effects of warm-ups on racing performance and suggests the following advice:

- Keep moving continuously at a moderate pace for at least 10 minutes during warm-up. At the end of this exercise your leg muscles will be warm and their contractions will become more efficient and forceful.

- During your warm-up, get the heart rate up to at least 70 percent of its maximum effectiveness. However, too high of a heart rate can be detrimental as you expend too much energy needed for the race.

- Find some way to keep moving until 60 seconds before the start of the race. With everyone standing around, jammed in at the starting line, try to find an open space near the start and then jump in during the last minute, or, if that is not practical, just jog in place. You will feel much more comfortable in the initial stages of the race.

We are all different and need to experiment to see what level of warm-up works best for each of us. Another expert on the subject, cross-country coach at the University of Wisconsin Martin Smith, says: "A good warm-up should do more than just get your muscles ready. You should also spend some time relaxing and thinking positive thoughts about the impending race. Develop a warm-up routine that you enjoy, and use that plan before all quality workouts during training ... never start a race in which you wish to do well without preparing the body for intense effort through an adequate warm-up ... ."

Cooling down after a race is nearly as important as warming up beforehand. Many competitors stop and do nothing except stand, sit or lie prone immediately afterward. This is not wise. It is important to keep moving around for three main reasons:

1. The metabolic waste products accumulated in the muscles during the race will be removed more rapidly and a faster recovery will happen if the heart rate does not drop too fast. The resulting better circulation is vital in the recovery process and the competitor will feel much better.
2. A competitor who ceases movement too rapidly may experience light-headedness or fainting. Those symptoms occur because the blood flow slows before blood vessels can constrict, which causes a rapid drop in blood pressure and a deficient supply of blood to the brain. A person should walk around for 5 to 10 minutes after a race to avoid these problems.
3. A body that is sweaty from the race will cool very rapidly afterward if activity immediately ceases, especially if it is cold outside or there is a breeze causing rapid evaporation of the perspiration. The body is no longer producing large amounts of heat, but the cooling process can cause a drop of body temperature to subnormal levels. If a person keeps moving, they can regulate the rate at which the body cools to a normal temperature. If the air temperature is cool, warm clothes should be donned as soon as possible after the race.

By paying strict attention to warming up before an event and cooling down gradually afterward, the performance, recovery and sense of well-being will be enhanced.

Emotional Factors

Sometimes racewalkers experience a high state of physical arousal before events. In endurance sports such as racewalking this anxiety can compromise a competitor's energy level according to some eminent exercise physiologists. Other research indicates that it can also interfere with an athlete's ability to focus on the event and think clearly. The focus instead tends to turn inward— an inappropriate focus of attention. Even if your form is almost automatically accomplished normally, you may be forced to use constant attention to perform legal racewalking form. The ability to make quick decisions can also be diminished. You may also experience self-doubt and have a preoccupation with what you can't do instead of what you must strive to do.

Nervousness and Performance

At competitive racewalking events that are important to you, it is normal to feel some nervousness prior to the start. This indicates readiness more than anything else and can be a positive arousal in contrast to the negative arousal previously mentioned. Many elite athletes can channel energy such as this to improve performance instead of diminishing it. Ask yourself the following questions to determine what kind of anxieties you may have. Do I have doubts of my own ability? Do I worry about things over which I have no control? If the answer is yes to these two questions, you are experiencing negative anxiety and it may interfere with your ability to race in a ready mental state. If you are nervous but still confident of your ability to perform well, it signifies readiness to do your best.

As you approach the starting line of a racewalking event each time you attend a race, make a mental note of your feelings. Do you feel confident or apprehensive that you can do your best? Can you remember how you felt before races in the past when you did well? What effect did either nervousness or anxiety have on performance—good or bad?

When you felt "psyched" and anxious to get going, what kind of performance ensued? Inexperienced competitors often feel anxiety, or even fear, of what they might encounter physically during a race. One of the differences between experienced and inexperienced competitors is that the experienced competitors tend to focus on every feeling they have both physically and mentally and then compensate for them, while the inexperienced try to disassociate so they can diminish discomfort caused by the exertion. The experienced have learned to capitalize on their strengths and concentrate on those things they can control while putting those they can't in the background. No matter where they place in an event, they are satisfied if they know that they have done their best in that particular race.

Psychology of Racing

Racewalking demands a certain amount of mental toughness for a competitor to do well. No matter how sound the athlete's technique or how good the conditioning, without mental toughness, that athlete will never give a truly optimal performance. In racewalking, mental toughness can be equated with consistency in performance and consists of a combination of attributes:

1. Discipline is most evident in a successful athlete's willingness to train with pride, diligence, focus and a commitment to performing well. Discipline also includes being able to sustain good technique and leg speed, even when feeling fatigued.
2. Tenacity is critical when those key decision points come up during a race either to put the pedal to the metal or back off. Often, it is only by conscious decision and force of will that an athlete can persevere and work through difficult spells in a race (i.e., stomach cramps, pain in the calves, overwhelming waves of fatigue, etc.).
3. Poise and emotional self-control are important prerequisites for success in racewalking. Athletes must learn how to gain control of themselves and their emotions before they can control their performance.

An athlete must have the desire, determination and inner drive to want to be the best. This involves a high degree of self-confidence, concentration and commitment. Mental toughness and a competitive attitude are necessary to stay focused on one's personal goals and race plans.

Peak Performers

The following list defines characteristics of those who perform very well at what they do.

- Peak performers always take responsibility for their own performances.
- Peak performers are effective thinkers.
- Peak performers look for reasons to keep performing at a high level.
- Peak performers are willing to ask for advice and constructive criticism.
- Peak performers learn from their mistakes and use the experiences to do better next time.
- Peak performers set realistic goals to attain.
- Peak performers do not abuse their bodies.
- Peak performers try to learn what their bodies are capable of and what they are not.
- Peak performers associate with any discomfort during a race or workout, while lesser athletes tend to disassociate.
- Peak performers do not overtrain and pay attention to adequate rest periods.
- Peak performers graciously accept defeat and congratulate the winners.
- Peak performers retain a cheerful attitude and optimistic thoughts.
- Peak performers do not procrastinate.

- Peak performers set priorities for the use of their time each day.
- Peak performers are constantly trying to increase their efficiency to maximize performance.
- Peak performers pay close attention to diet by eating very little fat, but a lot of complex carbohydrates.
- Peak performers do not allow themselves to become dehydrated.
- Peak performers endeavor to prepare adequately for all important future events.

Most people who try racewalking and its competitions truly like the sport, which is one main reason why there are comparatively fewer dropouts than most other sports after they achieve a certain level of competence.

24 Racewalk Judging

"The law is not a 'light' for you or any man to see by; the law is not an instrument of any kind. The law is a causeway upon which so long as he keeps to it, a citizen may walk safely."
—Robert Bolt

Without proper judging, racewalking events can be a painful experience for those who legally walk the entire event only to find out at the end that someone in their age group has beaten them by jogging or using a bent-legged, runner-type of push-off during part of the race. To maintain fairness to all competitors there must be, at the very least, monitors watching the event to see that no jogging takes place. Considering that racewalking is two-thirds as fast as running, it is easy to see how unfair it is to run. It can be compared to taking a shortcut to gain an unfair advantage.

In the more organized and important events, qualified judges who have passed certification tests must watch for violation of the two international rules that govern the sport. Again, the rules state that there must be constant contact with the ground, and the supporting (weight-bearing) leg must straighten as the heel strikes the ground and then remain straight until in the vertical upright position. These two rules were instituted to make a definite distinction between walking and running. At the slower speeds most people walk, violations are easily detectable by anyone who knows even a little about the sport. It is when high-level competitions are conducted and elite competitors are whizzing by at high speeds that experienced judges are necessary to keep the race under control. In important races such as road race championships, six to nine judges are usually on hand. In track events five judges are recommended. In smaller races, three is considered to be the minimum number. In any case, if three different judges consider a competitor to be walking unfairly, that competitor is automatically disqualified from the race.

The Role of USA Track & Field

The sport of racewalking, as all track and field events, is under the jurisdiction of USA Track & Field (USATF) nationally, and the International Amateur Athletic Federation (IAAF) on the international level. These organizations test, certify and supply racewalk judging officials. Racewalk judging is the most intense duty that a track and field official is faced with, demanding constant attention to the progression and legality of the competitors throughout the race.

Judges must begin by becoming apprentices, during which time they work independently beside more experienced officials for several times as nonscoring judges. By comparing their results with the experienced judges, they eventually become confident of their own judgments and are eligible to be association-level officials certified to judge local races. After two or three years of experience and a certain number of races, a judge can become eligible to be a National Judge in national championships, regional championships and other important races. Selected competent judges with extensive experience in important races can be promoted to Master Judge who can judge in international races as well. The top of the line is the IAAF Judge, which requires extensive experience in big events. These are the ones you will find at the Olympic Games and World Championships.

There are 56 associations in the USATF, many of them covering an entire state and even some covering more than a single state. Following is a list of these 56 associations. (Author's note: Associations are named, spelled out and italicized while states within associations are abbreviated. There are four USATF regions in the United States. For geographic administration, the North has "ceded" Kentucky and West Virginia to the South.)

EAST REGION: *Maine* • *New England* covers NH, VT, MA, RI • *Connecticut* • New York State has *Adirondack, Metropolitan* and *Niagara* • *New Jersey* • Pennsylvania has *Mid-Atlantic* and *Three Rivers* • *Virginia* covers south VA • *Potomac Valley* covers MD, District of Columbia and four counties in VA.

WEST REGION: *Alaska* • *Arizona* • *Colorado* • *Hawaii* • *Montana* • *New Mexico* • *Nevada* • *Oregon* • *Utah* • *Wyoming* • Idaho has *Snake River* • Washington has *Inland Empire* and *Pacific Northwest* • California has *Pacific, central CA, southern CA* and *San Diego-Imperial.*

NORTH REGION: *Dakotas* covers ND and SD • *Illinois* • *Indiana* • *Iowa* • *Michigan* • *Minnesota* • *Nebraska* • Ohio covers *western Ohio* and *Lake Erie* • *Wisconsin* • *Missouri Valley* covers KS and some of MO • *Ozark* covers some of MO and IL.

SOUTH REGION: *Alabama* • *Arkansas* • *Florida* • *Georgia* • *Kentucky* • *North Carolina* • *South Carolina* • *Oklahoma* • *Tennessee* • *West Virginia* • *Southern* covers Louisiana and Michigan • Texas has *Border, Gulf, West Texas, South Texas* and *Southwestern.*

See appendix 8 for who to contact about judging and racing in your area.

Judges are supplied with red disqualification cards that can be turned in with the competitor's name, reason for call and time of day on it. They are also issued caution paddles with a bent knee signal on one side and a loss of contact signal on the other, which the judge shows to a competitor if he or she is close to breaking a rule (e.g.,the paddle would read: "Number 66 caution— bent knee [or loss of contact]"). Cautions are noted on the judges' tally cards but do not count as a disqualification call.

In important races there is a "card runner" who collects disqualification cards (now called "warnings") from the judges and delivers them to a recorder near the Chief Judge who is selected before the event and usually stands close to the finish line. Disqualification calls are also posted on a tally board with a competitor's number and an "X" large enough so the athletes can see it as they pass by. Cards are turned in as soon as physically possible. If three separate judges agree that a competitor has broken one of the two rules, that walker is disqualified after verification by the Chief Judge. A judge may only turn in one disqualification call per competitor no matter how many times he sees that competitor violating one of the rules. It is required for the Chief Judge to notify those who have received three red cards as soon as possible by showing them a red paddle. Upon disqualification, notified walkers are required to leave the course or track at once. Sometimes such notification does not occur until the walker has crossed the finish line. Their time and finish postition are then removed from the final race results.

The following series of drawings shows the differences between legal and illegal techniques. The two series below show legal technique.

The following progressive series of diagrams shows illegal walking with the knees constantly bent.

The following progressive series of diagrams shows illegal walking as the walker fails to maintain contact with the walking surface.

Judging Less Important and Local Events

The judging methods just explained are used in championship events for elite athletes, but what about less important events that make up the vast majority of races with large numbers of people participating? A great number of events are held in this country with people of all ages who cannot do such an elaborate job of judging, and indeed they don't have to. In these cases the requirements can be more modest—similar but scaled down. There are currently not enough trained officials to go around. Most road races are not the multiloop courses used in championship events, so neither a card runner nor a disqualification board is used. In smaller races, efforts must be made to have three trained racewalk judges officiating the event. In the case where no official judges are available, there should at least be monitors to make sure that no running takes place in the event.

In the central Colorado region there are 40 to 50 races per year that give awards to walkers as well as runners. Accordingly, the judges cover every race in some fashion, and the competitors become conditioned to the fact that they must comply with the rules if they wish to see their name in the results. Fortunately, the race managers are trained to let the walkers leave the starting line well after the runners have left so that everyone knows who is in the walking division from the start. By handling events in this manner, only the fastest competitors catch up with the slow runners and are easily identified. Walkers starting at the same time as the runners makes officiating the event extremely difficult as the walkers start out hidden in a crowded group.

In Colorado a system has been instituted in which a large colored dot is placed on the tear-off tag on the numbers issued to the racers. These are used to identify those competing for awards. Those competitors without colored dots are classified as fitness walkers and are neither judged nor eligible for awards. At the starting line those with the dots start in front and those without begin in the back of the group. Sometimes the race managers allow the racewalkers to start two minutes before the fitness walkers. This method works quite well for the officials controlling the event.

In any case, if the event needs to be considered as legitimate competition, there must be officiating. To allow someone running to receive an award for walking is the height of absurdity. Competitors must use the form according to the international racewalking rules.

Judging Controversies

There have been some suggestions that the bent knee rule be relaxed somewhat for older competitors. In my teaching experience, however, I have yet to see one elderly pupil that cannot straighten his or her legs while standing still. This gives me reason to believe that there is no reason that they cannot, with proper relaxation of the legs—and the quadricep muscle in particular—straighten the legs while walking. I have been able to correct those who feel more comfortable walking bent-kneed by getting them to work on increased flexibility in the back of the leg and to pay attention to lifting their toes as their heels land. For those who do not wish to straighten their legs as they walk, or cannot because of some structural reason, separate fitness walking events should be held where outright running is the only reason for disqualification. Bent leg walking at high speeds uses a different set of driving muscles than legal walking technique and has a decidedly different appearance.

I know of cases where excellent competitors have been deprived of justly earned medals because their competitors were "given a break" by judges for their age. At the World Veteran's Games in Turku, Finland, in the 80 to 84 division, Gordon Wallace was unjustly denied medals when grossly bent-kneed walkers who were not disqualified finished ahead of him, literally running to the finish line. This was the reward Gordon got for training years to perfect his legal technique. Fortunately, Giulio dePetra of Carmel, California, also a very legal walker in his eighties, was so speedy that even the illegal walkers in his age division could not keep up with him in races (see role models in appendix 3).

The bent leg rule has been in force throughout the twentieth century, and I cannot think of any reasons for changing it. Luckily, very few people have complained as a result of being disqualified from races for badly bent knees because they cannot walk as fast if they try to comply with the rules. On the practical side, bent-kneed walking does nothing to promote flexibility of the hip, which is so vital to people as they age. In truth, the bent knee rule should not be tampered with because it is a big factor that separates walking from running.

The Contact Rule

The contact rule of racewalking has been under discussion. As athletes become stronger and faster, their increased speeds make it more difficult to maintain an instantaneous double support phase at full stride. The rule book says that judging must be done with the "naked eye," yet video cameras catch rapidly moving athletes with both feet off the ground for very small time periods that the human eye cannot see. The human eye apparently cannot detect a moving occurrence that does not last at least .05 seconds. The very good technique and smooth form makes world-class walkers appear as though their feet are firmly planted on the ground as long as the time off the ground does not exceed this short time period. This creates quite a challenge for the judges in elite events to make sure that the ones who are off the ground long enough to gain an advantage are disqualified.

From a practical matter it would be virtually impossible, extremely time consuming and financially out of the question to put every walker on videotape for the entire race. The solution would seem to find ways to make human eye judging as expert and fair as possible, and perhaps require athletes to wear shoes that have a lot of contrast with the surface they walk on.

In the past few years, RPC, a Canadian company specializing in high-tech sensing technology equipment, has developed an electronic device named Run-Alarm, which requires that sensors be installed in both shoes to tell when both feet are off the ground for any amount of time. The device emits a beeping sound when contact with the ground is lost. This may be one of the best training devices ever developed to help athletes get used to the feel of when their feet are touching the ground and when they are not. It is debatable, however, if and when this contact device will ever be used in racewalking championships.

Without enforced rules there would be chaos in racewalking competition and we would get a ridiculous-looking new sport that resembles running with a double contact phase. There is little argument that racewalk judging is one of the toughest assignments in sport officiating. However, the level of competency is very high in most national and international racewalking events because of the rigorous training required before judges are allowed to officiate them. Competency, consistency and fairness are the attributes that these judges must exhibit to remain as high-level officials in the sport.

Those who like to ridicule the sport, such as some uninformed television reporters, say that high-speed video proves that there is widespread cheating taking place in high-level events. This is an unfair assessment of the situation. The fact is that the highly trained racewalk judges must make judgment calls such as a baseball umpire or basketball referee. How many times do you see a second baseman or shortstop miss the bag as he is starting a double play yet be credited with the play? How many basketball superstars are ignored by the officials when blatantly traveling toward the basket? All sports are subject to competency and unprejudiced judgment of those officials in charge and the events would be in complete chaos without them.

Like many other sports where the judgment of the officials is the only way a sport can be held, racewalking always will depend on them. With enough knowledgeable officials and the increase of more people willing to help keep the sport of racewalking as fair as the other judged sporting events already so popular with the American public, I am certain that it can flourish.

25 | A Comparison of Walking and Running

> "Run only if you must. If running is an imperative that comes from inside you and not from your doctor. Otherwise, heed the inner calling to your own play. Listen if you can to the person you were and are and can be. Then do what you do best and feel best at. Something you would do for nothing. Something that gives you security and self-acceptance and a feeling of completion ... . When you find it, build your life around it.
> —George Sheehan, M.D.

If you are a runner but want to try a new form of aerobic exercise, you may wish to add speed walking into your workouts. Running is primarily a leg exercise and is far less intensive in technique than racewalking. Running is a falling, loading, pushing motion with the hamstring, Achilles tendon and calf muscles as its driving forces. The legs never straighten during the running movement, and for that reason hip action is not pronounced or even apparent except in very fast running. The slower you go the flatter your feet land. Running or jogging slowly, such as 12 to 13 minutes per mile or slower, is less efficient than walking at the same speed. From about 12 minutes per mile and faster, however, jogging or running becomes more efficient than walking because it becomes harder to keep the feet on the ground while walking at higher speeds—therefore, walkers are getting a better workout.

Differences in Body Types

Long-distance runners often develop a gaunt, skinny look that helps them run faster. They strive for a light frame with a large motor that increases their efficiency. Walkers on the other hand do not need to concern themselves with such a light frame. There have been many top-level walkers with fully developed bodies that come into play because of the overall muscle use so characteristic of the sport.

The Differences in Muscle Use between Walking and Running

Since racewalking uses more muscles than most other sports, walkers can get into better overall body condition than runners who primarily use just the leg muscles. Runners, cyclists and swimmers, for example, do not get the same overall body capillary enlargement that a racewalker does. Certainly a superbly trained marathon runner would have the same or slightly better cardiovascular capacity and leg strength, but would lack the necessary capillary enlargement in the hips, arms, front of the legs and shoulders to allow the legal movements of racewalking. Running is almost entirely a bent leg–driving exercise. Conversely, the world's leading racewalkers could, with a small amount of running training, compete fairly well in running because they would have the necessary cardiovascular endurance and capillary buildup in the legs similar to top runners. Some of the world's elite racewalkers do use running as a method of cross training to put variety into their training programs. It is practically unheard of, however, for runners to cross train by racewalking. They don't know that the increased hip flexibility gained would increase their efficiency of stride. Actually, the world's top racewalkers try to make walking as close as possible to running by still maintaining legal walking techniques. After all, running is the fastest way to go.

Anyone who watches runners and racewalkers moving along can readily distinguish significant differences in how muscles are being used in each activity. Running is mainly a pushing/falling activity, which is due to the fact that the leg usually lands under the center of gravity with each stride. This leaves the body in a continuously unstable situation. This instability, along with the magnitude of forces that are needed to counter it, are what makes running such an injury-prone sport. The human knee was simply not designed to withstand the sort of eccentric loading that you find in running. This is accentuated by running on concrete in shoes with soles made out of unstable "marshmallow fluff." Running is, in fact, a very "one-sided" sort of activity in that it uses the muscles in the back of the leg to a greater degree than those in the front. It takes a fairly athletically inclined person to withstand the forces of a lot of running.

In racewalking there is a better balance of activity between the muscles being used. This is due to the fact that they must not only drive to the body but also start from a position of heel strike that is slightly in front of the body and progress to the classic straight leg through the rest of the stride. This provides a stiff lever from start to finish. It also makes racewalking more energy intensive for distance moved since the body cannot rely on the stretch reflex of the tendons and muscle groups as much for propulsion as in running. This is one thing that makes walking so injury-free—less use of ballistic stretching of muscle groups to get energy back into the system. Therefore, racewalking is a combination of a pulling from the point of heel contact until the foot is directly under the center of gravity—and pushing/falling from that point to the rear where the toes leave the ground. These factors make walking a better overall body workout than running. Specifically, the differences in muscle activity used in racewalking and running are as follows:

1. In running the arms are essentially used for balance and timing. In walking there is greater use of many of the upper body muscles that are used to

swing the arms from front to back (not side to side or back to front) to counteract the hip motion and stay in balance. Pushing the arms forward is counterproductive because it pushes the upper body backward.

2. The muscles of the back and hips are moved more vigorously in racewalking, which helps the legs propel the body forward. It also allows for greater leg length, causing them to act as if the apex or the triangle created by the legs and the ground is significantly higher. In other words, the hip rotating action increases stride length by moving to the front and back with each stride, which allows the racewalker a smooth and characteristic hip motion without any bobbing up and down. The hips are used to a lesser extent in running, although one of the most noticeable differences between an elite runner and the average jogger is that the elite runner will use the hips more, and thus get more propulsion in a more fluid manner.

3. The leg muscles, of course, are the primary propulsive muscles in both running and walking. There are three major differences in the way that various muscles are used:

    a) Whereas in running the foot is brought forward until the foot is placed under the center of gravity, in racewalking the foot continues on to a short distance in front of the body. This means that the muscles in the hip and also the quadriceps must work to straighten the leg. This also causes more use of the vastus medialis—the innermost quadriceps muscle, which is instrumental in the final 15 degrees of the straightening of the knee.

    b) The tibialis anterior (shin muscle) is used much more in walking than in running. It holds the toe up so that the shoe and foot create a "rocker" for the athlete to roll over. Since a runner doesn't put the foot down in front of the body and lands more or less flat footed, there is no need for the development of this muscle.

    c) The gastrocnemius group (back of leg muscles) acts more forcefully in a walker than in a runner. The racewalker must generate all ground reaction forces of propulsion from the contraction of this muscle with some help of hip muscles, which forces the weight-bearing leg backward, whereas the runner can use the muscle-tendon stretch reflex to bound forward into each stride.

When you watch a walker and runner going along there is much more noticeable muscle activity happening in the racewalker from the neck down through the toes. This is mainly due to the fact that it does take more effort to stay on the ground at all times at racing speed than to lift off with each step. This is the reason for the no-lifting rule in racewalking. The bent leg rule was instituted in walking because a bent leg gives a powerful "runners push-off" utilizing normal running muscles instead of walking muscles, and it makes both running and walking look strange if the competitor keeps one foot on the ground at all times.

Converting Runners to Walkers

Efficient runners do not land on the toes—that is only for sprinters. They don't overstride but try to keep the feet under the body. Foot contact should be directly under the knee with the knee flexed. The upper body is essentially relaxed and the arms are used mainly as timing devices. Good runners generally stay erect with a straight back. Too pronounced of a forward lean will cause more work for the leg muscles to push forward. The head is kept erect, which results in an upright, balanced stance, the head in line with the trunk and the trunk in line with the legs. The elbow should not be locked at a right angle as it is in racewalking, and the arms are not used to the same extent. If the elbows are locked while running it creates tension and causes the shoulders to sway. Using the upper body too much causes a runner to work harder to go slower.

A good runner, in order to learn efficient walking technique, needs to work on racewalking form and technique for a fairly lengthy period unless expert instruction is available. Their conditioning would be superb, but the muscles and coordination necessary to walk fast would be lacking at first. Runners seem to have a difficult time adapting to the straight-legged technique required for legal walking. Longtime runners seem to have an automatic reflex of flexing the knee as the foot strikes the ground on each stride. They could learn very rapidly if they would make a special effort to lift their toes as much as possible at heel strike. Their walking speed would be limited because they would be relying on leg strength and cardiovascular conditioning alone—an extremely inefficient way to go. They are usually very immobile in their hips, displaying little horizontal or vertical movement. Runners new to the walking technique seem to be constantly in danger of being illegal as far as the rules of walking are concerned. However, these difficulties are greatly diminished if they are taught to change their motor patterns by a competent racewalking instructor. There are many experienced and competent instructors who have converted good runners into excellent racewalking competitors in a short period of time.

26 Cross-Training Activities

"The most delightful pleasures cloy without variety."
—Publilius Syrus

European racewalkers, who are among the best in the world, do a lot more cross training between different sports than U.S. athletes. They claim that it makes them less resistant to "burnout" and overstress as they work hard to stay in optimum physical condition. A 1968 study by Menier and Pugh established a high oxygen uptake for Olympic-level walkers, although no one picked up on the fact that these athletes had a double-gaited fitness and could transfer their walking fitness to the running gait. Many studies have shown that when duration and intensity are increased, the injury rate for runners also has a dramatic increase. Dr. George Sheehan in *The Physician and Sports Medicine* pointed out that, "Runners are now encouraged to substitute some of their running time with cycling, swimming or weight lifting. But when we think about alternative types of training, we should consider walking. It is possible that walking will enhance our running more than any of our current alternative sports."

Let's look at some alternate activities that may be employed in your exercise program to help keep you in condition, remembering that the main emphasis in your training should be on racewalking:

- *Cross-country skiing* has been used successfully by many racewalking athletes in the winter as an enjoyable activity to stay in excellent aerobic condition. This is an overall body exercise just as racewalking is, but develops the arm and shoulder strength more than walking does. The diagonal stride technique is a bit more related to walking than the skating technique, but skating is so much more fun and efficient that it should be learned as well. I never get tired or bored of this fun exercise.

- *Swimming* is very good for the upper body but doesn't do much for the legs. Since it is a nonweight-bearing activity, it does little to strengthen the skeletal system or help prevent osteoporosis. It is a good aerobic sport if you swim at least 45 minutes a day. If you are a typical swimmer, you rest a lot more than you swim and the activity is nowhere near continuous. It requires a fairly long pool to give you maximum benefit. Swimming is an okay adjunct to a walking program. Either swim in addition to walking or on days when you cannot walk for a particular reason. Often, it is inconvenient or hard to find a pool to swim in when it fits into your schedule, unless you have one at home. Many find that doing repeated laps for a half hour or more in a pool somewhat boring.

• *Running* does use some of the same muscular systems as racewalking but is not an overall body exercise like racewalking. It is as good as any exercise for aerobic conditioning and leg strengthening. As I discuss elsewhere in the book, there is a certain amount of risk of injury unless you are one of those few lucky ones that seem to be immune to running injuries. See chapter 25 on the differences between walking and running.

• *Bicycling* is good if you can do it in a place where you can stay at a steady pace to get a decent workout. If you pedal hard enough to keep your pulse at your ideal level and don't coast it's good, but you'll have to ride a long way—maybe 20 or more miles. Again, it is a nonweight-bearing activity and is fairly dangerous (if done in traffic or on slippery or gravely surfaces) and expensive. It provides very good leg exercise especially for the quadriceps. The stationary bike is better in that you don't tend to coast and will keep up a steady pace. Bicycling is an excellent aerobic adjunct to your walking program for days when you can't walk. A caveat: Bicyclists tend to walk bent-kneed because the knee is taught not to straighten while riding.

• *Rowing* is an excellent aerobic exercise, but doing it on a machine may be as tedious as stationary bicycling or swimming. If you can row on a lake, it is one of the best possible activities, but few have this luxury. It should be done for 30 minutes or more at a time. Good cross training for walking for both the arms and legs. A caveat: Don't overdo this exercise at first because of potential back strain problems.

• *Rope jumping* is a very strenuous and strong aerobic workout and for that reason is extremely difficult to maintain for more than a few minutes. Because it requires a great deal of coordination and causes almost as much pounding on the legs as running, it is not highly recommended.

• *Roller skating/roller blading* is a very good aerobic activity as well as being lots of fun, but it can be rather dangerous because of the inability to dodge things quickly or brake adequately unless you are very good. It should be done in flat, unobstructed areas while wearing protective elbow and knee pads. The surfaces used for skating are very unyielding. Roller blading skates offer such little resistance that you can get into deep trouble by going too fast for your ability to be able to stop or bail out if something gets in the way. Realistically speaking, if you put a lot of effort into it, you can build up dangerous speeds.

- *Court sports (racquetball, handball, volleyball, tennis, etc.)* are all fun games and good exercise activities as long as they are played hard with people of somewhat equal ability. The fact remains that most people do them for fun and don't put a lot of effort into them. They are stop and start exercises. The movements, while sometimes vigorous, are not constant enough and may be classed as "anaerobic" (without oxygen) in nature. The pulse is not maintained at the steady heart rate required for aerobic improvement. Pulse rates vary between 90 and 170 with the elevated rates being too brief. The sports are a good adjunct to your walking program, but there is a relatively high risk of minor injuries.

- *Team sports (softball, flag football, bowling, etc.)* are also loads of fun, but too much time is spent waiting for something to happen. They are not very good cardiovascular exercises because of their anaerobic nature, and are fraught with a dangerous amount of injuries. Soccer is probably the best aerobic game followed by basketball. These are good adjuncts to walking because they are fun and likely to be continued because of their social nature.

The Impact of Running

An average runner hits the ground at a minimum of at least three times their body weight and much more in very fast running. A walker loads their weight on the foot at one and one-quarter to one and one-half times their body weight. Any analysis of the two gaits must take into account the way the foot makes contact with the ground. A runner is airborne and the heel or entire foot strikes the ground, which introduces shock to the musculoskeletal system. By contrast, a walker is always in contact with the ground, and the heel is placed on the ground with very low impact, a significant difference.

Let's assume a 154-pound man runs 40 miles a week including interval training. He decides to shift 20 of the miles to high-intensity walking. He has a 4-foot running stride, which means he takes 1,320 steps per mile (5,280 feet/4=1,320). Because of the horizontal springing action of running, fewer strides per mile are taken than a walker. The numbers look like this:

2 x 154 = 308 extra running-impact pounds per step over walking

308 x 1,320 steps = 406,560 extra running-impact pounds per mile over walking

406,560 x 20 miles = 8,131,200 extra running-impact pounds per week over walking

It stands to reason that over the many years of a runner's racing career, a reduction of impact of this magnitude would be a significant mitigating factor in injury prevention. Indeed, high-intensity walking could not only contribute to injury prevention in runners but could very well extend some running careers. It is probably the most overlooked, underrated training option available to runners. Creative coaches should get their runners out of the swimming pools, off the bicycles and out on the road or track doing high-intensity walking for the best cross-training exercise possible.

PART 4

Appendices

A Layperson's Guide to Exercise Physiology

It often fills me with wonder how so many people know less about the inner workings of their own bodies and so much more about other things. Doesn't it make some sense to learn more about the place you live—and will live 24 hours a day for your entire life—your own body? Perhaps a little rudimentary description of the environment within your envelope of skin will whet your interest and curiosity for further knowledge on just what goes on in there during exercise.

All physical movement depends on a very complex set of instructions sent out to various body functions by the brain. The movers and shakers are the muscles acting on the skeletal system that supports them. There are, however, many other body functions that must aid the working muscles as they spring into action. When you decide to make a certain movement, the nervous system is directed by the brain to activate a great number of bodily functions that are necessary to support the actions of the musculoskeletal system. Oxygen and fuels such as glucose must be delivered in the bloodstream to provide the necessary energy to the muscles and various cells. The circulatory system is also responsible for removing waste products and carbon dioxide as exercise continues. Many hormones, such as adrenaline, are needed to assist in force and energy production. I will address these complicated functions in a very simplified fashion and you needn't be a scientist to understand them.

The Musculoskeletal System

There are 215 muscles and 205 bones in the human body and many tendons and cartilage binding the whole system together. The joints where bone systems meet are articulated or moved by the muscles and tendons. There are three types of joints: *fibrous*, which have little or no movement and are connected by fibrous elastic connective tissue, such as those in the skull; *cartilaginous*, which are similar to fibrous but have very limited motion (e.g., the vertebrae); and *synovial*, which articulate our joints involved in movement. This latter joint type has a thin layer of cartilage that covers the ends of the bones and a fibrous capsule that covers the joint. It is lined on the inside with a membrane called the synovial membrane. This membrane produces a synovial fluid, which provides a natural "lube job" for reducing friction as the joints move. The knee has several fibrous disks between the femur and tibia called menisci that compensate for additional strain on this joint.

As a general rule, muscle size and strength go together. There are three types of muscle strength: iso*metric strength*, the force that can be exerted against an immovable object; *isotonic strength*, the maximum weight that can be lifted at one time; and *isokinetic strength*, the maximal force output throughout a range of motion. Every movement we make requires force by a prime mover muscle called an *agonist*, but this must not be interfered with by the antagonist opposing muscles that must be relaxed if the prime movers are to work efficiently. This is a main reason why the body must be relaxed when racewalking. When muscles shorten it is called *concentric contraction*. If a muscle contracts without shortening, the contraction is called *isometric*. If a muscle lengthens, as the biceps would do when the elbow extends when lowering a heavy weight, the motion is known as *eccentric*. (An explanation of these functions can be found in chapter 22, "The Roles of Muscles in Walking.") There are two muscle fiber types—*slow twitch* and *fast twitch*. Those muscles with a predominance of slow twitch fibers have endurance characteristics that allow them to operate over a longer period of time. Those walkers who have mostly this type of fiber do well in long-distance events. Fast twitch fibers, on the other hand, help sprinters and those who must use rapid or explosive movements, but endurance capability is lower.

Energy for Movement

Foods that we eat contain protein, carbohydrate and fat molecules, but protein is little used in energy production and mainly used for providing the amino acid building blocks for repairing tissues and to synthesize essential enzymes and hormones. The energy comes mainly from carbohydrates and secondarily from fats. In order for the energy from foods to be used by the body, the foods must be broken down into a form that can be stored in the muscles and the liver. The body requires that the energy that bonds food molecules together must be released and stored as a*denosine triphosphate*, commonly referred to as ATP, a high-energy phosphate. *Enzymes* are organic catalysts that speed specific body chemical reactions. Enzymes assimilated from foods must chemically act on ATP to release energy in a form far more potent than originally contained in the foods consumed. The specific enzyme assigned to release energy to the muscles and brain is called *ATPase*, the suffix *"ase"* denoting *enzyme*. Glucose is formed in the transformation process and its storage form in muscles and the liver is called *glycogen*. Muscle contractions receive the needed energy when a nerve impulse triggers the splitting of the ATP. Glycogen is broken down in a process called *glycolysis* to form lactic acid and ATP. A series of enzymes then breaks down glucose, glycogen or free fatty acids and combines with oxygen to form carbon dioxide and water. Energy released from this action is used to form more ATP. The first stages of this process are done without oxygen (anaerobically) but the final step requires oxygen (aerobically).

The anaerobic process yields only 3 molecules of ATP while the final one yields 39 molecules. For this reason you can only exercise anaerobically for about a minute, but can exercise a long time in an aerobic state. Enzyme activity is enhanced when muscles are warm, which is a good reason why you should warm up before exercising strenuously. Strenuous exercise produces lactic acid, a waste product that reduces enzyme activity and causes fatigue. Enzymes work more rapidly when there is more food available that can be processed. The trick is to eat the right foods to enhance the process. See chapter 4 on nutrition and health. For the processing of oxygen see chapter 10.

APPENDIX 2

Loosening and Flexibility Exercises

Knee Bend. Bend down with both feet firmly planted on the floor, keeping the back straight and the arms stetched outward. Repeat 10 to 20 times. Good for stretching the muscles around the knee and front of the thigh.

Table Stretch. Alternately place legs on a low table or chair. Slowly bend body forward several times. Good for stretching the rear of the legs to increase their flexibility.

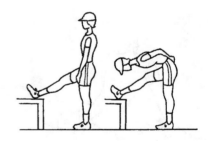

Ilipsoas Stretch. Crouch over one leg and keep the shin vertical with the other behind, placing hands on floor. Gently lower the hip up and down to create a mild stretch. Hold for 20 to 30 seconds. Stretches the muscles in the front of the hip. Also good for hamstrings, groin and lower back.

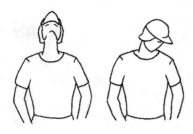

Neck Roll. Roll your head slowly in a full circle. Hold in a stretch where desired for a few seconds. Good for neck flexibility and aids in attaining better posture.

Prone Stretch. Lie flat on back and bring one leg over to the opposite side, keeping shoulders and arms flat on floor. Good stretch for hip and torso muscles. Hold for 20 to 30 seconds and repeat several times on each side.

Quad Stretch. Sit on floor with one leg tucked under the buttocks. While sitting, bend hip forward and back. Good for stretching quadricep muscle. Can also be done with opposite leg straight in front.

Hop Rotation. Hop from side to side and twist the arms and hips from one side to the other, keeping the feet together. Good for loosening hip, stomach and diaphragm muscles. Do for 15 to 20 seconds and repeat several times.

Side Leg Raise. Lay on side and raise leg in the air to a 90-degree angle from resting leg. Hold for 10 seconds and repeat several times on each side. Also reach upper hand toward raised leg at times. Good for stretching and strengthening the torso and hip muscles.

Toe Lift. Stand with toes on a 2- to 3-inch object and flex ankle up and down. Repeat 20 to 30 times. This flexes and strengthens the tibialis anterior and tendon and reduces shin pain often experienced by beginners.

Upward Reach Stretch. Clasp hands above head. Hold for 10 seconds or more. Good for stretching the shoulder and arm muscles.

Bent Leg Sit-Up. Lie on floor and do partial bent leg sit-ups. Excellent strengthening exercise for abdominal muscles.

Windmill Stretch. Move arms in a back stroke motion and let the body rotate while walking. Practice in a stationary postition first. Do this until you feel a loosening effect. Excellent for loosening the shoulders and upper torso. Increases coordination.

Knee Lifts. Stand and lift knee to inside of opposite leg and place hands behind neck. Do this as a dynamic exercise and repeat several times on each side. A good conditioner for waist and hip flexors.

Sitting on Feet Knee Stretch. Sit on floor with feet under the buttocks. Get into this position gradually so as not to strain the knee. Hold for 15 to 20 seconds and repeat several times. Good for stretching the quads and knee joint.

Leg Figure 8s. Brace yourself for balance and move foot in a figure 8 movement. Repeat several times with each leg. This aids in leg coordination and ability to swing the leg freely from the hip joint.

Neck Exercise. Place hand behind head and rotate head side to side slowly. Good for loosening and strengthening the neck muscles.

Gastrocnemius Stretch. Keep back leg straight
with heel on floor turned slightly outward. Lean
into wall until stretch is felt in the calf. Good
stretch for gastrocnemius in the rear of the legs
and the Achilles tendon.

Seated Thigh Stretch. Sit with knees out and
soles of feet together. Grasp ankles and pull body
foreward. Hold for 15 to 20 seconds and repeat
several times. Stretches the groin muscles.

Modified Hurdler Stretch. Sit on floor with one
leg straight and the other tucked in. Use towel
over bottom of foot so stretch can be adjusted.
Good stretch for hamstring and calf muscles.

Seated Torso Stretch. Sit on the floor and cross one leg over the other, turning head and torso in opposite direction. Place elbow on inside of opposite knee. Stretch a few times to each side. Good stretch for spinal and torso muscles.

Hamstring Stretch. Lie on your back and lift leg straight up to a 90-degree angle from the ground. Place hand under the knee of lifted leg. Hold for 10 to 15 seconds and repeat. Good for stretching the hamstring muscle.

Soleus Stretch. Keep back leg slightly bent with heel on floor turned slightly outward. Lean into wall and flex knees until stretch is felt in calf. A good stretch for the soleus muscle in back of the lower leg.

Walking on Edge of Feet. Walk on edges of feet until muscles tire and repeat several times with rest periods in between. Good for strengthening ankle and foot muscles that aid in foot push-off at the rear of the stride.

Toe Touch. Bend forward with the legs straight and gently stretch the hands toward the floor. Good for stretching the muscles on the rear of the legs and the lower back. Don't strain—let stretch happen gradually.

Quadricep Stretch. Steady yourself against a solid object and grasp one ankle with your hand. Pull heel toward buttock until the quadricep muscle (front of thigh) is stretched. Hold each leg for 30 seconds.

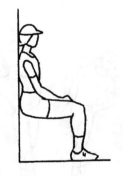

Sitting against Wall. Place back against a wall and assume a sitting position. Hold for 10 seconds or more. Good for strengthening the quadricep muscles.

Side Stretch. Bend sideways and reach toward foot. Hold for 10 seconds and alternate to each side several times. Good for stretching the side torso muscles.

Shoulder Stretch. With arms overhead, grasp the elbow of one arm with the other hand and pull elbow behind head. Hold each side for 15 to 20 seconds. Good for stretching back of arm and shoulder muscles. Can also be done while walking.

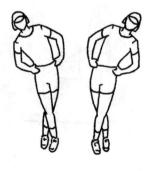

Squat. Squat with toes pointed slightly outward and heels 5 inches apart. Hold for upward of 30 seconds as you become more flexible. Good stretch for knees, back, ankles, Achilles tendons and deep groin.

Tensor Stretch. Cross one leg in front of the other and lean to opposite side until stretch is felt on outside of hip. Stretch to each side a few times. Called the tensor stretch, this is good for stretching the side muscles.

Arm Swing. Step forward on one foot and swing arms and torso as far as possible in that direction. Exhale as body twists to one side and inhale as arms come to forward position. Repeat on each side several times. Good for stretching the abdominal and lower back regions.

Towel Swivel. Hold a towel in each hand behind the buttocks and use it to rotate the hips
as though you were drying them. This is helpful
in rotating the hips in the same action as when
racewalking. Do it after showering as well.

Prone Knee Bend. Lie on floor and pull knee
toward chest. Alternate each leg for 10 seconds
or more and repeat several times. Good stretch
for lower back and buttocks.

Walking Crossover. Walk with an exaggerated
crossover step, hands clasped and swinging opposite to the hip girdle. Repeat the crossover a
dozen or more times. This gives added flexibility to the torso, shoulders and hips.

Role Models

Howard Channell

Born in 1918, Howard Channell is one of the best and most dedicated athletes in his somewhat mature age group. He grew up in Kansas where his early athleticism was dedicated mostly to basketball. Having had a successful high school career in the sport, he was awarded an athletic scholarship to Kansas State University. He also ran the quarter mile in track. At the start of World War II he was in the U.S. Air Force where he ran on an Air Force track team and did an impressive 4:15 mile. In the 1950s and 1960s he was relatively inactive as far as athletics were concerned.

After retirement from the service in 1970 he began to do some systematic exercise including jogging. In 1981 he moved to the Denver area to be closer to his children. Eventually his knees began to hurt from running. After consulting with a physician, he found that he had damaged knee cartilage and that he needed to have two pairs of vertebrae fused in his back. In early 1985, at age 66, his doctor told him to walk for exercise and to avoid jarring exercises. At that time he started his gradual rise in walking efficiency and became a student of the racewalking technique. He joined the Front Range Walkers Club in its first year of operation in 1985, and in that same year won a silver medal in the Senior Games.

Since that time he has won many gold medals in his age group as his times have steadily declined with age—seemingly fooling mother nature. Apparently he has not fully reached his potential yet at a time of life when most of his peers are becoming crippled and doing the old-age shuffle. Some times, accomplished in his early to mid-seventies have been 29:40 for 5K, 17:39 for 3,000 meters and 8:29 for 1,500 meters—marks that many people half his age would be delighted with.

He watches his diet scrupulously and carefully takes supplemental vitamins that seem to help him remain strong. He supplements his walking training with weight training and is extremely strong for a man his age. He has been certified as a racewalking judge and regularly helps in this activity. He will certainly carry on for many more years as an excellent role model for walkers in the Denver, Colorado, area.

Judy Coffee

Judy Coffee's story is an amazing one of determination, perseverance, hard work and success. What she accomplished is very hard to believe except for those who saw it happen. Experts say that losing the weight she did as fast as she did is highly improbable.

Overweight as a child, she never participated in athletics, although she pursued equestrian sports for five years, training and cross-country jumping her own horses. Judy's problem with weight persisted until April of 1988 when she decided to join Weight Watchers. Those of us who have seen this slim, attractive, 5-foot, 9-inch-tall lady striding past us during a race will find it hard to believe that Judy weighed 289 pounds when she made that decision to change her life.

During the 16 months it took to lose 145 pounds, Judy walked a lot of miles, able to cover only a half mile at first at a very slow pace. Fitness walking helped stabilize her metabolism, relieve stress and provide the psychological boost she needed to increase her self-esteem. After gradually increasing her endurance to 45 minutes of walking five times a week, she entered her first race—the 5K Colorado racewalk championship at Evergreen on July 4, 1989. She finished, walking without any particular technique background on a hilly course at 7,000 feet of altitude in the respectable time of 35:12. It was there she observed Viisha Sedlak racing and became very excited about the possibility of learning how to become efficient at racewalking. With my encouragement, she began the learning process in one of my classes one month later. She was also given some instruction by the "Olympic God" Carl Schueler after the Summerwalk 5K event two months later in Littleton. She made rapid progress in speed and efficiency during the last half of that year. The results of her first eight competitions speak for themselves: 7/4/89, 5K—35:12; 8/19/89, 5K—34:16; 9/4/89, 5K—33:15; 9/17/89, 5.34 miles—60:00; 10/7/89, 5K—32:00; 10/28/89, 5K—33:53; 11/23/89, 4 miles—41:28; and 12/30/89, 2 miles—19:47.

Judy says she tries to lead a well-balanced life. Friends like being around her because they rely on and appreciate her stability. Walking provides a solitude she uses to get her thoughts organized and to focus on positive things. Her hints for better nutrition are to reduce intake of fats, drink lots of water and eat foods high in complex carbohydrates. She hopes her future includes becoming a leader with Weight Watchers and that continued racewalking will provide her a fit and healthy older adulthood (she's now in her mid-40s). Judy's success is fueled by the philosophy printed on a cup given to her by husband Rob, "If you believe you can, you are halfway there." Her story is an inspiration to all, especially those who aspire to improve their life through exercise, diet and weight loss.

Don Denoon

This women's track coach (in his early fifties in 1996) at Southern Illinois University in Carbondale, Illinois, is a remarkable athlete and deserves a lot of credit for his excellence in racewalking. Don Denoon started out as a runner at the age of 13, but his father had jobs that kept the family moving around the country. In high school he ran for the track team with good success in Rapid City, South Dakota. After high school he entered the U.S. Air Force (1962–1966) where he joined their track team as a runner. This track team entered meets where there were team points scored for racewalking. The head coach persuaded Don and another runner to learn racewalking technique and represent the Air Force team in track meets. Don seemed to have an aptitude for the event because after an initial effort of around 21 minutes for 2 miles he soon brought the time down below 16 minutes for the distance. In 1966 he had become so adept that he was able to lower the world 1-mile racewalking record from 6:17.3 to 6:10.2 at the indoor *Los Angeles Times* track meet. He credits encouragement from southern California coach Charles Silcock to be one of his main motivators to excel in the sport.

He found a women's team that needed coaching in 1964 while still in the Air Force, and this became the start of a 30-year career of coaching others— mostly women. After leaving the Air Force in 1966, he became a student at Long Beach State as he continued coaching and training. He was able to coach such luminaries as the world-famous runner Mary Decker (later Slaney) up to the time she entered college at age 18. He qualified to attend the racewalking Olympic Trials in 1968 and 1972 and nearly made both Olympic teams. Later he coached at various colleges and universities, including Drake, and culminated with his present job at Southern Illinois University in 1984.

He currently works out both on his own and with his athletes as an aid to staying in fantastic condition. He trains hard and stays in remarkable shape, routinely beating athletes half his age. He incorporates both running and racewalking into his training and finds that they are complementary to each other.

Since entering the 50+ division he not only leaves those in his own age group in the dust, but those in the 40+ division as well. He has set U.S. masters records for his age in the 5K (21:48), 10K (44:59), 15K (1:08:37) and 20K (1:32:15). Only a few athletes in the prime of their lives can duplicate these times. At the time of this writing, he holds U.S. records for all distances on both road and track events, some of which are also world records. He established himself as the fastest 50+ racewalker in the world at the World Veteran's Games in Japan in 1993 where he prevailed over the 40+ athletes as well. He repeated that feat in a 1994 World Masters Championship in Toronto, Canada, where he again beat every other entrant. He was named to the USA Track & Field National Racewalking Team in 1993, which is quite an honor even for young athletes in their prime. His athletic career can be characterized as one of dedication, enthusiasm and perseverance, elements that any walker can be proud of.

Giulio De Petra

Here is a story of one man's remarkable persistence and dedication to the sport of racewalking for over 70 years. Born in a small mountain town in southern Italy, Giulio De Petra was sent by his family to Naples each year to receive a better education. One day in 1924 at the age of 14, he was sitting sullenly on the infield of a school's running track discouraged by his inability to compete favorably with the other youngsters in the running and jumping events. Suddenly an approaching figure on the track caught his eye—it was a competitive racewalker cruising around the track in a style he had not seen before. Intrigued, he walked onto the track, pulled in behind the walker and proceeded to mimic his form. The man noticed him and began to pick up the pace but for lap after lap was unable to leave young Giulio behind. In frustration the racewalker finally left the track, leaving a youngster excited about learning the beginnings of a new athletic skill. Within three months of this episode, Guilio won the student racewalking championship for the Campania region of southern Italy.

He started training harder and began competing nationally at the age of 16, gaining the reputation as a young superstar in the sport. The year 1928 brought realistic expectations of competing in the Amsterdam Olympiad, but international disputes regarding the rules of racewalking resulted in the event being canceled. When the event distance was increased to 50K in 1932, Giulio found that he could not excel at this longer distance. He did very well for half that distance, but at the time he was self-coached and not aware of the detrimental effects of dehydration—he did not drink adequate fluids to do well in such a race.

In 1933 he began training for the 1933 Olympics in Berlin. He attended a 25K race called "Quer durch Berlin" (Tour of Berlin) and finished second behind Swiss walker Arthur Schwab. He attended the same race the next year and finished third. He traveled to Hamilton, Canada, to compete in the 50K Canadian Championship where he led for much of the race, but again faded because of dehydration and finished second. Unfortunately, his dream to compete in the Berlin Games was not realized because he was drafted into the Italian Army to fight in Ethiopia where he remained from late 1935 until early 1937. When he returned to civilian life he moved to Pescara where he resumed training and organizing events. In 1938 he won the 25K Italian Racewalking Championship and entered in all the national events until he was again pressed into the army as the clouds of war began to develop over Europe. His training was interrupted until the war's end.

In 1948, at 37 years old, he emigrated to the United States to study English at Pasadena City College as job opportunities in his beleaguered home country were few. In 1951 he was employed teaching Italian at the Army Language School at the Presidio of the Monterey where he soon became chairman of the Italian Language department. He retired from teaching in 1976 and resumed his racewalking career, promoting a sport not yet well known on the Monterey Peninsula. He taught the sport at the Monterey Peninsula College and created a club known to this day as the Monterey Peninsula Walk Walk Walk Club. He obtained a nonprofit status for the club and organized five racewalking national championships in ensuing years.

He jumped back into competition again and won numerous age group awards both nationally and internationally. From 1983 to 1993 he participated in all the world masters championships garnering three gold, six silver and two bronze medals. Two of these gold medals were at the 1993 championships in Miayazaki, Japan. While preparing for the 1995 World Championships in Buffalo, New York, he unexpectedly was striken with a fatal heart attack. Giulio De Petra will be fondly remembered by his legions of racewalking friends all over the world.

Bob DiCarlo

Bob DiCarlo is a master athlete—he exemplifies what walking can do for health and what serious training can do to improve performance in racewalking. Bob grew up in Crawford, New Jersey, but his athletic career didn't begin until he attended the University of Michigan as a 2-miler. He modestly suggests that his time for the event (9 minutes, 32 seconds) was not very good, but those who have tried this demanding event know this is an excellent time. He studied medicine and chose anesthesiology as his specialty. After finishing his medical training he moved to Denver where he currently practices his specialty at a local hospital. Bob joined the running community as a Rocky Mountain Road Runner and became prominent in the activity, achieving a 2:40 marathon and a 34:52 10K as a 40+ runner.

Little did he know in April 1986 that a traumatic and dramatic event would change him from a runner to a walker. While out training in the evening after work in his neighborhood, he collapsed from a severe heart attack. He was extremely lucky that someone nearby trained in cardiopulmonary resuscitation found him in time to save his life. Diagnosis revealed clogged arteries and the medical decision was that a cardiac bypass operation was necessary to give Bob further quality of life. Bob's physician recommended a walking program as rehabilitation therapy, not realizing that Bob's old competitive spirit had not waned. Instead of just strolling around as a normal patient would do, Bob wisely consulted Front Range Walker member Leonard Jansen, an expert racewalking coach at the Olympic Training Center. He started training for racewalking in earnest and began entering some local races as he got stronger and stronger.

A rigorous training program has yielded some impressive times as he gets faster over 60 years old—an 8:26 mile and 57:54 10K. A real highlight of his new athletic career was a 27:39 5K at the World Veteran's Championships in Eugene, Oregon, which placed him sixth in the 55–59 division. Then, at the next World Veterans Games he did even better at 26:48. Now in his sixties he is still cruising along at a high speed (in the upper 26-minute range for 5Ks) and winning some races overall against younger people.

During the winter season, Bob trains indoors at his health club, alternating speed work and endurance sessions, considering a 10:30 mile as his slow pace—a pace that many of us would be very satisfied with. He includes weight training for upper body strength in his regimen, knowing what it takes to compete at a high level. With his impeccable form, Bob probably has not yet reached his full potential. Future years will certainly see even more amazing racewalking times for this might-have-been "cardiac cripple."

George Dyer Jr.

It is exciting when we meet someone who is born less than genetically perfect and who has the courage and enthusiasm to overcome many obstacles. Born in June 1967, George Dyer Jr. was afflicted with Rubinstein Tabes Syndrome, a rare and potentially debilitating condition that normally causes profound retardation. In his early years he had no coordination and could neither walk nor talk. Up to the age of six there was little hope that he could escape an institutional life.

When George was very young, his father died, leaving his mother Ellen faced with the task of raising George by herself. Gradually, with his mother's loving attention, George responded well to medical treatment and he was soon able to attend public junior high school. Ellen and the doctors familiar with the case considered George's continuing progress to be a minor miracle.

Since those junior high school years, George has been interested in athletic activities. He began participating in Special Olympics' events at about the age of 12 and made such impressive progress that in 1983 at age 16, he was selected to represent Colorado in the International Special Olympics in Baton Rouge, Louisiana. In those days, his special interests were swimming, bowling, basketball and track and field. He became a regular at the North Jeffco Recreation Center where he developed many skills that earlier would otherwise have seemed impossible for someone of his handicap. The center hired him to be a recreation aide in its summer "Tiny Tot" program. George said of those years that nothing discouraged his desire to partake in any programs offered by the Special Olympics. Sports were and still are the special passion of his life.

In 1988 George was introduced to racewalking by Front Range Walker member John Lyle and Ron Dunsmore of the Colorado Governor's Council for Physical Fitness, a coach for the Special Olympics. Although they both encouraged George to participate in racewalking events, he did not enter any of the metro Denver local open races until the Governor's Cup 5K in 1994. Since that time he shows up regularly at races with great enthusiasm.

His exercise routines have become a big part of his life and consist of regular bowling leagues four times a week, swimming one night a week and racewalking as many times as he can during the daytime. In summer he regularly participates in softball and track and field events. He credits this lifestyle with helping him lose a lot of weight, which, in turn, helped cure bad knee and ankle problems. Although he feels very tired at times, he does not let that deter him from continuing his extensive exercise programs—he enjoys them too much to give them up. He feels a lot of improved self-esteem as he views the 100+ medals and other awards he has received over the past 13 years. He now adds his racewalking awards to this treasure trove. His goal is to decrease his mile time in racewalking into the 10-minute range. It won't be surprising if he accomplishes this goal over the next few years as his technique improves. If we were to award a medal to the most enthusiatic person about the sport of racewalking, it would likely go to this inspirational athlete.

Katherine Greenamyre

"Have lots of outdoor exercises, make many friends, enjoy a variety of activities, don't blame others for your troubles, don't fall for diet fads but follow a sensible diet." This did not come from a page in a fitness magazine but from the lips of Katherine Greenamyre, a 100-year-old wonder who resides in Longmont, Colorado.

Born in 1896 at a farm in Cheney, a small town of 47 people, 10 miles south of Lincoln, Nebraska, Katherine moved with her family to Colorado when she was eight, where they lived on a farm south of Fort Collins. A teacher for most of her life, Katherine has taught girls athletics, creative writing, American history and Latin. Her autobiography, *Let Me Take You Back with Me*, traces her childhood to 1988 when she wrote the book. It also traces the Greenamyre family tree whose branches spread across the country. The annual family reunion, which she started many years ago, drew 32 in 1994, including great-nieces and -nephews from as far away as California, Arizona and Ohio.

Katherine is a lean and sprightly lady. She exercises and eats sensibly, enjoying her meat baked, not fried. She also eats potatoes, green vegetables, bread and butter, dessert and coffee or tea in her daily meals. She had always been a good walker, having walked much throughout her life. Many of those miles were from walking to her school job daily 1.5 miles each way. Many times she and some of her friends used to walk from Timnath into Fort Collins (about 6 miles) just for the fun and exercise. Today, despite fading eyesight and hearing, Katherine continues to walk around her neighborhood every morning when the weather is good. Her family has had a history of bad hearts, and as the sole survivor of four children, she is determined to stay out of the wheelchair by motivating herself to get out and walk whenever she can. Katherine is also active in community affairs. Her vigorous longevity has been featured in the local newspaper. In 1995 she signed up for a two-year membership in the Front Range Walkers. She surely keeps an active lifestyle that belies her chronological age. Katherine must be the oldest active walking club member in the United States. She is certainly an inspiration to all who want to live a long and healthy life.

Dan Immesoete

Dan Immesoete grew up in Peoria, Illinois, the eldest of six children. He had a fairly normal life as an athletically inclined child. He played all the usual Little League sports, finding competitive swimming as his forte. When he was in eighth grade, though, he started having trouble with one of his legs. The problem was diagnosed as osteogenic sarcoma, a rare degenerative bone cancer that can strike rather suddenly. Two years before Dan got the cancer, the same ailment was publicized heavily because one of Ted Kennedy's children also lost a leg to the disease.

Normally this would be a crushing blow to a superactive 14 year old, but Dan's spirit and desire to be a competitive athlete would not wane despite his entire leg being amputated just below the hip. Between problematic chemotherapy treatments, he kept on swimming, and in high school he worked out with the swim team on a regular basis.

After graduating from high school, he spent some time with the National Institutes of Health in Washington, D.C. Later he learned of a program at Colorado State University that leads to a degree in sports medicine and wellness management. He felt that this course of study fitted him very well and he matriculated there in 1987. In 1989 he took a year off from his university studies to join the Vail disabled ski team and did well in this sport as he competed with some of the best disabled skiers in the United States. He met the love of his life, Leann, at CSU and dated her all the way through college. They graduated in 1991 and married in January of 1992.

He got subsequent employment as an exercise physiologist with Associated Healthfocus in Stockton, California, and spent almost a year with them. The lure of the mountains was great, however, and in late 1992 he wangled a transfer to the Associated Healthfocus office in Denver.

Dan began entering triathlons, and, because of his constant training to stay in shape, found he could do quite well in the swimming and biking parts but was left in the dust in the running event because of the need to locomote on two crutches and one leg. He decided that entering running events would be another good way to stay in superb physical shape. Since swimming is a nonweight-bearing activity, he thought a weight-bearing exercise would help in his overall training.

He read about the Jingle Bells 5K in the Washington Park neighborhood in mid-December of 1992 and decided to enter the run. When he arrived at the park too late to enter the running event, he still had time to go in the walk. What happened next was a source of amazement when he cruised across a very icy, slippery course in 34:04, beating many seasoned racewalkers in the process. As a judge I devised a rule that he had to keep either one foot or two crutches on the ground at all times, and I noticed that neither his leg nor crutches were bent as they passed under his body. He then entered the 5K on Superbowl Sunday on dry streets and walked an astounding 31:24. In a Valentine's Day event he came back with a 31:34 5K.

With the cancer-oriented Qualife Wellness Community so heavily involved in our National 5K USA Track & Field Championship in Denver on August 29, 1993, it was only natural that we made a special effort to enter Dan. His crowning achievement came in this event where he amazed everyone by breaking 30 minutes at 29:48—well under 10 minutes per mile. This is a very good time for a normal person with two good legs. We doubt that any total-leg amputee in the world has attained such speed in a sanctioned event with IAAF world-class officials as witnesses.

In early 1994 he was offered a better position as a physical therapist in North Carolina, and he and Leann decided to move. I am sure that he continues to partcipate in athletics in his new location and inspire new walkers with his great character and courage.

Sally Richards

In all my years of watching people take up the sport of racewalking, I have never seen such a quick adaptation to legal technique and speed as Sally Richards showed in 1991 when she broke into the racewalking scene. In her very first race in Littleton, Colorado, on August 17, 1991, which was unjudged, she had virtually no idea what the rules were or how to comply with them. Consequently, in the opinion of some of the other competitors she was guilty of lifting as most runners tend to do at first. Sally decided to take a lesson from me to find out about this new and fascinating sport and shortly thereafter learned the rules and how to relax properly to attain legal technique. She bought a copy of Elaine Ward's *Introduction to the Technique of Racewalking* to use as a guide. On August 31 she entered the Masters 5K Track Championship in Boulder and, according to the judges, looked about as good as anyone else in the event with the exceptions of Peggy Miller and Viisha Sedlak, both very experienced competitors. Her time in the event was 29:08! How can a rank beginner do this sort of thing? Perhaps her athletic background is the key.

Sally grew up in Denver where she was always involved in athletic events. She was an elite skiing competitor in downhill and slalom. She attended the University of Grenoble in France, and represented the United States in the FIS university circuit for ski racing in the early 1970s. This was a very interesting interlude in her life, being able to race at many of the great ski areas in the Alps. After marrying a Frenchman and moving to Phoenix, Arizona, in 1980, her marriage subsequently fell apart and she moved again to Aspen, Colorado, in 1981. At this time she became a competitor in cross-country skiing and running. She competed in about a dozen marathons and many ski races while living there and did fairly well in 5K and 10K road races.

In the late 1980s she remarried and moved to Evergreen where she presently resides. She has done a lot of hiking and trail running in the hills and has found that she likes the mental stimulation she gets from these activities. The idea of walking and its less traumatic effect on her body began to enter her thoughts more as time passed. This led her to enter her first race in Littleton (previously mentioned). Since her recent indoctrination into the sport she has become very excited about racewalking and wants to get the rest of her family involved.

As of 1996 she is the top woman masters racewalker in the United States and is rated second in the World Masters competition. She is very close to 24 minutes flat in the 5K and 49 minutes flat in the 10K event. She was renamed to two USA Track & Field teams (1993–1994 and 1994–1995) to represent the United States in international events. Sally now does extensive training and coaching of others in the United States and the United Kingdom. She is truly a dynamic ambassador for the sport of racewalking as well as a very personable and pleasant person.

Gus Theobald

This truly remarkable gentleman, born in Australia in March 1897, was predicted by many to become the first participant in racewalking in the 100+ division. Gus Theobald became interested in competitive walking in 1931 when, by chance after a soccer match, he met some walking athletes of the Glenhuntly Athletic Club. At age 35 he was considered "too old" to compete in any of their events besides walking. Little did anyone in those days suspect that this would result in nearly 60 years of competitive success and officiating. He became a superb athlete and was the overall winner in both the Open Victorian and Australian 50K walks in 1949 at age 52.

His career as a racewalk official paralleled his athletics. He was a racewalk judge at the 1956 Olympics and 1962 Commonwealth Games, having been an accredited official since 1935. He holds all age group records for Australia from the age of 60 and over in all the regular competitive distances. In addition, he was on the General Committee of the Glenhuntly Athletic Club for 58 years and served in many official positions including 14 years as president. He was instrumental in the formation of the Caulfield Little Athletics Centre and in helping form the World Veteran's Association at its inception in the 1970s. In 1982 he was awarded the British Empire Medal for his enormous contribution to his sport since 1935.

By the age of 90 he was by far one of the fastest walkers in the world in his age group, walking times that many men a third his age would be proud of (around 35 minutes for a 5K). Tragically, however, while out on a training walk on August 8, 1990, he was struck down by a speeding automobile and killed instantly. At the time of his death the Australian athletic world mourned the loss of a great athlete. He had provided inspiration and encouragement to aspiring athletes, young and old. His impact on the sport of racewalking is sadly missed by veteran walkers all over the world.

Gordon Wallace

The saga of Gordon Wallace began in May of 1976 at the age of 66. His fairly active life as a forest ranger had kept him in excellent health, but disturbing sensations had started to beset him—the classic symptoms of heart disease—a strange pressure in the chest, pain, numbness and weakness radiating through the shoulders and arms and into the jaw. Many adults react to such news by ignoring the symptoms, but Gordon took the symptoms seriously and consulted his friend, cardiologist Dr. Charles Trahern. An exercise EKG showed abnormalities. A heart catheterization, which entails running a probe through the arteries to detect blockages, showed that two of his main arteries were totally occluded and a third was 50 percent blocked. The doctors said that only an active previous life that provided collateral circulation around the blockages had saved him. Gordon was offered two choices: He could take pills for the rest of his life, medication that would not permit strenuous activity since the blockages would still be there; or he could undergo triple-bypass surgery, which carried more risks but would allow more blood flow and the opportunity for vigorous activity. He decided that surgery was his only viable option since he did not want to give up an active life. In retrospect he realized that it was his normal diet of eggs, fatty meats and dairy products that had caused the problem—certainly not lack of exercise.

After the operation Gordon did everything in his power to become the strongest and most active human being possible. Recovery was rapid and he was released after just 10 days in the hospital. Three weeks after the operation he was able to take an extended drive of several hundred miles with his wife, and just a month after he began to swim on a regular basis. Jogging seemed to be the exercise recommended by most knowledgeable physicians of the day, but it was an exercise Gordon found boring, tedious and painful, and he gave it up after three months. He then read that aerobics expert Dr. Ken Cooper had a brisk walking program along with his running programs that were just as beneficial for the cardiovascular system. A friend's daughter-in-law, who was a former racewalking champion, happened to visit Gordon's home in Prescott, Arizona, and agreed to give some coaching in this sport, which he had never heard of. He liked everything about it and took it up with a vengeance.

Gordon had found his niche. Racewalking was an effective means of attaining and maintaining superior physical fitness without being inconvenient, expensive or dangerous. Through persistence, dedication, strength and endurance, he rapidly improved and none of the troubling symptoms recurred even in the most strenuous workouts. The 5K distance was the standard to measure progress and at the end of 1977 he entered his very first race, recording a time of 31:34 for 3 miles, which amazed all who knew about his former condition. Being newly semiretired he began searching out and attending racewalks all around the country. It became his passion and the joy of his life. He decided to try to do well in his age group in the Arizona 1978 Senior Olympics. Eventually, he became acquainted with most of the luminaries of the sport, which whetted his appetite to improve. The admiration and encouragement for what he was doing by those promoting the sport gave him further impetus. His times began to plummet and he was rapidly approaching national class in his age group, which was 65–69 at the time. At age 70 his conditioning was superb and the idea of entering the upcoming European championships in August 1980 in Helsinki, Finland, entered his mind. He decided to give it his best shot against the best Europe had to offer. To his delight, the new septuagenarian won both the 10K and 20K events.

His performances that year earned him second place in the voting as the outstanding U.S. master walker of the year in 1979, behind veteran Ron Laird who became his mentor. Gordon then proceeded to win that same award in 1980. Under Ron's guidance he became the world's best by 1981—and proved it by winning gold medals in the 5K track walk (30:06) and 20K road walk (2:08) in the Fourth World Veterans Games in Christchurch, New Zealand. The long, grueling hours of training had paid off. He had left the best over-70 racewalkers in the world in the dust and had beaten most of the over-60 crowd as well. At the Athletics Congress Convention in December 1981 he was voted the outstanding walker in the United States. The life-threatening event of five years before had become a distant memory. He continued racing at a very high level through the 1980s, last competing at the World Veterans Games in Turku, Finland, in 1991 in the 80–84 age division.

In 1982 Gordon wrote and published a book covering his remarkable walking career, entitled *Valiant Heart—From Cardiac Cripple to World Champion*. During the 1980s he entered the University of Texas as a doctoral candidate and, after a vast amount of research, wound up with a doctoral dissertation entitled *Racewalking in America: Past and Present*, which is undoubtedly the most comprehensive writing available on the subject. His remarkable career ended when he died of cancer in late 1993.

Racewalking Speed

One of the troubles with racewalking in the United States is that it is extremely hard to recruit world-class athletes into the sport. Up to this point proper respect for the sport has been lacking. There are precious few youth programs coaching and teaching racewalking to youngsters. Until recently New York State had been the only one with interscholastic competition, but it is being phased out because of the lack of competent coaching available. The state of Maine, however, has a fledgling program started under the guidance of coach Tom Eastler. At the university level there are only a few NAIA colleges that offer varsity training, competition and letters. Star athletes naturally gravitate to running events since that is all there is in most locales. This leads to tremendous competition in running and only a select few can expect to rise to the top in those events. What many athletes do not know is that there are far better odds of making a national or international team in the sport of racewalking. Good running athletes, especially those who are unfortunately susceptible to injuries from running, should ask themselves: "Just what is my potential performance in racewalking after proper training?"

Since athletes who are trying to excel at either racewalking or running very seldom compete in both at a high level, I decided to come up with some standard of predicted performance if an athlete were to switch to the other sport and train exclusively for it. It was decided that if ultimate performances—the world records in each sport for various distances—were compared that some sort of rule of thumb based on a ratio of these times might be the most logical predictor. For instance, if we compare the running world record for 5K at 12:50 with the walking world record of 18:11, we come up with a ratio of walking speed that is .713 that of running or around seven-tenths. Then someone who runs a certain time in the 5K might figure that the same effort might produce a walking time in the neighborhood of seven-tenths as fast. Let's see what happens at various distances for both men and women:

Women's Records

DISTANCE	RUNNING	WALKING	RATIO
One Mile	4:15.6	6:16.7	.678
3K	8:06.1	11:44.0	.691
5K	4:36.5	20:17.9	.723

DISTANCE	RUNNING	WALKING	RATIO
10K	29:31.8	41:29.0	.711
15K	47:53	1:11:13.0	.672
20K	1:07:51	1:29.40	.753
Marathon	2:21:06	3:35 (est.)*	.657

Women's 20K racewalking record is outstanding.
*Seldom competed

Men's Records

DISTANCE	RUNNING	WALKING	RATIO
One Mile	3:44.4	5:33.5	.672
3K	7:25.1	10:47.1	.690
5K	12:44.4	18:07.1	.704
10K	26:43.5	38:02.6	.700
15K	42:28	57:47.0	.735
20K	56:55.6	1:17:25	.735
30K	1:29:18.8	2:01:44	.735
Marathon	2:06:50	3:04 (est.)*	.690
50K	2:50:55*	3:37.41	.785

Men's 20K, 30K and 50K racewalking marks are outstanding.
*Seldom competed

It is significant that the men's 20K and 50K and the women's 10K are the most important championship distances contested on a worldwide basis. Perhaps the lower ratios (with the exception of the sprint distances of 2 miles or less where the limitations of the sport are more of a factor) indicate that there is room for improvement in that particular walking event as far as world records go. Those somewhat above .700, on the other hand, may indicate that world record potential is probably being approached. Keep in mind that the 50K distance has been run by very few world-class marathoners, which suggests that the .785 figure is higher than it would be otherwise. The 50K world record probably would be under 2:40 in that case.

It would be interesting to discover if runners of all speeds who have shifted to walking have similar ratios to the world record performances. On all records that I can compare on a personal basis the ratio falls between .667 and .700.

It must be remembered that there is a great deal of training required to approach maximum efficiency in racewalking performances. The sport is much more technically oriented than running. The ratios above should serve as an approximate guide to what an athlete switching from one sport to another might possibly achieve through proper training and dedication. There is, however, another factor that I have noticed in my experience of watching people develop in racewalking. Some people are such naturals in racewalking that the ratio can be .900 or more. I have seen people who never jog below 8 minutes per mile dip well below 9 minutes per mile in walking.

Guide for a Runner to Predict Potential Racewalking Speed

Based upon the empirical data above, there appears to be a straight line relationship between running and racewalking times for people who are fairly proficient in both disciplines. This makes it possible to give running athletes and fitness joggers alike an idea of their potential in racewalking. The following listed times are an approximation of running times related to racewalking times. For instance, if your running time for a 5K is 18:00, you could potentially racewalk the distance somewhere around 25:43, plus or minus a minute depending on efficiency and style. The speeds shown are not possible with "legal" walking technique until after several months of racewalking training for most people.

5K RUNNING TIME	5K WALKING TIME	10K RUNNING TIME	10K WALKING TIME
13:00	18:34	27:00	38:34
13:15	18:56	27:30	39:17
13:30	19:17	28:00	40:00
13:45	19:38	28:30	40:43
14:00	20:00	29:00	41:26
14:15	20:22	29:15	41:47
14:30	20:43	29:30	42:08
14:45	21:04	29:45	42:30
15:00	21:26	30:00	42:52
15:15	21:47	30:15	43:13
15:30	22:08	30:30	43:34
15:45	22:30	30:45	43:56
16:00	22:52	31:00	44:17
16:15	23:13	31:15	44:38
16:30	23:34	31:30	45:00
16:45	23:56	31:45	45:22
17:00	24:17	32:00	45:43
17:15	24:38	32:15	46:04
17:30	25:00	32:30	46:26
17:45	25:22	32:45	46:47
18:00	25:43	33:00	47:08
18:15	26:04	33:15	47:30
18:30	26:26	33:30	47:52
18:45	26:47	33:45	48:13
19:00	27:08	34:00	48:34
19:15	27:30	34:15	48:56
19:30	27:52	34:30	49:17
19:45	28:13	34:45	49:38
20:00	28:34	35:00	50:00
20:15	28:56	35:15	50:22

5K RUNNING TIME	5K WALKING TIME	10K RUNNING TIME	10K WALKING TIME
20:30	29:17	35:30	50:43
20:45	29:38	35:45	51:04
21:00	30:00	36:00	51:26
21:15	30:22	36:15	51:47
21:30	30:43	36:30	52:08
21:45	31:04	36:45	52:30
22:00	31:26	37:00	52:52
22:15	31:47	37:15	53:13
22:30	32:08	37:30	53:34
22:45	32:30	37:45	53:56
23:00	32:52	38:00	54:17
23:15	33:13	38:15	54:38
23:30	33:34	38:30	55:00
23:45	33:56	38:45	55:22
24:00	34:17	39:00	55:43
24:15	34:38	39:15	56:04
24:30	35:00	39:30	56:26
24:45	35:22	39:45	56:47
25:00	35:43	40:00	57:08
25:15	36:04	40:15	57:30
25:30	36:26	40:30	57:52
25:45	36:47	40:45	58:13
26:00	37:08	41:00	58:34
26:15	37:30	41:15	58:56
26:30	37:52	41:30	59:17
26:45	38:13	41:45	59:38
27:00	38:34	42:00	60:00
27:15	38:56	42:15	60:22
27:30	39:17	42:30	60:43
27:45	39:38	42:45	61:04
28:00	40:00	43:00	61:26
28:15	40:22	43:15	61:47
28:30	40:43	43:30	62:08
28:45	41:04	43:45	62:30
29:00	41:26	44:00	62:52
29:15	41:47	44:15	63:13
29:30	42:08	44:30	63:34
29:45	42:30	44:45	63:56
30:00	42:52	45:00	64:17
30:15	43:13	45:15	64:38
30:30	43:34	45:30	65:00
30:45	43:56	45:45	65:22
31:00	44:17	46:00	65:43
31:15	44:38	46:15	66:04

5K RUNNING TIME	5K WALKING TIME	10K RUNNING TIME	10K WALKING TIME
31:30	45:00	46:30	66:26
31:45	45:22	46:45	66:47
32:00	45:43	47:00	67:08
32:15	46:04	47:15	67:30
32:30	46:26	47:30	67:52
32:45	46:47	47:45	68:13
33:00	47:08	48:00	68:34
33:15	47:30	48:15	68:56
33:30	47:52	48:30	69:17
33:45	48:13	48:45	69:38
34:00	48:34	49:00	70:00
34:15	48:56	49:15	70:22
34:30	49:17	49:30	70:43
34:45	49:38	49:45	71:04
35:00	50:00	50:00	71:26

Age-Graded Tables for Racewalking

The Florida Race Walkers have come up with a comprehensive system of grading racewalkers as to ability from open competition (ages 20 to 30 up through 84 years old). When using the following table, 900 or more points would denote world class, 800 or more national class, 700 or more regional class, 600 or more local class, 400 to 599 average competitors and less than 400 below average. This will give you a good idea where you stand against other walkers of your own age and may provide an incentive to move up the ladder a little. The table could be useful in recognizing outstanding performances in age group events. You can interpolate with the 5K and 10K times for other distances and compare it with your best times to see if you have done your best at the different distance. In some areas of the country they have special races in which they give awards solely on the number of age-graded points, which certainly levels the playing field for all age groups.

To use the following table, find your current age and read the appropriate time (which is faster than the world record in practically all cases). Note that the male times are considerably faster than the female times. These virtually unattainable times are equal to 1,000 points. Convert the 1,000 points into seconds. Take your actual time from a 5K or 10K, convert it also into seconds and divide it into the 1,000-point conversion. Remove the decimal point and that will be your age-graded performance level. For example, suppose you are a 53-year-old woman with excellent racewalking form. Your 1,000 points = 25:12 on the table. Therefore, 25 min. x 60 = 1,500 seconds plus 12 = 1,512. If you walk a 5K in 29:01, the performance is 29 x 60 = 1,740 plus 1 = 1,741. Dividing 1,512 by 1,741 = .868, a figure that places you high up in the national class category. A time of 28 minutes flat would give 900 points and place you in the world-class category for age 53.

	5K WALK		10K WALK	
Age	MEN	WOMEN	MEN	WOMEN
open	19:25	21:33	40:24	44:30
30	19:32	21:42	40:37	44:50
31	19:36	21:43	40:42	45:02
32	19:40	21:45	40:49	45:16
33	19:44	21:48	40:58	45:32
34	19:48	21:52	41:09	45:48
35	19:53	21:57	41:20	46:04
36	19:58	22:03	41:31	46:20
37	20:04	22:10	41:42	46:36
38	20:10	22:18	41:53	46:52
39	20:16	22:27	42:05	47:08
40	20:22	22:36	42:18	47:25
41	20:28	22:45	42:31	47:43
42	20:34	22:57	42:45	48:01
43	20:40	23:08	43:00	48:19
44	20:46	23:20	43:16	48:38
45	20:53	23:32	43:32	48:58
46	21:00	23:44	43:49	49:19
47	21:08	23:56	44:06	49:40
48	21:16	24:08	44:24	50:01
49	21:24	24:20	44:43	50:23
50	21:32	24:33	45:02	50:45
51	21:41	24:46	45:21	51:07
52	21:50	24:59	45:40	51:29
53	21:59	25:12	45:59	51:52
54	22:08	25:26	46:18	52:16
55	22:18	25:40	46:37	52:40
56	22:28	25:54	46:57	53:05

	5K WALK		10K WALK	
Age	MEN	WOMEN	MEN	WOMEN
57	22:38	26:08	47:17	53:31
58	22:48	26:23	47:37	53:58
59	22:59	26:38	47:57	54:25
60	23:10	26:53	48:17	54:52
61	23:21	27:08	48:37	55:19
62	23:32	27:24	48:58	55:46
63	23:44	27:40	49:19	56:23
64	23:56	27:56	49:40	56:51
65	24:08	28:12	50:01	57:21
66	24:20	28:21	50:23	57:52
67	24:33	28:46	50:45	58:24
68	24:46	29:03	51:07	58:57
69	24:59	29:20	51:29	59:31
70	25:12	29:38	51:52	60:06
71	25:26	29:56	52:16	60:42
72	25:40	30:14	52:40	61:19
73	25:54	30:32	53:05	61:57
74	26:08	30:50	53:31	62:36
75	26:23	31:08	53:58	63:16
76	26:38	31:26	54:25	63:57
77	26:53	31:44	54:52	64:38
78	27:08	32:02	55:19	65:19
79	27:24	32:20	55:46	66:00
80	27:40	32:38	56:23	66:40
81	27:56	32:56	56:51	67:20
82	28:12	33:14	57:21	68:00
83	28:21	33:33	57:52	68:40
84	28:46	33:52	58:24	69:20

USATF Age-Graded Standards of Excellence

Those who meet or exceed the following marks in judged races on sanctioned courses can apply for all-American status and receive a certificate.

Age-F	1.5K	Mile	3K	5K	8K	10K	15K	20K	25K	30K	40K	50K
F-30	7:13	7:47	14:50	25:38	42:04	52:43	1:21:56	1:52:06	2:24:43	2:59:15	4:08:45	5:37:30
F-35	7:22	8:03	15:18	26:27	43:11	53:56	1:23:29	1:53:32	2:26:51	3:01:53	4:12:21	5:42:23
F-40	7:37	8:21	15:53	27:25	44:47	55:56	1:26:37	1:58:06	2:32:33	3:08:56	4:22:13	5:55:48
F-45	8:03	8:43	16:32	28:33	46:35	58:10	1:30:08	2:03:00	2:38:56	3:17:00	4:33:31	6:11:25
F-50	8:25	9:05	17:15	29:49	48:36	1:00:51	1:34:24	2:08:30	2:48:11	3:26:08	4:46:23	6:29:09
F-55	8:55	9:31	18:05	31:14	50:54	1:03:33	1:38:40	2:14:48	2:54:26	3:36:33	5:01:03	6:49:24
F-60	9:17	10:01	19:01	32:51	53:32	1:06:50	1:43:51	2:21:54	3:03:54	3:48:29	5:17:54	7:12:43
F-65	9:48	10:35	20:08	34:43	56:33	1:10:37	1:49:50	2:30:12	3:14:51	4:02:20	5:37:25	7:39:46
F-70	10:26	11:15	21:22	36:54	1:00:02	1:15:01	1:56:49	2:39:54	3:27:38	4:18:30	6:00:18	8:11:30
F-75	11:10	12:01	22:51	39:28	1:04:10	1:20:14	2:05:05	2:51:18	3:42:50	4:37:46	6:27:35	8:49:28
F-80	12:03	12:58	24:41	42:37	1:09:13	1:26:38	2:15:15	3:05:24	4:01:36	5:01:39	7:01:26	9:47:35
F-85	13:13	14:15	27:05	46:45	1:15:50	1:35:01	2:28:37	3:24:00	4:26:20	5:33:10	7:46:16	10:39:15
F-90	14:56	16:06	30:36	52:14	1:25:30	1:47:18	2:48:13	3:51:12	—	—	—	—

Age-M	1.5K	Mile	3K	5K	8K	10K	15K	20K	25K	30K	40K	50K
M-30	6:31	7:01	13:21	23:05	37:57	47:49	1:13:10	1:38:18	2:06:12	2:32:17	3:27:30	4:31:00
M-35	6:43	7:14	13:47	23:46	38:55	48:53	1:14:28	1:39:43	2:06:56	2:34:14	3:30:17	4:34:53
M-40	6:58	7:29	14:16	24:24	40:15	50:32	1:17:03	1:43:13	2:11:29	2:39:47	3:37:53	4:44:49
M-45	7:13	7:46	14:47	25:31	41:44	52:25	1:19:58	1:47:10	2:16:35	2:46:05	3:46:36	4:56:24
M-50	7:33	8:05	15:23	26:33	43:25	54:32	1:23:14	1:51:37	2:22:20	2:53:13	3:58:29	5:09:29
M-55	7:50	8:26	16:04	27:43	46:19	56:55	1:26:56	1:56:38	2:28:52	3:01:19	4:07:41	5:24:22
M-60	8:13	8:51	16:50	29:02	47:28	59:38	1:31:10	2:02:23	2:36:20	3:10:33	4:20:30	5:41:23
M-65	8:38	9:19	17:43	30:33	49:56	1:02:45	1:36:01	2:08:58	2:44:53	3:21:11	4:35:15	6:01:01
M-70	9:08	9:50	18:44	32:18	52:46	1:06:21	1:41:37	2:16:35	2:53:56	3:33:31	4:52:23	6:23:51
M-75	9:43	10:28	19:55	34:20	56:04	1:10:35	1:48:13	2:25:34	3:05:02	3:48:06	5:12:40	6:50:54
M-80	10:26	11:14	21:22	36:50	60:06	1:15:44	1:56:15	2:36:31	3:20:50	4:05:57	5:37:34	7:24:11
M-85	11:21	12:13	23:14	40:04	65:20	1:22:26	2:06:43	2:50:48	3:39:31	4:29:18	6:10:11	8:07:50
M-90	12:41	13:39	25:58	44:46	72:52	1:32:08	2:21:52	3:11:28	4:06:38	5:03:17	6:57:43	9:11:37

Age-graded time/.8 for mid-point of each 5-year interval (e.g., age 32, 37, 42, 47, etc.)

The Regional Ladder System

Racewalking competitors can now be involved in a Regional Ladder System coordinated by the Southern California Walkers and USATF and supported by the North American Racewalking Foundation. This is a postal ladder designed to stimulate competition throughout the United States. Those who subscribe receive quarterly issues of *4 Regions Newsletter* by sending $7 to Elaine Ward, North American Racewalking Foundation, Box 50312, Pasadena, CA 91115-0312. Include name, birth date and address. Make check payable to USATF RW Postal. I am sure that some of you who compete regularly will want to subscribe. Here are the requirements to be scored in the ladders:

- Course must be certified as to accurate length.
- There must be certified judges.
- Both road and track courses can be accepted.
- Submitted ladder times do not need to be made in a USATF-sanctioned race, but records must be made in a sanctioned race.
- Age of competitor and address in first ladder submission in calendar year will establish his/her age group and region for the year.
- All competitors who qualify can be ranked in the ladders, but only those who subscribe to *4 Regions Newsletter* will be sent ladders and be eligible for medals, placement certificates, raffle drawings and cash prizes.
- Results will be accepted until December 15 of each year.

Time Qualifications for Inclusion in Ladders

AGE	5K	10K	20K
Youth	35:00 B/G		
Intermed.	34:00 B/G		
Young	29:00 M/W	58:00 M/W	
19–21	28:00 M/W	58:00 M/W	1:55 M/W
22–29	27:00 M 28:00 W	55:00 M 58:00 W	1:50 M 1:58 W
30–34	28:00 M 30:00 W	58:00 M 61:00 W	1:55 M 2:15 W
35–39	28:00 M 31:00 W	59:00 M 63:00 W	2:00 M 2:15 W
40–44	29:00 M 32:00 W	59:00 M 65:00 W	2:05 M 2:20 W
45–49	30:00 M 33:00 W	61:00 M 67:00 W	2:10 M 2:25 W
50–54	31:00 M 34:00 W	65:00 M 69:00 W	2:15 M 2:30 W
55–59	32:00 M 35:00 W	66:00 M 72:00 W	2:20 M 2:35 W
60–64	34:00 M 38:00 W	70:00 M 78:00 W	2:30 M 2:45 W
65–69	37:00 M 40:00 W	76:00 M 82:00 W	2:40 M 2:55 W
70–74	39:00 M Open W	Open M & W	Open M & W
75–79	Open M & W	Open M & W	Open M & W
80–84	Open M & W	Open M & W	Open M & W

Racewalking
History and Records

Unbeknownst probably to many, racewalking has a long and rich tradition. Walking races have existed as far back as the sixteenth century. In the eighteenth and nineteenth centuries, walking races were held on a regular basis in Europe, including organized national championship events. For many years the famous American walker, Thomas Payson Weston, competed with and defeated the best in the world. The sport was called "pedestrianism" or "go as you please," and the form was not judged. Many of the events were tests of endurance and included six-day events and others for hundreds and even thousands of miles. Wagering on the contestants was common to add spice to the contests. True racewalking, as we know it today, really began around the turn of this century with the modern Olympic Games, and the emergence of George Larner of England as the walking maestro of the day and father of modern racewalking technique. As Larner brought a degree of respectability to the sport, his style was universally regarded as flawless. Racewalking was included in the 1906 Olympics in Athens, Greece, the only interim games ever held. George Bonhag unexpectedly represented the United States and won by default as all the competitors in front of him were disqualified for "unfair walking." George, who was a mediocre 1,500-meter runner, entered the walk on a whim after learning only the basics of technique before the event. The result was the only American Olympic gold medal for racewalking in history.

In the early years, the Olympic events vied with ultra long-distance walks for popularity. Britain, the United States and Canada dominated early competitions, but the three-nation mastery was broken with the emergence of Italy's Ugo Frigerio, one of the most flamboyant and colorful characters in track and field history. Frigerio's crowd-pleasing antics included leading applause on his own behalf, giving lap-long fascist salutes to the crowd and trading comments with the spectators. He brought a lot of attention to racewalking, winning two Olympic gold medals in 1920 and one in 1924. Although his times fall short of today's standards, he clearly dominated other walkers of the era.

Walking was dropped from the Olympics in 1928 but reemerged in 1932 with the 50K event. British walkers again rose to the top of the heap in the

1930s with occasional strong competition from the rest of Europe. During and after World War II, Swedish walkers were very dominant and some of their times are still considered to be quite good today. Among them, some of the best were John Mikkaelsson, who had impeccable form and won the newly adopted 10K in the 1948 and 1952 Olympics, and John Ljunggren, who won the 50K in 1948, 1956 and 1960.

During the forties, fifties and early sixties, U.S. racewalking sank to the very bottom of the athletic barrel with few real athletes in the sport. A notable exception from this period was Henry Laskau, a German refugee and new citizen of the United States, who competed quite well internationally and is now a vigorous promoter of the sport in Florida. Ron Zinn, who was killed in the Vietnam "police action," was a leading U.S. walker in the early sixties, and is memorialized by awards given each year at USA Track & Field National Conventions to outstanding competitors and promoters of racewalking.

In the sixties the Soviet Vladimir Golubnichiy emerged as the outstanding competitor in the world. He won Olympic gold medals in 1960 and 1968, a bronze in 1964 and a silver in 1972, all in the 20K (12.4-mile) event, which became the official distance for world championships along with the 50K (31 miles). He remained dominant in the 20K worldwide for about 15 years. The United States had a breakthrough in the 1968 Olympic Games when Larry Young from Missouri won a bronze in Mexico City in the 50K, a feat he repeated in 1972 in Munich. Young's amazing accomplishments out of a relatively weak program, along with some outstanding results by Rudy Haluza and Ron Laird, gave impetus for a resurgence of the sport in the United States during the early seventies. Many of today's competitors have emerged from the New York State school system, which is about the only one in the United States that has competitive racewalking. Others have emerged from the Parkside College of Wisconsin at Kenosha, which offers some scholarships to young racewalkers. Women began competing in this country in the early seventies and their participation has been increasing ever since. Women have been firmly ensconced in the Olympic Games since 1992.

To enhance a racewalking program in Mexico, eminent Polish coach Jerzy Hausleber was hired in the late sixties. Through his efforts competitors have achieved international success ever since. Such outstanding competitors and world record holders as Raul Gonzales (one of the world's greatest stylists), Ernesto Canto, Domingo Colon and Daniel Bautista Carlos Mercenario have emerged from this excellent Mexican program over the past two decades. The mid-1990s generation of outstanding international competitors in the United States includes Herman Nelson, Allen James, Tim Seaman, Curt Clausen and Andrzej Chylinski. The best U.S. women competitors include Teresa Vaill, Victoria Herazo, Michelle Rohl, Debbi Lawrence and Debora VanOrden. Some current notable foreign world giants in racewalking are Giovanni de Benedictis and Arturo Di Mezza of Italy, Nick A'Hern of Australia, Robert Korzeniowski of Poland, Bernardo Segura and Daniel Garcia of Mexico, Axel Noack of Germany, Rene Piller of France, Jefferson Perez of Ecuador, Mikhail

Shchennikov and Ilya Markov of Russia, Daniel Plaza and Valentin Massana of Spain and Tim Berrett of Canada. Some outstanding competitors on the female side are Kerry Junna-Saxby of Australia, Yan Wang of China, Elizabetta Perrone of Italy, Yelena Ninikolayeva of Russia, Beate Anders-Gummelt of Germany, Sari Essayah of Finland and Madelein Svensson of Sweden.

Official World Records as Kept by the International Athletic Federation

As you read the following list, you may be amazed by some of the racewalking records. Many good recreational runners would be hard-pressed to run as fast. Much of the following data comes from Bob Bowman's *U.S. Racewalking Handbook*, published yearly by USA Track & Field. Readers can be kept current by purchasing any of these yearly record books from 1997 on. Official records are kept only in a few events and must be set on a track. Road records are called best performances. Unofficial marks and American records are kept at many other distances both indoor and outdoor.

Event	Time/Distance	Name	Citizen of	Date Set
		OUTDOOR MEN		
20,000 meters	1:17.25.6	Bernardo Segura	Mexico	5/7/94
2 hours	29,572 m.	Maurizio Damilano	Italy	10/3/92
30,000 meters	2:01.44.1	Maurizio Damilano	Italy	10/3/92
50,000 meters	3:41.28.2	Rene Piller	France	5/7/94
		OUTDOOR JUNIOR MEN		
10,000 meters	38:54.75	Ralf Kowalsky	Germany	6/24/81
		INDOOR MEN		
5,000 meters	18:07.8	Mikhail Shchennikov	Russia	2/14/95
		OUTDOOR WOMEN		
5,000 meters	20:13.26	Kerry Junna-Saxby	Australia	2/25/96
10,000 meters	41:56.23	Nadezhda Ryashkina	USSR	7/24/90
		OUTDOOR JUNIOR WOMEN		
5,000 meters	20:37.7	Jin Bingjie	China	3/3/90
		INDOOR WOMEN		
3,000 meters	11:44.0	Alina Ivanova	Ukraine	2/7/92

Event	Time/Distance	Name	Citizen of	Date Set
		WORLD OUTDOOR TRACK RECORDS (MEN)		
1,500 meters	5:12	Antanas Grigaliunas	USSR	5/12/90
1 mile	5:36.9	Antanas Grigaliunas	USSR	5/12/90
3,000 meters	10:47.11	Giovanni de Benedictis	Italy	5/19/90
2 miles	11:47.02	Giovanni de Benedictis	Italy	7/29/81
5,000 meters	18:17.22	Robert Korzeniowski	Poland	7/3/92
5 miles	31:23.1	Maurizio Damilano	Italy	8/22/82
10,000 meters	38:02.6	Jozef Pribilinec	Czechoslovakia	8/10/85
7 miles	45:13.0	Daniel Bautista	Mexico	7/5/79
15,000 meters	57:47.0	Bernardo Segura	Mexico	5/7/94
10 miles	1:05.07.6	Domingo Colin	Mexico	5/26/79
20,000 meters	1:17.25.5	Bernardo Segura	Mexico	5/7/94
15 miles	1:42.18	Reima Salonen	Finland	9/1/79
25,000 meters	1:44.27	Guillaume Leblanc	Canada	6/16/90
30,000 meters	2:01.44	Maurizio Damilano	Italy	10/4/92
20 miles	2:22.10	Raul Gonzales	Mexico	5/19/78
35,000 meters	2:33.25	Raul Gonzales	Mexico	5/2/80
40,000 meters	2:55.54	Raul Gonzales	Mexico	5/2/80
25 miles	2:57.02	Raul Gonzales	Mexico	5/25/79
30 miles	3:34.17	Raul Gonzales	Mexico	5/25/79
50,000 meters	3:41.28.4	Rene Piller	France	5/7/94
50 miles	7:38.49	Florimond Cornet	France	6/25/39
100,000 meters	9:16.33	Frederic Marie	France	4/19/87
150,000 meters	16:07.00	Hector Nielson	England	10/14/60
100 miles	17:18.51	Hector Nielson	England	10/14/60
200,000 meters	22:16.40	Hector Nielson	England	10/14/60
1 hour	15,477 m.	Jozef Pribilinec	Czechoslovakia	9/6/86
2 hours	29,572 m.	Maurizio Damilano	Italy	10/4/92
3 hours	25 mi. 739 yds.	Raul Gonzales	Mexico	5/25/79
12 hours	73 mi. 1,584 yds.	Ted Richardson	England	10/16/38
24 hours	133 mi.	Hector Nielson	England	10/14/60
		WORLD INDOOR TRACK RECORDS (MEN)		
1,500 meters	5:13.52	Tim Lewis	USA	2/13/88
1 mile	5:33.52	Tim Lewis	USA	2/07/88
3,000 meters	10:56.9	Reima Salonen	Finland	2/5/84
2 miles	12:05.9	Jim Heiring	USA	2/28/86
3 miles	18:05.3	Mikhail Shchennikov	Russia	2/2/93
5,000 meters	18:15.25	Grigori Kornev	Russia	2/7/92
10,000 meters	38:31.4	Werner Heyer	East Germany	1/12/80
15,000 meters	1:00.03	Valdas Kazlauskas	USSR	1/24/87

Event	Time/Distance	Name	Citizen of	Date Set
20,000 meters	1:20.40	Ronald Weigel	East Germany	1/27/80
1 hour	14,906 m.	Hartwig Gauder	East Germany	2/8/86

WORLD BEST ROAD PERFORMANCES (MEN)

Event	Time/Distance	Name	Citizen of	Date Set
5,000 meters	18:21.0	Robert Korzeniowski	Poland	9/16/90
10,000 meters	38:19.0	Pavol Blazek	Czechoslovakia	9/16/90
	38:19.0	Stefan Johansson	Sweden	5/9/92
15,000 meters	59:43.0	Josef Pribilinec	Czechoslovakia	4/17/83
	59:43.0	Jose Marin	Spain	4/17/83
20,000 meters	1:18.13.0	Pavol Blazek	Czechoslovakia	9/16/90
25,000 meters	1:45:52.0	Hartwig Gauder	East Germany	7/20/80
30,000 meters	2:07.29.0	Raul Gonzales	Mexico	9/30/79
35,000 meters	2:30.43.0	Raul Gonzales	Mexico	9/30/79
40,000 meters	2:56.09.0	Raul Gonzales	Mexico	9/30/79
50,000 meters	3:37.41	Andrey Perlov	USSR	8/5/89
100,000 meters	9:07.00	Zbigniew Klapa	Poland	7/31/38
24 hours	142 mi. 458 yds	Jesse Castaneda	USA	9/18/76

WORLD JUNIOR RECORD (MEN 19 AND UNDER)

Event	Time/Distance	Name	Citizen of	Date Set
10,000 meters	38:54.75	Ralf Kowalski	East Germany	6/24/81

WORLD BEST OUTDOOR TRACK PERFORMANCES (WOMEN)

Event	Time/Distance	Name	Citizen of	Date Set
1,500 meters	5:50.41	Kerry Junna-Saxby	Australia	1/19/91
1 mile	6:19.39	Ileana Salvador	Italy	6/15/91
3,000 meters	11:48.24	Ileana Salvador	Italy	8/29/93
2 miles	13:23.04	Ileana Salvador	Italy	9/12/89
5,000 meters	20:17.9	Kerry Junna-Saxby	Australia	1/14/90
5 miles	36:41.9	Sue Cook	Australia	9/14/83
10,000 meters	41:56.23	Nadezhda Ryashkina	USSR	7/24/90
15,000 meters	1:15.37.9	Ann Jansson	Sweden	10/25/87
20,000 meters	1:41.33.9	Ann Jansson	Sweden	10/25/87
25,000 meters	2:22.04.4	Lucyne Rokitowska	Poland	10/9/83
30,000 meters	2:56.36.0	Cinzia Ghiandra	Italy	10/18/86
35,000 meters	3:33.35.4	Zofia Turnosz	Poland	10/12/85
40,000 meters	4:06.21.8	Zofia Turnosz	Poland	10/12/85
50,000 meters	5:13.49.8	Zofia Turnosz	Poland	10/12/85
75,000 meters	8:42.46.0	Beverly LaVeck	USA	11/5/83
50 miles	9:23.03.0	Beverly LaVeck	USA	11/5/83
100,000 meters	11:17.42	Sandra Brown	England	10/27/90
150,000 meters	22:35.44	Giuliana de Gobbi	Italy	10/31/78
100 miles	21:42.14.0	Beverly LaVeck	USA	11/5/83
200,000 meters	29:23.54.0	Ann Sayer	England	4/11/82
150 miles	37:17.17.0	Ann Sayer	England	4/11/82

Event	Time/Distance	Name	Citizen of	Date Set

WORLD BEST OUTDOOR TRACK PERFORMANCES (WOMEN) (cont'd)

Event	Time/Distance	Name	Citizen of	Date Set
1 hour	13,194 m.	Victoria Herazo	USA	12/6/92
2 hours	22,239 m.	Jane Zarubova	Czechoslovakia	10/12/85
3 hours	18 mi. 1,559 yds.	Lucyne Rokitowska	Poland	10/9/83
24 hours	116 mi. 40 yds.	Ann Sayer	England	6/20/82

WORLD BEST INDOOR TRACK PERFORMANCES (WOMEN)

Event	Time/Distance	Name	Citizen of	Date Set
1,500 meters	5:53.41	Debbi Lawrence	USA	1/15/93
1 mile	6:16.72	Sada Endekite	USSR	2/24/90
3,000 meters	12:05.5	Olga Krishtop	USSR	3/6/87
2 miles	14:49.1	Sue Liers	USA	2/8/81
5,000 meters	21:22.6	Tamara Kovalenko	Russia	2/26/92
10,000 meters	45:26.5	Irina Tolstik	USSR	3/4/88

WORLD BEST ROAD PERFORMANCES (WOMEN)

Event	Time/Distance	Name	Citizen of	Date Set
5,000 meters	20:25	Kerry Junna-Saxby	Australia	6/10/89
10,000 meters	41:29	Larisa Ramazanova	Russia	6/3/95
15,000 meters	1:12.10.0	Sue Cook	Australia	12/19/82
20,000 meters	1:29.30.0	Kerry Junna-Saxby	Australia	5/13/88
25,000 meters	2:12.38.0	Sue Cook	Australia	6/20/81
30,000 meters	2:45.52.0	Sue Cook	Australia	9/5/82
35,000 meters	3:22.17.0	Sue Liers	USA	9/26/82
40,000 meters	3:52.24.0	Sue Liers	USA	9/26/82
50,000 meters	5:01.52.0	Lillian Millen	England	4/16/83
50 miles	8:54.53.0	Aaf de Rijk	Holland	5/22/82
100,000 meters	11:40.07.0	Aaf de Rijk	Holland	10/17/81
100 miles	18:28.01.0	Aaf de Rijk	Holland	5/22/82
200,000 meters	23:33.24.0	Annie Meer-Timmermann	Holland	4/10/82
24 hours	124 mi. 493 yds.	Annie Meer-Timmermann	Holland	4/10/82

AMERICAN OUTDOOR TRACK RECORDS (MEN)

Event	Time/Distance	Name	Date Set
1,500 meters	5:39	Ray Funkhouser	8/5/84
1 mile	6:09.9	Ray Funkhouser	7/6/85
3,000 meters	11:26.7	Jonathan Matthews	5/15/93
5,000 meters	20:01.9	Jim Heiring	5/6/84
10,000 meters	40:20.6	Tim Lewis	6/29/85
15,000 meters	1:02.34.0	Marco Evoniuk	5/5/84
20,000 meters	1:24.26.9	Allen James	5/7/94
25,000 meters	1:51.43.3	Allen James	10/9/94

Event	Time/Distance	Name	Citizen of	Date Set
30,000 meters	2:21.40.0	Herman Nelson	9/7/91	
20 miles	2:23.52.0	Robert Kitchen	3/21/71	
35,000 meters	2:47.36.0	Robert Kitchen	11/21/71	
40,000 meters	3:13.58	Herman Nelson	10/29/89	
50,000 meters	4:04.23	Herman Nelson	10/29/89	
100,000 meters	9:36.33	Dan Pierce	12/20/87	
100 miles	18:46.13	Alan Price	9/30/84	
1 hour	14,058 m.	Jonathan Matthews	11/14/93	
2 hours	26,661 m.	Allen James	10/9/94	

AMERICAN INDOOR RECORDS (MEN)

Event	Time/Distance	Name	Date Set
1,500 meters	5:13.2	Tim Lewis	2/13/88
1 mile	5:33.5	Tim Lewis	2/7/88
3,000 meters	11:16.3	Ray Sharp	2/3/84
2 miles	12:05.94	Jim Heiring	2/28/86
3 miles	19:40.0	Todd Scully	3/4/77
5,000 meters	19:18.4	Tim Lewis	3/7/87
10,000 meters	44:36.0	John Knifton	2/9/74

AMERICAN ROAD RECORDS (MEN)

Event	Time/Distance	Name	Date Set
5,000 meters	20:12	Jonathan Matthews	9/17/94
10,000 meters	40:55	Tim Lewis	9/24/89
15,000 meters	1:01.31	Tim Lewis	9/24/89
20,000 meters	1:22.17	Tim Lewis	9/24/89
25,000 meters	1:49.36	Tim Lewis	4/5/84
30,000 meters	2:14.31	Allen James	10/31/93
35,000 meters	2:41.26	Carl Schueler	3/17/84
40,000 meters	3:13.57	Carl Schueler	9/23/84
50,000 meters	3:55.39	Allen James	3/13/94

AMERICAN JUNIOR RECORDS (MEN 19 AND UNDER)

Event	Time/Distance	Name	Date Set
3,000 meters	11:54.4	Tim Seaman	7/20/91
5,000 meters	21:13.5	Tim Seaman	6/13/91
10,000 meters	43:03.37	Tim Seaman	4/27/91
1 hour	12,554 m.	Curt Clausen	10/25/86

AMERICAN OUTDOOR TRACK RECORDS (WOMEN)

Event	Time/Distance	Name	Date Set
1,500 meters	6:46.6	Lisa Metheny	6/28/75
1 mile	6:51.7	Maryanne Torrellas	7/9/83
3,000 meters	13:19.1	Maryanne Torrellas	7/7/89
5,000 meters	21:32.87	Debbi Lawrence	4/25/92
10,000 meters	44:41.87	Michelle Rohl	7/26/94

Event	Time/Distance	Name	Date Set

AMERICAN OUTDOOR RECORDS (WOMEN) *(cont'd)*

Event	Time/Distance	Name	Date Set
15,000 meters	1:12.30.0	Debbi Lawrence	2/12/93
20,000 meters	1:48.18.6	Sue Liers	3/20/77
1 hour	13,194 m.	Victoria Herazo	12/6/92

AMERICAN INDOOR TRACK RECORDS (WOMEN)

Event	Time/Distance	Name	Date Set
1,500 meters	5:53.41	Debbi Lawrence	1/15/93
1 mile	6:18.03	Debbi Lawrence	2/9/92
3,000 meters	12:20.79	Debbi Lawrence	3/12/93

AMERICAN ROAD RECORDS (WOMEN)

Event	Time/Distance	Name	Date Set
5,000 meters	22:15	Debbi Lawrence	9/8/91
10,000 meters	44:17	Michelle Rohl	8/7/95
15,000 meters	1:11.13	Victoria Herazo	5/12/91
20,000 meters	1:35.40	Victoria Herazo	5/21/95

AMERICAN JUNIOR RECORDS (WOMEN 19 AND UNDER)

Event	Time/Distance	Name	Date Set
3,000 meters	13:53.71	Anya-Maria Ruoss	7/15/94
5,000 meters	23:00.78	Anya-Maria Ruoss	7/23/94
10,000 meters	51:32.96	Deidre Collier	7/16/88
1 hour	11,490 m.	Gretchen Eastler	10/20/91

AMERICAN JUNIOR ROAD RECORDS (WOMEN 19 AND UNDER)

Event	Time/Distance	Name	Date Set
5,000 meters	24:16	Deborah Iden	9/26/93
10,000 meters	48:44	Susan Armenta	4/12/92

Masters World Best
Age Group Times in Selected Distances

Many of the following times seem incredible, and even world class in open events. These times are presumed to have been set in a legitimate racewalking event under the recognized rules. World records, to be recognized as such, must be competed on a curbed track, but most of these marks were set in road events. Accordingly, these times are called "WORLD BEST" for each 5-year age group. Data is supplied by Beverly LaVeck—record keeper for World Association of Veteran Athletes.

Event	Age Group	Name	Time	Citizen of
		MENS' WORLD BESTS		
3,000 meters	Men 40–44	W. Sawall	11:28.2	Australia
	Men 45–49	H. Lankinen	12:37.1	Finland
	Men 50–54	D. DeNoon	12:34.9	United States
	Men 55–59	A. Nokela	13:21.2	Finland
	Men 60–64	G. Chaplin	14:37.0	Great Britain
	Men 65–69	C. Colman	15:58.3	Great Britain
	Men 70–74	C. Colman	16:58.7	Great Britain
	Men 75–79	J. Grimwade	16:19.5	Great Britain
	Men 80+	A. Strang	20:39.0	Finland
5,000 meters	Men 40–44	M. Balek	20:13.0	Yugoslavia
	Men 45–49	G. Little	20:54.4	New Zealand
	Men 50–54	G. Little	21:01.0	New Zealand
	Men 55–59	V. Golubnichiy	22:44.5	Russia
	Men 60–64	G. Weidner	24:07.7	Germany
	Men 65–69	T. Daintry	25:44.0	Australia
	Men 70–74	T. Daintry	27:02.0	Australia
	Men 75–79	J. Grimwade	27:40.0	Great Britain
	Men 80–84	J. Grimwade	29:24.1	Great Britain
	Men 85–89	G. Theobald	33:15.1	Australia
	Men 90+	G. Theobald	35:18.5	Australia
10,000 meters	Men 40–44	M. Jobin	40:39	Canada
	Men 45–49	G. Little	43:44	New Zealand
	Men 50–54	G. Little	42:20	New Zealand
	Men 55–59	A. Nokela	47:56	Finland
	Men 60–64	C. Bomba	47:48	Italy
	Men 65–69	R. Jones	55:24	Australia
	Men 70–74	T. Daintry	54:17	Australia
	Men 75–79	J. Grimwade	55:01	Great Britain
	Men 80–84	J. Grimwade	61:25.4	Great Britain
	Men 85+	G. Conway	82:44	United States
20,000 meters	Men 40–44	W. Sawall	1:21.36	Australia
	Men 45–49	W. Sawall	1:25.03	Australia
	Men 50–54	G. Little	1:26.32	New Zealand
	Men 55–59	G. Weidner	1:37.04	Germany
	Men 60–64	C. Bomba	1:43.50	Italy
	Men 65–69	T. Daintry	1:51.18	Australia
	Men 70–74	J. Grimwade	1:56.19	Great Britain
	Men 75–79	J. Grimwade	1:56.19	Great Britain
	Men 80–84	J. Grimwade	2:04.09	Great Britain
	Men 85–89	G. Theobald	2:26.07	Australia
	Men 90+	G. Theobald	2:34.01	Australia

Event	Age Group	Name	Time	Citizen of
30,000 meters	Men 40–44	J. Marin	2:10.26	Spain
	Men 45–49	B. Bingelli	2:33.06	Switzerland
	Men 50–54	E. Whiteman	2:47.55	United States
	Men 55–59	B. Caudron	2:38.54	France
	Men 60–64	M. Green	2:51.36	United States
	Men 65–69	R. Mimm	3:09.02	United States
	Men 70–74	C. Bomba	3:21.11	Italy
	Men 75–79	H. Drazin	3:46.22	United States
50,000 meters	Men 40–44	J. Marin	3:49.06	Spain
	Men 45–49	W. Sawall	3:59.08	Australia
	Men 50–54	G. Weidner	4:14.37	Germany
	Men 55–59	G. Weidner	4:25.47	Germany
	Men 60–64	M. Gould	4:59.58	Canada
	Men 65–69	L. Creo	5:32.55	Great Britain
	Men 70–74	C. Colman	5:33.21	Great Britain
	Men 75+	J. Grimwade	5:19.34	Great Britain

WOMENS' WORLD BESTS

Event	Age Group	Name	Time	Citizen of
3,000 meters	Women 35–39	A. Manning	12:43.2	Australia
	Women 40–44	S. Griesbach	13:26.5	France
	Women 45–49	V. Heikkila	14:26.2	Finland
	Women 50–54	V. Heikkila	15:11.9	Finland
	Women 55–59	M. Worth	16:31.0	Great Britain
	Women 60–64	M. Worth	16:28.5	Great Britain
	Women 65–69	B. Tibbling	17:08.3	Sweden
	Women 70–74	B. Tibbling	18:05.0	Sweden
	Women 75–79	A. Forbes	21:23.6	New Zealand
	Women 80–84	N. Jeffreys	24:00.0	Australia
	Women 85+	N. Jeffreys	27:36.0	Australia
5,000 meters	Women 35–39	A. Manning	21:37.5	Australia
	Women 40–44	S. Griesbach	22:49.4	France
	Women 45–49	V. Heikkila	24:31.3	Finland
	Women 50–54	V. Heikkila	25:20.0	Finland
	Women 55–59	J. Albury	26:46.9	Australia
	Women 60–64	O. Meyer	27:04.0	Germany
	Women 65–69	J. Albury	27:57.0	Australia
	Women 70–74	B. Tibbling	29:16.0	Sweden
	Women 75–79	B. Tibbling	32:44.8	Sweden
	Women 80–84	P. Clarke	37:41.0	United States
	Women 85+	D. Robarts	44:43.9	United States
10,000 meters	Women 35–39	A. Manning	44:28	Australia
	Women 40–44	S. Griesbach	47:07	France
	Women 45–49	G. Johnson	50:58	United States

Event	Age Group	Name	Time	Citizen of

WOMENS' WORLD BESTS (*cont'd*)

Event	Age Group	Name	Time	Citizen of
	Women 50–54	V. Heikkila	52:02	Finland
	Women 55–59	O. Meyer	57:00	Germany
	Women 60–64	O. Meyer	56:38	Germany
	Women 65–69	B. Tibbling	58:41	Sweden
	Women 70–74	B. Tibbling	60:18	Sweden
	Women 75–79	B. Tibbling	67:46	Sweden
	Women 80–84	M. Lindgren	78:26	Sweden
	Women 85+	N. Jeffreys	92:41	Australia
20,000 meters	Women 35–39	V. Herazo	1:35.39	United States
	Women 40–44	H. McDonald	1:42.22	Australia
	Women 45–49	V. Heikkila	1:45.25	Finland
	Women 50–54	H. Maeder	1:52.16	Switzerland
	Women 55–59	E. Richardson	2:00.39	United States
	Women 60–64	M. Worth	2:04.34	Great Britain
	Women 65–69	O. Meyer	2:12.02	Germany
	Women 70–74	M. Gordon	2:27.57	United States
	Women 75+	A. Crocker	2:49.18	United States
50,000 meters	Women 35–39	L. Millen	5:01.52	Germany
	Women 40–44	S. Brown	4:50.51	Great Britain
	Women 45–49	S. Brown	4:56.27	Great Britain
	Women 50–54	M. Hoernecke	5:37.24	Spain
	Women 55–59	E. Petterson	6:50.15	United States
	Women 60–64	M. Henry	7:27.49	United States
	Women 65+	R. Scott	6:31.12	Great Britain

Racewalking in the Olympics

The following paragraphs outline each racewalking event in the modern Olympic Games—noting the number of competitors (**C**) and nations (**N**), the world record for that distance at the time (**wr**), the top three finishers (and their country code) and the performances of all American competitors that participated. Other codes used below are: * = new Olympic record; **DNF** = did not finish; **DQ** = disqualified and **n/a** = not available. Because many of the competitions were road events and world records must be set on a track, most Olympic times are not eligible for world record consideration. They can, however, be classified as "world best performances."

1896—Athens (no racewalks)

1900—Paris (no racewalks)

1904—St. Louis

An 800-yard walk was one of the 10 events in the "All Round Championship"—forerunner of the modern decathlon. All 10 events were held on the same day.

800-YARD WALK (C-7, N-2)
1-Thomas Kiely IRL 3:59
2-Adam Gunn USA 4:13
3-Thomas Truxtun Hare USA 4:20
5-Ellery Clark USA 4:31
6-John Grieb USA 4:49

1906—Athens

The Intercalated (or "Interim") Games were to be held by the Greeks every four years between the Olympics. This was, however, the only time they were held. It was the first time racewalking appeared (although considered unofficial by the International Olympic Committee [IOC]). Bonhag, failing to win his 5-mile and 1,500-meter running races, entered the 1,500-meter race having never competed in a walking race before. Using a few prerace instructions, he won the race and became the only U.S. racewalking gold medalist in history.

MEN'S 1,500-METER RACEWALK (C-9, N-6)
1-George Bonhag USA 7:12.6
2-Donald Linden CAN 7:19.8
3-Konstantin Spetsiotis GRE 7:24.0

MEN'S 3,000-METER RACEWALK (C-8, N-5)
1-Gyorgy Sztantics HUN 15:13.2
2-Hermann Muller GER 15:20.0
3-Georgios Saridakis GRE 15:33.0

1908—London

The first "official" racewalks in the modern Olympics were held at these Games. Great Britain took the top five spots in the 10-miler. There were no entries from the United States.

MEN'S 3,500-METER RACEWALK (C-24, N-9)
1-George Larner GBR 14 55.0
2-Ernest Webb GBR 15:07.4
3-Harry Kerr AUS/NZE 15:43.4

MEN'S 10-MILE RACEWALK (C-25, N-8)
1-George Larner GBR 1:15.57
2-Ernest Webb GBR 1:17.31
3-Edward Spencer GBR 1:21.20

1912—Stockholm

These games were very well run and significantly helped to establish the modern Olympic Games. Americans Sam Schwartz, Edward Renz and Arthur Voelmeke were eliminated in the preliminaries.

MEN'S 10K RACEWALK (C-22, N-11)
wr-Ernest Webb GBR 45:15.6
1-George Goulding CAN 46:28.4
2-Ernest Webb GBR 46:50.4
3-Fernando Altimani ITA 47:37.6
Frank Kaiser USA DNF

1916—Berlin

This Olympiad was canceled due to war. In ancient times, all warfare ceased for major athletic events. Since the beginning of the modern Olympics, the Games have been canceled three times due to war.

1920—Antwerp

Ugo Frigerio, a most colorful character, gave the midfield band conductor several pages of sheet music that he requested be played during the race. He won easily, even pausing once to admonish the band's selection of tempo. In honor of their war effort, women were allowed to participate in a few events for the first time—against IOC president, Pierre de Coubertin's wishes.

MEN'S 3,000-METER RACEWALK (C-22, N-12)
wr-Gunnar Rasmussen DEN 12:53.8
1-Ugo Frigerio ITA 13:14.2*
2-George Parker AUS 13:20.6
3-Richard Remer USA 13:23.6
5-Thomas Maroney USA 13:26.8
8-William Roelker USA n/a

MEN'S 10K RACEWALK (C-23, N-13)
wr-Gunnar Rasmussen DEN 45:26.4
1-Ugo Frigerio ITA 48:06.2
2-Joseph Pearman USA 49:40.8
3-Charles Gunn GBR 49:44.4
6-Thomas Maroney USA 50:20.6

1924—Paris

At the request of Pierre de Coubertin, who was planning to retire, the Games were moved from Amsterdam to Paris. The first Winter Games were also held in France.

MEN'S 10K RACEWALK (C-23, N-13). Harry Hinkel was the only American in the finals. Charles Foster was eliminated in the preliminaries.

wr-Gunnar Rasmussen DEN 45:26.4
1-Ugo Frigerio ITA 47:49.0
2-George Goodwin GBR 48:37.9
3-Cecil McMaster SAF 49:08.0
9-Harry Hinkel USA n/a

1928—Amsterdam
No racewalks due to judging controversies. Women's track and field events were included for the first time.

1932—Los Angeles
The depression and isolation of California resulted in the lowest level of participation in the Games since 1906. Automatic timing and photo-finish cameras were introduced at this Olympiad.

MEN'S 50K RACEWALK (C-15, N-10)
wr-Paul Sievert GER 4:34.03
1-Thomas Green GBR 4:50.10
2-Janis Dalinch LAT 4:57.20
3-Ugo Frigerio ITA 4:59.06
8-Ernest Crosbie USA 5:28.02
9-William Chisholm USA 5:51.0
Harry Hinkel USA DNF

1936—Berlin
The torch relay was introduced at these Games.

MEN'S 50K RACEWALK (C-33, N-16)
wr-Paul Sievert GER 4:34.03
1-H. Harold Whitlock GBR 4:30.41*
2-Arthur Schwab SWI 4:32.09
3-Adalberts Bubenko LAT 4:32.42
21-Albert Mangan USA 5:12.0
23-Ernest Koehler USA 5:20.18
26-Ernest Crosbie USA 5:31.44

1940—Tokyo
Canceled due to war.

1944—London
Canceled due to war.

1948—London

Germany and Japan were not invited to participate. With the first participation by communist countries came the first defections by participants. The United States had no qualifiers for the 10K finals (though Henry Laskau was seventh in the preliminary heats in which both Ernest Weber and Fred Sharage were disqualified).

MEN'S 10K RACEWALK (C-19, N-10)
wr-Verner Hardmo SWE 42:39.6
1-John Mikaelsson SWE 45:13.2
2-Ingemar Johansson SWE 45:43.8
3-Fritz Schwab SWI 46:00.2

MEN'S 50K RACEWALK (C-23, N-11)
wr-Paul Sievert GER 4:34.03
1-John Ljunggren SWE 4:41.52
2-Godel Gaston SWI 4:48.17
3-Tebbs Lloyd-Johnson GBR 4:48.31
12-Ernest Crosbie USA 5:15.16
15-John Deni USA 5:28.33
16-Adolph Weinecker USA 5:30.14

1952—Helsinki

The Soviet Union made its first appearance at these Games. In the 10K, both Schwab and Junk began running 30 yards from the finish, making the judges (who had disqualified seven men in the heats and final) look foolish. Schwab barely edged out Junk in a photo finish. The controversies that resulted from this race led Olympic officials to replace the 10K with the 20K in 1956.

MEN'S 10K RACEWALK (C-23, N-12)
wr-Verner Hardmo DEN 42:39.6
1-John Mikaelsson SWE 45:02.8*
2-Fritz Schwab SWI 45:41.0
3-Bruno Junk SOV 45:41.0
Henry Laskau USA DQ
Price King USA DQ

MEN'S 50K RACEWALK (C-31, N-16)
wr-Antal Roka HUN 4:31.21
1-Giuseppe Dordoni ITA 4:28.07*
2-Josef Dolezal CZE 4:30.17
3-Antal Roka HUN 4:31.27
22-Adolf Weinecker USA 5:01.0
Leo Sjoegren USA DNF
John Deni USA DNF

1956—Melbourne

Remote location and several boycotts led to a very low number of competitors. So many disputes had developed over the judging of the comparatively fast-paced 10K racewalk in 1952 that it was replaced by the less controversial 20K event in these Games.

MEN'S 20K RACEWALK (C-21, N-10)
wr-Mikhail Lavrov SOV 1:27.58
1-Leonid Spirin SOV 1:31.27
2-Antanas Mikenas SOV 1:32.03
3-Bruno Junk SOV 1:32.12
12-Henry Laskau USA 1:38.47
16-Bruce MacDonald USA 1:43.26
17-James Hewson USA 1:46.25

MEN'S 50K RACEWALK (C-21, N-10)
wr-Ladislav Moc SOV 4:21.07
1-Norman Read NZE 4:30.42
2-Yevgeny Maskinskov SOV 4:32.57
3-John Ljunggren SWE 4:35.02
7-Adolf Weinacker USA 5:00.16
11-Elliott Denman USA 5:12.14
12-Leo Sjogren USA 5:12.34

1960—Rome

MEN'S 20K RACEWALK (C-36, N-18)
wr-Vladimir Golubnichiy SOV 1:27.05
1-Vladimir Golubnichiy SOV 1:34.07
2-Noel Freeman AUS 1:34.16
3-Stanley Vickers GDR 1:34.56
19-Ronald Zinn USA 1:42.47
23-Robert Mimm USA 1:45.09
24-Rudy Haluza USA 1:45.11

MEN'S 50K RACEWALK (C-39, N-20)
wr-Sergei Lobastov SOV 4:16.08
1-Donald Thompson GBR 4:25.30*
2-John Ljunggren SWE 4:25.47
3-Abdon Pamich ITA 4:27.55
19-Ronald Laird USA 4:53.22
23-Bruce MacDonald USA 5:00.48
24-John Allen USA 5:03.15

1964—Tokyo

MEN'S 20K RACEWALK (C-30, N-15)
wr-Vladimir Golubnichiy SOV 1:27.05

1-Kenneth Matthews GBR 1:29.34*
2-Dieter Lindner GDR 1:31.13
3-Vladimir Golubnichiy SOV 1:31.59
6-Ronald Zinn USA 1:32.43
17-John Mortland USA 1:36.35
Ronald Laird USA DQ
(Ron Zinn died in Vietnam nine months later.)

MEN'S 50K RACEWALK (C-34, N-19)
wr-Abdon Pamich ITA 4:14.02
1-Abdon Pamich ITA 4:11.12*
2-Paul Nihill GBR 4:11.31
3-Ingvar Pettersson SWE 4:14.17
21-Chris McCarthy USA 4:35.41
26-Bruce MacDonald USA 4:45.10
29-Michael Brodie USA 4:57.41

1968—Mexico City

These Games were famous for a Black Power protest by two U.S. sprinters and the impact of high altitude. The rarefied air helped short-distance athletes set records but slowed long-distance athletes not properly trained at altitude. Sex tests were added for women athletes.

MEN'S 20K RACEWALK (C-33, N-20)
wr-Vladimir Golubnichiy SOV 1:27.05
1-Vladimir Golubnichiy SOV 1:33.58
2-Jose Pedraza Zuniga MEX 1:34.0
3-Nikolai Smaga SOV 1:34.03
4-Rudy Haluza USA 1:35.0
17-Thomas Dooley USA 1:40.08
25-Ronald Laird USA 1:44.38

MEN'S 50K RACEWALK (C-36, N-18)
wr-Christoph Hohne GDR 4:10.41
1-Christoph Hohne GDR 4:20.13
2-Antal Kiss HUN 4:30.17
3-Larry Young USA 4:31.55
10-Goetz Klopfer USA 4:39.13
26-David Romansky USA 5:38.03

1972—Munich

These Games were marked by the kidnap and murder of 11 Israeli athletes by eight Palestinian terrorists. Full-scale drug testing was begun.

MEN'S 20K RACEWALK (C-24, N-12)
wr-Peter Frenkel and Hans Georg Reimann GDR 1:25.19

1-Peter Frenkel GDR 1:26.42*
2-Vladimir Golubnichiy SOV 1:26.55
3-Hans Georg Reimann GDR 1:27.16
10-Larry Young USA 1:32.53
15-Thomas Dooley USA 1:34.59
19-Goetz Klopfer USA 1:38.34

MEN'S 50K RACEWALK (C-36, N-18)
wr-Bernd Kannenberg GER 3:52.44
1-Bernd Kannenberg GER 3:56.11*
2-Veniamin Soldatenko SOV 3:58.24
3-Larry Young USA 4:00.46
17-William Weigle USA 4:22.52
27-Steve Hayden USA 4:36.07

1976—Montreal

African nations boycotted these Games over New Zealand having played rugby in South Africa.

MEN'S 20K RACEWALK (C-38, N-21)
wr-Bernd Kannenberg GER 1:24.45
1-Daniel Baudsta Rocha MEX 1:24.40*
2-Hans-Georg Reimann GDR 1:25.13
3-Peter Frenkel GDR 1:25.29
20-Ronald Laird USA 1:33.27
22-Larry Walker USA 1:34.19
29-Todd Scully USA 1:36.37

1980—Moscow

The Americans boycotted these Games to protest the Soviet invasion of Afghanistan. The canceled U.S. team included Jim Heiring, Todd Scully and Larry Walker (20K); and Marco Evoniuk, Dan O'Conner and Carl Schueler (50K).

MEN'S 20K RACEWALK (C-34, N-20)
wr-Daniel Baudsta MEX 1:20.06
1-Maurizio Damilano ITA 1:23.35*
2-Pyotr Pochinchuk SOV 1:24.45
3-Roland Wieser GDR 1:25.58
7-Bohdan Bulakowski POL 1:28.36
(Bulakowski now lives in LaGrange, Georgia, where he coaches some of the top U.S. racewalkers.)

MEN'S 50K RACEWALK (C-27, N-14)
wr-Raul Gonzalez MEX 3:41.38

1-Hartwig Gauder GDR 3:49.24*
2-Jorge Liopart SPA 3:51.25
3-Yevgeny Ivchenko SOV 3:56.32

1984—Los Angeles

In retaliation for the 1980 U.S. boycott, the Soviets boycotted these Games.
For the first time in Olympic history, not one walker was disqualified for improper technique.

MEN'S 20K RACEWALK (C-38, N-22)
wr-Ernesto Canto MEX 1:18.39
1-Ernesto Canto MEX l:23.13*
2-Raul Gonzalez MEX 1:23.20
3-Maurizio Damilano ITA 1:23.26
7-Marco Evoniuk USA 1:25.42
23-Jim Heiring USA 1:30.20
33-Dan O'Connor USA 1:35.12

MEN'S 50K RACEWALK (C-31, N-16)
wr-Raul Gonzalez MEX 3:41.38
1-Raul Gonzalez MEX 3:47.26*
2-Bo Gustafsson SWE 3:53.19
3-Alessandro Bellucci ITA 3:53.45
6-Carl Schueler USA 3:59.46
14-Vincent O'Sullivan USA 4:22.51
Marco Evoniuk USA DNF

1988—Seoul

The speed of racewalkers improved dramatically in these Games. In the 20K,
17 walkers beat the 1984 Olympic record. In the 50K, 11 walkers beat the
1984 record.

MEN'S 20K RACEWALK (C-53, N-28)
wr-Ernesto Canto MEX 1:18.39
1-Jozef Pribilinec CZE 1:19.57*
2-Ronald Weigel GDR 1:20.0
3-Maurizio Damilano ITA 1:20.14
36-Gary Morgan USA 1:27.26
37-Jim Heiring USA 1:27.30
44-Tim Lewis USA 1:31.0

MEN'S 50K RACEWALK (C42, N-22)
wr-Raul Gonzalez MEX 3:41.38
1-Vyacheslav Ivanenko SOV 3:38.29*
2-Ronald Weigel GDR 3:38.56
3-Hartwig Gauder GDR 3:39.45

22-Marco Evoniuk USA 3:56.55
23-Carl Schueler USA 3:57.44
34-Andy Kaestner USA 4:12.49

1992—Barcelona

Television used freeze-framing to repeatedly point out "lifting" not called by the judges. Steep hill leading to stadium on final lap was exhausting.

WOMEN'S 10K RACEWALK (C-44, N-21)
wr-Nadezhda Ryashkina USSR 41:56.2
1-Chen Yueling CHN 44:32.0
2-Elena Nikolayeva EUN 44:33.0
3-Li Chunxiu CHN 44:41.0
20-Michelle Rohl USA 46:45.0
26-Debbi Lawrence USA 48:23.0
27-Victoria Herazo USA 48:26.0

MEN'S 20K RACEWALK (C-42, N-19)
wr-Stefan Johahsson SWE 1:18.35
1-Daniel Plaza ESP 1:21.45
2-Guillaume LeBlanc CAN 1:22.25
3-Giovanni de Benedictis ITA 1:23.11
30-Allen James USA 1:35.12

MEN'S 50K RACEWALK (C-42, N-19)
wr-Raul Gonzales MEX 3:41.38
1-Andrey Perlov EUN 3:50.13
2-Carlos Mercenario MEX 3:52.09
3-Ronald Weigel GER 3:53.45
23-Carl Schueler USA 4:13.38
33-Herman Nelson USA 4:25.49
Marco Evoniuk USA DNF

1996—Atlanta

Heat and humidity were big factors in these Games, causing many competitors to drop out. Ecuador won its first Olympic medal ever in the men's 20K, and it was gold.

WOMEN'S 10K RACEWALK (C-61, N-31)
wr-Nadezhda Ryashkina USSR 41:56.2
1-Yelena Ninikolayeva RUS 41:49
2-Elisabetta Perrone ITA 42:12
3-Yan Wang CHN 42:19
15-Michelle Rohl USA 44:29
21-Debbi Lawrence USA 45:32
Victoria Herazo USA DQ

MEN'S 20K RACEWALK (C-27, N-17)
wr-Bernardo Segura MEX 1:17.25.6
1-Jefferson Perez ECU 1:20.07
2-Ilya Markov RUS 1:20.16
3-Bernardo Segura MEX 1:20.23
50-Curt Clausen USA 1:32.11

MEN'S 50K RACEWALK (C-51, N-28)
wr-Rene Piller FRA 3:41.28.2
1-Robert Korzeniowski POL 3:43.30
2-Mikhail Shchennikov RUS 3:43.46
3-Valentin Messana ESP 3:44.19
24-Allen James USA 4:01.18
26-Andrzej Chylinski USA 4:03.13

Glossary of Physiological Terms

ACCELERATION: Rate of increased change in velocity.

ACCLIMATION: A laboratory adaptation to an environmental stress.

ACCLIMATIZATION: Adaptation to a particular environmental stress.

ACID-BASE BALANCE: The proper balance of H and OH ions in the blood.

ACIDOSIS: The situation in which the acid-base balance shifts to the acid side, due either to increased levels of unbuffered acids in the blood or to a reduction in the blood bicarbonates.

ACTIN: Thin muscle protein filament that works with the protein filament myosin to produce muscular contraction movement.

ACTION POTENTIAL: The change in the electrical potential across the cell or tissue membrane.

ACUTE: Referring to something immediate or of short duration (e.g., a treadmill run to the point of exhaustion would be an acute bout of exercise).

ADENOSINE DIPHOSPHATE (ADP): A high energy phosphate compound from which ATP is synthesized.

ADENOSINE TRIPHOSPHATE (ATP): A high-energy compound formed from oxidation of fat and carbohydrates from which the body derives its energy.

ADIPOSE TISSUE: Connective tissue in which fat is stored.

ADRENAL GLANDS: Endocrine glands located directly above each kidney, composed of the medulla (the hormones epinephrine and norepinephrine) and the cortex (cortical hormones).

ADRENALINE: See epinephrine.

ADRENOCORTICOTROPHIC HORMONE (ATCH): A pituitary hormone responsible for controlling the hormones released by the adrenal cortex.

AEROBIC: In the presence of air or oxygen.

AEROBIC FITNESS: Synonymous with the terms maximal oxygen uptake, maximal oxygen consumption and cardiovascular endurance capacity.

AEROBIC METABOLISM: A process that occurs in the cells (mitochondria) that uses oxygen to produce energy and is also known as cellular respiration.

AFFERENT NERVE: Sensory nerve that carries impulses from the sensory receptors (i.e., skin, eyes, ears) to the central nervous system.

AGILITY: The ability to change directions rapidly while maintaining total body control.

ALDOSTERONE: Hormone from the adrenal cortex responsible for sodium retention.

ALKALINE RESERVE: The amount of bicarbonate in the blood available for buffering acids.

ALKALOSIS: The situation in which the acid-base balance shifts to the alkaline, or basic, side.

ALVEOLAR AIR: The air present in the alveoli that is involved in the exchange of gases with the blood in the pulmonary capillaries.

ALVEOLI: Small air sacs, located at the termination of the pulmonary tree, in which the exchange of respiratory gases takes place with the blood in the adjacent capillaries.

AMINO ACIDS: The 22 basic building blocks of proteins for muscles, enzymes, hormones, etc.

AMPHETAMINE: Prescription drug that stimulates the central nervous system.

ANABOLIC STEROID: A prescription drug that has the anabolic or growth-stimulating characteristics of the male androgen, testosterone. Frequently taken by athletes to increase body size and muscle bulk. Illegal in national and international competitions.

ANABOLISM: The building up of body tissue or the constructive phase of metabolism.

ANAEROBIC: In the absence of oxygen.

ANAEROBIC THRESHOLD: That point at which the metabolic demand of exercise cannot be met totally by available aerobic sources and an increase in anaerobic metabolism occurs, as reflected by an increase in the blood lactate.

ANDROGEN: Male sex hormone from the testes and, in limited amounts, from the adrenal cortex.

ANEMIA: Inadequate number of red blood cells, or low hemoglobin levels, limiting oxygen transport.

ANGINA PECTORIS: Chest pain associated with narrowed coronary arteries and a lack of blood to the heart.

ANOXIA: Inadequate oxygen in the blood or tissues.

ANTHROPOMETRY: The study of body measurements.

ANTIDIURETIC HORMONE: Hormone from the posterior pituitary gland that promotes water retention through its action on the kidneys.

ARTERIOLE: A small artery that regulates the flow of blood from the arteries to the capillaries.

ARTERIOSCLEROSIS: Loss of elasticity of the arteries, or hardening of the arteries. The precursor to various diseases of the cardiovascular system (e.g., stroke and coronary artery disease).

ARTERY: A vessel that transports blood away from the heart.

ASPARTATES: Potassium and magnesium salts of aspartic acid, which some athletes believe has ergogenic properties.

ATHEROSCLEROSIS: Narrowing of the coronary arteries caused by cholesterol buildup.

ATHLETE'S HEART: An enlarged heart, typically found in endurance athletes due primarily to hypertrophy (enlargement) of the left ventricle through extensive training. It is no longer considered to be a pathological or diseased condition, as it once was.

ATRIUM: One of the chambers of the heart. The right atrium receives blood from the systemic circulation, and the left atrium receives blood from the pulmonary circulation.

ATROPHY: Loss of size, or mass, of body tissue (e.g., muscle atrophy with disuse).

AUTOGENIC INHIBITION: Reflex inhibition of a motor neuron in response to excessive tension in the muscle fibers it supplies.

AUTONOMIC NERVOUS SYSTEM: That portion of the nervous system that controls involuntary activity (e.g., smooth muscle and the myocardium) and includes both sympathetic and parasympathetic nerves.

AUTOREGULATION: Local control of blood distribution through vasodilatation in response to a tissue's changing needs.

AXIS CYLINDER: The central core of the axon of the nerve fiber.

AXON: The fiberlike extension of the nerve cell, which transmits the nerve impulse away from the cell body.

BALANCE: The ability to have complete control of the body as it is in motion.

BASAL METABOLIC RATE (BMR): The rate of body metabolism under the most optimal conditions of quiet, rest and relaxation. The lowest rate of metabolism compatible with life.

BETA BLOCKERS: A class of drugs that blocks the transmission of neural impulses from the sympathetic nervous system. Some think they have ergogenic properties.

BETA CELLS: Cells in the pancreas that secrete insulin.

BLOOD LIPIDS: Blood-borne fats (i.e., triglycerides and cholesterol).

BLOOD PRESSURE: The force that blood exerts against the walls of the blood vessels, arteries or heart.

BODY COMPOSITION: The chemical composition of the human body comparing the fat-free mass and fat mass of the body.

BODY DENSITY: The density of the body is equal to the body weight divided by the body volume.

BODY MASS INDEX (BMI): Measurement of body weight determined by dividing weight in kilograms by height in meters squared, and is highly correlated with body composition.

BORG SCALE: A numerical scale used to rate perceived exertion.

BRONCHIOLE: A small branch airway that may undergo spasm, making breathing difficult (e.g., as in exercise-induced asthma).

BRONCHUS: The subdivision of the trachea as it splits into two branches.

BUFFER: A substance in the blood that combines with either acids or bases to maintain a constant acid-base, or pH, balance.

CALORIE: A unit of heat energy defined as the amount of heat required to raise the temperature of 1 kilogram of water 1°C from 15 to 16°C.

CALORIMETER: A device for measuring the heat production of the body or of specific chemical reactions.

CAPACITY: The term used to define overall body endurance or stamina. See maximal oxygen uptake.

CAPILLARIES: The smallest vessels in the vascular system that connect the arterioles and venules, where all exchanges of gases or materials between the circulatory system and the tissues or lungs take place.

CAPILLARY-TO-FIBER RATIO: The number of capillaries per muscle fiber.

CARBOHYDRATE: A food substance, either simple like sugar or complex like potatoes, beans, etc., that includes various sugars and starches and is stored in the liver and muscles in the form of glucose and glycogen. Excess is stored as fat.

CARDIAC: Relating to the heart (e.g., cardiac muscle and cardiac output).

CARDIAC CYCLE: The period that includes all heart functions between two consecutive heartbeats.

CARDIAC MUSCLE: The myocardium, or muscle, of the heart.

CARDIAC OUTPUT: Output, or volume, of blood pumped by the heart per minute. The product of heart rate and stroke volume.

CARDIOVASCULAR DECONDITIONING: A decrease in the cardiovascular system's ability to deliver sufficient oxygen and nutrients.

CARDIOVASCULAR DRIFT: Increase in heart rate during exercise to compensate for a decrease in stroke volume, thus maintaining a constant cardiac output.

CARDIOVASCULAR ENDURANCE: Synonymous with aerobic fitness and maximal oxygen uptake.

CATABOLISM: The tearing down, or destruction, of body tissue.

CATALYST: A chemical substance that initiates or accelerates a chemical action without being altered as a result of the action.

CATECHOLAMINES: Active amines such as epinephrine and norepinephrine having powerful effects similar to those of the sympathetic nervous system.

CENTRAL NERVOUS SYSTEM: That division of the nervous system that includes the brain and spinal cord.

CEREBELLUM: The hindbrain, responsible for the smooth coordination of body movements.

CEREBRAL CORTEX: The portion of the brain that contains the primary and supplementary motor areas that control all movement patterns of a voluntary nature.

CEREBRUM: The large forebrain.

CHOLESTEROL: A lipid or fatty substance essential for life and found in various tissues and fluids. Elevated levels in the blood have been associated with an increased risk of cardiovascular disease.

CHRONIC ADAPTATION: Referring to training of an extended or long-term nature (e.g., physical training program of six months' duration causing changes that improve the body's efficiency both at rest and during exercise).

CIRCUIT TRAINING: Selected exercises or activities performed in sequence as rapidly as possible.

CLO UNITS: The insulating value of clothing.

COLLAGEN: A protein substance found in bones, cartilage and white fibrous tissues.

CONCENTRIC CONTRACTION: A muscular contraction in which shortening of the muscle occurs, or the movement of an electrical impulse through a neuron.

CONDITIONED REFLEX: A nervous reflex pattern that is learned.

CONDUCTION: Transfer of heat or cold through direct contact with an object or medium.

CONNECTIVE TISSUE: Specialized tissue, such as ligaments and tendons, that connects various body structures.

CONTRACTION: Development of tension by muscle that is concentric (muscle shortens), eccentric (muscle lengthens under tension) or static (contracts without length change).

CONVECTION: The transfer of heat or cold from a body to a moving liquid or gas.

COORDINATION: The act of movement in an organized, controlled and precise manner.

CORONARY ARTERIES: Those arteries that supply the heart muscle or myocardium.

CORTEX: Refers to the outer layer (e.g., cerebral cortex is the outer layer of the brain).

CORTISOL: A hormone from the adrenal cortex.

CREATINE PHOSPHATE: An energy-rich compound that plays a critical role in providing energy for muscular contraction.

CROSS INNERVATION: Innervation of a fast twitch motor unit by a slow twitch motor neuron, or vice versa.

DEAD SPACE: The volume of the various parts of the respiratory system in which no gas exchange occurs.

DEHYDRATION: Loss of body fluids.

DELAYED ONSET MUSCLE SORENESS (DOMS): Muscle soreness that develops 24 hours or more after strenuous exercise.

DENDRITE: The projection of the nerve cell that transmits impulses toward the cell body.

DETRAINING: Body changes in response to ceasing or reducing physical training.

DIAPHRAGM: The major muscle of respiration that separates the thorax from the abdomen.

DIAPHYSIS: The shaft of a long bone such as the femur.

DIASTOLE: The relaxation phase of each cardiac cycle, immediately following the contraction, or systole, of the heart.

DIASTOLIC PRESSURE: The lowest pressure of the arterial blood against the walls of the vessels or heart resulting from the diastole of the heart.

DIRECT CALORIMETRY: A method of gauging the body's rate and quantity of energy production by direct measurement of heat produced by the body.

DIURETIC: A substance that increases kidney function leading to a loss of body fluids through frequent urination.

DIURNAL VARIATION: Fluctuations in physiological responses that occur in a single day.

DYNAMIC ACTION: A muscle action that produces movement in a joint.

DYNAMOMETER: A device for measuring muscular strength.

DYSPNEA: Labored breathing.

ECCENTRIC CONTRACTION: Lengthening of the muscle under tension, as when lowering a heavy object.

ECTOMORPHY: One of three categories of the somatotype in which the body is rated for the degree of linearity.

EDEMA: A body part filled with fluid.

EFFECTIVE BLOOD VOLUME: That volume of blood available to supply the exercising muscles.

EFFERENT NERVE: Also referred to as a motor nerve or motoneuron conducting impulses from the central nervous system to the various end organs, such as the muscles.

EJECTION FRACTION: Fraction of blood pumped out of left ventricle with each contraction of the heart; measured by dividing the stroke volume by the end-diastolic volume and dividing by 100.

ELECTROCARDIOGRAM (EKG): A recording of the electrical activity of the heart.

ELECTROCARDIOGRAPH: An instrument that picks up and produces a record of the electrical activity of the heart.

ELECTROLYTE: Any solution that conducts electricity by means of its ions.

ELECTROMYOGRAM (EMG): A recording of the electrical activity of a muscle or a group of muscles.

END-DIASTOLIC VOLUME (EDV): Volume of blood remaining in the left ventricle of the heart at the end of the diastole just before contraction.

ENDOCRINE GLAND: A ductless gland that produces and/or releases hormones directly into the bloodstream.

ENDOMORPHY: One of three categories of the somatotype in which the body is rated for corpulence or obesity.

ENDURANCE: The ability to resist fatigue. Includes muscular endurance, which is a local or specific endurance, and cardiovascular endurance, which is a more general, total body endurance.

ENERGY BALANCE: Balance of caloric intake and expenditure.

ENGRAM: A learned, memorized motor pattern stored both in sensory and motor portions of the brain that can be replayed on request.

ENZYME: An organic catalyst that speeds the velocity of specific chemical reactions such as in the digestive process.

EPIMYSIUM: Outer connective tissue that surrounds an entire muscle binding it together.

EPINEPHRINE: One of the hormones of the adrenal medulla secreted during times of stress to help mobilize energy. Also referred to as adrenaline.

EPIPHYSIS: That part of the long bone that ossifies separately before uniting with the main shaft, or diaphysis, of the bone.

ERGOGENIC AID: Substance or phenomenon that elevates or improves physical performance.

ERGOGRAPH: An instrument or device used for recording muscular work.

ERGOLYTIC: Able to impair work or performance.

ERGOMETER: A device for exercising the subject in a manner in which the physical work performed can be measured (e.g., a bicycle ergometer).

ERYTHROPOIETIN: The hormone that stimulates red blood cell production.

ESSENTIAL AMINO ACIDS: The nine amino acids necessary for human growth that must be part of the human diet since the body cannot synthesize them.

ESTROGEN: Female sex hormone.

EVAPORATION: The loss of heat through the conversion of the water in sweat to a vapor.

EXCESS POST-EXERCISE OXYGEN CONSUMPTION (EPOC): Excess oxygen consumption above resting levels after exercise also known as oxygen debt.

EXERCISE PHYSIOLOGY: The study of how body structure and function is altered by exercising the body regularly.

EXERCISE PRESCRIPTION: Individualizing the exercise program on the basis of the duration, frequency, intensity and mode of exercise.

EXTERNAL RESPIRATION: The process of bringing air into the lungs and the resulting exchange of gas between the alveoli and the capillary blood.

EXTRACELLULAR FLUID: The 35 to 40 percent of the body's water that is outside the cells, including blood plasma, interstitial fluid, lymph, cerebrospinal fluid and others.

EXTRINSIC NEURAL CONTROL: Redistribution of blood controlled by neural mechanisms.

FARTLEK TRAINING: Speed play, where the athlete varies his or her pace at will from fast sprints to slow jogging; normally performed in the country, using hills.

FASCIA: Connective tissue surrounding and connecting muscle.

FASCIULUS: A small bundle of muscle fibers wrapped in a connective tissue sheath within a muscle.

FAST TWITCH MUSCLE FIBER: One of several types of muscle fibers that have low oxidative capacity, high glycolytic capacity and are associated with speed or power activities.

FAT: An energy source food substance that is composed of glycerol and fatty acids.

FAT-FREE MASS: The mass or weight of the body that is not composed of fat such as bone muscle, skin and organs.

FATIGUE: Diminished work capacity due to any one or a combination of factors, including short intense exercise or long duration effort, low blood sugar, etc.

FATTY ACID: Along with glycerol, the product of the breakdown of fats.

FATTY STREAKS: Early lipid deposits within blood vessels.

FAT WEIGHT: Absolute amount of body fat. Fat weight plus lean body weight equals total body weight.

FLEXIBILITY: The range of movement of a specific joint or group of joints, influenced by the associated bones and bony structures, muscles, tendons and ligaments.

FORCED EXPIRATORY VOLUME (FEV): The volume of air exhaled in the first second after maximum inhalation.

FREE FATTY ACIDS: The components of fat that are used by the body for metabolism.

GASTRIC EMPTYING: The movement of food mixed with gastric secretions from the stomach into the duodenum.

GLUCAGON: A hormone from the pancreas that acts to increase blood glucose, or sugar, levels.

GLUCONEOGENESIS: The conversion of glucose into glycogen.

GLUCOSE: A simple sugar that is transported in the blood and metabolized in the tissues. Essential energy source for brain and nervous tissue.

GLYCEROL: A substance that combines with fatty acids to form fat.

GLYCOGEN: The storage form of glucose or carbohydrates in the body, found predominantly in the muscles and liver.

GLYCOGEN LOADING: Manipulating exercise and diet to optimize the total amount of glycogen stored in the body.

GLYCOGENOLYSIS: The metabolic breakdown of glycogen into glucose.

GLYCOLYSIS: The breakdown of glycogen into lactic acid.

GOLGI TENDON ORGAN: A proprioceptor located in series with muscle tendons.

GONADS: Endocrine glands responsible for reproduction (i.e., the testes in males and ovaries in females).

GROWTH HORMONE (GH): A pituitary hormone responsible for controlling tissue growth. Also referred to as somatotrophic hormone.

HEART RATE: Frequency of contraction of the heart muscle; also called pulse rate.

HEART RATE RECOVERY PERIOD: The time it takes for the heart rate to return to a normal resting rate following exercise.

HEAT CRAMP: Severe cramping of the skeletal muscles, due to excessive dehydration and the associated salt 1088.

HEAT EXHAUSTION: A disorder due to an excessive heat load on the body, characterized by breathlessness, extreme tiredness, dizziness and rapid pulse; usually associated with a decrease in sweat production.

HEAT STROKE: The most serious heat disorder, characterized by a body temperature above 105°F, cessation of sweating and total confusion or unconsciousness, which can lead to death.

HEMATOCRIT: The relative contribution, or percentage, of the blood cells to the total blood volume.

HEMOCONCENTRATION: Used in reference to an apparent increase in red blood cell number due to a plasma volume reduction (i.e., there is a relative, but not an absolute, increase).

HEMODILUTION: An increase in blood plasma, resulting in a dilution of the blood's cellular contents.

HEMOGLOBIN: Iron pigment of the red blood cells that has a high affinity for oxygen.

HIGH ALTITUDE CEREBRAL EDEMA: A condition of unknown cause in which fluid accumulates in the cranial cavity at high altitude characterized by mental confusion, which can be fatal in severe cases.

HIGH ALTITUDE PULMONARY EDEMA: A condition of unknown cause in which fluid accumulates in the lungs at high altitude, interfering with ventilation and resulting in shortness of breath, fatigue and characterized by impaired blood oxygenation, mental confusion and unconsciousness.

HIGH DENSITY LIPOPROTEIN (HDL): A cholesterol carrier regarded as a scavenger that removes cholesterol from the arterial wall and transports it to the liver to be metabolized.

HOMEOSTASIS: The ability of the body to maintain an environment of organic stability even when natural functions are disrupted.

HORMONE: A chemical substance produced or released by an endocrine gland and transported by the blood to a specific target tissue.

HYDROSTATIC WEIGHING: A method of measuring body volume in which a person is weighed while submerged underwater—the difference between the scale weight on land and the underwater weight equals body volume; the value must be corrected to account for any air trapped in the body.

HYPEREMIA: An excessive amount of blood in a part of the body.

HYPERGLYCEMIA: Elevated levels of glucose in the blood.

HYPERPLASIA: Increase in size, due to an increased number of cells.

HYPERTENSION: Abnormally high blood pressure, usually defined in adults as a systolic pressure in excess of 140 mmHg and/or diastolic pressure in excess of 90 mmHg.

HYPERTHERMIA: Overheating of the body temperature.

HYPERTROPHY: Increase in the size, or mass, of an organ or body tissue.

HYPERVENTILATION: Breathing rate and/or tidal volume increased above levels necessary for normal function.

HYPOGLYCEMIA: Abnormally low glucose levels in the blood.

HYPONATREMIA: A blood sodium concentration below the normal values of 136 to 143 mmol/l.

HYPOTENSION: Abnormally low blood pressure.

HYPOTHALAMUS: That region of the brain involved in controlling or releasing many of the hormones of the pituitary gland.

HYPOTHERMIA: Life-threatening heat loss brought on by rapid cooling, energy depletion and exhaustion.

HYPOXIA: A lack of oxygen in the blood or tissues.

INDIRECT CALORIMETRY: A method of estimating energy expenditure by measuring respiratory gases.

INFRARED INTERACTANCE: A procedure for measuring body composition using a probe that emits electromagnetic radiation through the skin; the amount of energy reflected back from the tissues indicates tissue composition.

INHIBITION: Negative nervous control to restrict, or limit, the amount of force generated.

INNERVATION RATIO: The ratio of the number of muscle fibers per motoneuron.

INSPIRATION: The active process involving the diaphragm and the intercostal muscles that expands the lungs, which causes decreased pressure in the lungs allowing outside air to rush in.

INSULIN: A hormone produced by the pancreas that assists in the control of the blood sugar, or glucose, levels.

INTERNAL RESPIRATION: The exchange of gases between the blood and tissues.

INTERVAL TRAINING: A training program that alternates bouts of heavy or very heavy work with periods of rest or light work.

INTESTINAL ABSORPTION: The movement of nutrients through the intestinal wall into the blood.

INTRACELLULAR FLUID: The approximately 60 to 65 percent of total body water that is contained in the cells.

IN VITRO: Functioning outside of, or detached from, the body.

IN VIVO: Functioning within the body.

ION: An electrically charged atom or group of atoms.

ISCHEMIA: A temporary deficiency of blood to a specific area of the body.

ISOKINETIC CONTRACTION: A contraction in which the muscle generates force against a variable resistance where the speed of movement is constantly maintained.

ISOMETRIC CONTRACTION: A contraction in which the muscle generates force, but there is no observable movement (e.g., pushing against a building).

ISOTONIC CONTRACTION: A contraction in which the muscle generates force against a constant resistance and movement results, either shortening (concentric) or lengthening (eccentric).

KARVONEN METHOD: The calculation of training heart rate by adding a given percentage of the maximal rate reserve to the resting rate, giving an adjusted heart rate that is equivalent to the desired percentage of VO_2 max.

KINESTHESIS: A sense, or awareness, of body position.

LACTATE THRESHOLD: The point during exercise of increasing intensity at which blood lactate begins to accumulate above resting levels.

LACTIC ACID: The end product of glycolysis, or anaerobic metabolism.

LATENT PERIOD: A period of time between the stimulus and the response to that stimulus.

LEAN BODY WEIGHT: That weight of the body that is not fat (e.g., bone, muscle, skin, organ weights, etc.); determined by subtracting the fat weight from the total body weight.

LIGAMENT: Connective tissue that binds bone to bone to maintain the integrity of a joint.

LIPID: A fat, or fatlike, substance.

LIPOPROTEIN LIPASE: The enzyme that breaks down triglycerides to free fatty acids and glycerol, allowing the free fatty acids to enter the cells for use as fuel or storage for energy.

MANOMETER: An instrument for measuring pressure.

MAXIMAL EXPIRATORY VENTILATION (VE MAX): The highest ventilation that can be achieved during exhaustive exercise.

MAXIMAL OXYGEN UPTAKE (VO_2 MAX): The best physiological index of total body endurance; also referred to as aerobic power, maximal oxygen intake, maximal oxygen consumption or cardiovascular endurance capacity.

MAXIMUM HEART RATE: The highest heart rate attainable from maximal exercise to the point of exhaustion.

MEAN BODY TEMPERATURE: A weighted average of skin and internal body temperatures.

MENSTRUATION: The periodic cycle in the uterus associated with preparation of the uterus to receive a fertilized egg.

MENTAL PRACTICE: Mental rehearsal of the athletic event or sport.

MESOMORPHY: One of three categories of the somatotype in which the body is rated for the degree of muscularity.

METABOLIC EQUIVALENT (MET): One met is resting metabolism and equals about 3.5 ml O_2/kg./min.

METABOLISM: The sum total of the energy-producing and absorbing processes in the body (i.e., the energy used by the body).

MICROMINERALS: Known as trace elements of which the body needs less than 100 mg. per day.

MICRON: Unit of measure equal to 0.001 mm.

MITOCHONDRIA: Energy-producing bodies within the cell; the site of all oxidative energy production.

MORPHOLOGY: The form and structure of the body.

MOTOR AREA, OR MOTOR CORTEX: That area of the cerebral cortex that controls voluntary muscle movement.

MOTOR END PLATE: The area where the efferent, or motor nerve, attaches to the muscle fiber.

MOTOR NERVE OR MOTONEURON: The efferent nerve that transmits impulses to muscles.

MOTOR REFLEX: An involuntary response to a given stimulus.

MOTOR UNIT: The motor nerve and the group of muscle fibers it supplies.

MUSCLE FIBER: The structural unit of muscle; a single cell with multiple nuclei composed of a number of smaller units called myofibrils (i.e., fast twitch type contracts rapidly but fatigues quickly and slow twitch contracts slowly and is fatigue resistant).

MUSCLE SPINDLE: A sensory receptor located in the muscle itself, that senses changes in muscle tension.

MUSCULAR FITNESS: The strength, muscular endurance and flexibility a person needs to carry out daily tasks without injury.

MYELIN SHEATH: The inner covering of the medullated nerve fiber.

MYOCARDIUM: The muscle of the heart.

MYOFIBRIL: The small elements that comprise the muscle fiber, and is composed of the proteins actin and myosin.

MYONEURAL JUNCTION: The junction between the muscle fiber and its nerve.

MYOSIN: A muscle protein that acts with actin, another muscle protein, to allow the muscle to contract.

NEGATIVE FEEDBACK SYSTEM: The primary mechanism through which the endocrine system supplies hormones to provide homeostasis and stops when this is achieved.

NERVE IMPULSE: An electrical signal conducted along a neuron to another neuron or group of muscle fibers.

NEURILEMMA: The outermost covering of a nerve fiber.

NEURON: The nerve cell; the basic structural unit of the nervous system that conducts nervous impulses to and from various parts of the body.

NEUROTRANSMITTER: A chemical used for communication between a neuron and another cell.

NONESSENTIAL AMINO ACIDS: The 11 or 12 amino acids the body synthesizes.

NOREPINEPHRINE: A hormone produced by the adrenal medulla, and a chemical transmitter substance at peripheral sympathetic nerve endings.

OBESITY: An excessive amount of body fat considered to be greater than 25 percent above normal in men and 35 percent in women.

OSSIFICATION: The process of calcification or hardening of the bone during the growth process.

OSTEOPOROSIS: Decreased bone mineral content that causes decreased bone density and an enlargement of bone spaces, producing fragility and porosity.

OVERLOAD: Stressing the body or parts of the body to levels above that normally experienced; sometimes referred to as overtraining and is characterized by decreased performance.

OXIDATIVE SYSTEM: The body's most complex energy system that generates energy by disassembling fuels with the aid of oxygen, and has a very high energy yield.

OXYGEN DEBT: The quantity of oxygen above normal resting level used in the period of recovery from any specific exercise or muscular activity.

PACINIAN CORPUSCLE: A proprioceptor located in muscle and tendon sheaths adjacent to joints.

PANCREAS: An endocrine gland that produces both the hormones insulin and glucagon that control blood glucose levels.

PARASYMPATHETIC NERVOUS SYSTEM: A major subdivision of the autonomic nervous system whose fibers arise from the midbrain, medulla or sacral region of the spinal cord.

PARATHORMONE: Hormone produced by the parathyroid glands that assists in controlling calcium and phosphorus levels.

PARATHYROIDS: Endocrine glands that are located on or embedded in the thyroid glands and that produce parathormone.

PERCEIVED EXERTION: Personal estimate of exercise difficulty.

PERICARDIUM: The fibrous sac that encapsulates the heart.

PERIOSTEUM: The fibrous membrane that surrounds bone.

PERIPHERAL NERVOUS SYSTEM: That part of the nervous system that lies outside the central nervous system (i.e., spinal cord and brain).

pH: A system for expressing the degree of acidity or alkalinity of a solution in which a value of 7.0 is neutral, greater than 7.0 alkaline and less than 7.0 acidic.

PHOSPHOCREATNINE: An energy-rich compound that plays a critical role in providing energy for muscle action by maintaining ATP concentration.

PLAQUE: A build up of lipids, smooth muscle cells, connective tissue and debris that forms at the site of injury to an artery.

PLASMA: The liquid fraction of the whole blood.

PLYOMETRICS: A type of dynamic action resistance training based on the theory that use of the stretch reflex during jumping will recruit additional motor units.

PONDERAL INDEX: Defined as height divided by the cube root of weight.

POWER: The product of force and velocity divided by time; probably far more important than absolute strength alone.

PRECAPILLARY SPHINCTER: A small band of smooth muscle controlling the flow of blood to the true capillaries.

PRINCIPLE OF SPECIFICITY: The principle that a training program must stress the physiological systems critical for optimal performance in a given sport in order to achieve desired training adaptations.

PROGRESSIVE OVERLOAD: Gradually increasing the training stimulus in a systematic manner.

PROGRESSIVE RESISTANCE EXERCISE (PRE): The resistance used in training is progressively increased systematically as the body adapts to the training stimulus.

PROPRIOCEPTOR: A sensory receptor sensitive to pressure, stretch, tension, pain, etc.

PROTEIN: A food substance formed from amino acids; it forms muscle tissue, hormones, enzymes, etc.

PULMONARY DIFFUSION: The exchange of gases between the lungs and the blood.

PULSE: A wave that travels down the artery after each contraction of the heart, or periodic expansion of the artery resulting from the systole of the heart.

PULSE PRESSURE: The mathematical difference between the systolic and diastolic pressures.

RADIATION: The transfer of heat through electromagnetic waves.

RATING OF PERCEIVED EXERTION (RPE): A person's subjective assessment of how hard he or she is working.

REACTION TIME: The period of time between the presentation of a stimulus and the subsequent reaction to that stimulus.

RECIPROCAL INHIBITION: The inhibition of the antagonist muscles, which allows the agonists to move.

REFLEX: An automatic, involuntary, unlearned response to a given stimulus.

RELATIVE BODY FAT: The ratio of fat weight to total body weight, expressed as a percentage.

RELATIVE HUMIDITY: A ratio expressing the degree of moisture in the surrounding air.

RELEASING FACTORS: Hormones transmitted from the hypothalamus to the anterior pituitary that promote release of some other hormones.

REPETITION RACEWALKING (REPEATS): Similar to interval training but with long work intervals and long periods of recovery.

RESIDUAL VOLUME: That volume of air remaining in the lung following a maximal expiration; vital capacity plus residual volume equal total lung capacity.

RESISTANCE TRAINING: Training designed to increase strength, power and muscular endurance.

RESPIRATION: The exchange of gases at both the level of the lung and tissue—intake of oxygen from the atmosphere into the lungs and then via the blood to the tissues, and exhale of carbon dioxide from tissues to the atmosphere.

RESPIRATORY CENTERS: Autonomic centers located in the medulla oblongata and the pons in the brain at the top of the spinal cord that establish breathing rate and depth.

RESPIRATORY EXCHANGE RATIO (R or RER): The ratio of carbon dioxide expired to oxygen consumed at the level of the lungs.

RESPIRATORY QUOTIENT (RQ): The ratio of the carbon dioxide produced in the tissues to the oxygen consumed by the tissues.

RESTING HEART RATE: Heart rate at rest—normally between 60 to 80 beats per minute, but has been recorded in trained athletes as low as in the 30s.

RESTING METABOLIC RATE (RMR): The amount of calories burned if you remained still for 24 hours; it gives an indication of how many more calories are needed to accomplish a day's activities, or to figure those necessary to accomplish weight loss or weight gain.

RUFFINI RECEPTOR: A proprioceptor located in the joint capsule.

SARCOLEMMA: The membrane surrounding the muscle fiber.

SARCOMERE: The functional contractile unit of muscle, which is a part of the myofibril.

SARCOPLASM: The fluid portion of the muscle fiber, or the muscle protoplasm.

SARCOPLASMIC RETICULUM: Network of tubules and vesicles within muscle fibers that stores calcium and is necessary to allow excitation of the muscle fibers.

SENSORY MOTOR INTEGRATION: The process by which the sensory and motor systems communicate and coordinate with each other.

SENSORY NERVE: Afferent, or sensory, nerves that transmit impulses from the sensory organs to the central nervous system.

SHIVERING: A rapid involuntary cycle of contraction and relaxation of skeletal muscles that generates heat when the body is cold.

SKELETAL MUSCLE: A muscle-controlling skeletal movement that is normally under voluntary control.

SKIN FOLD FAT THICKNESS: The most widely applied field technique used to estimate body density, relative body fat and fat-free mass involving caliper measurement of skin folds at various points on the body.

SLOW-TWITCH MUSCLE FIBER: One of several types of muscle fibers that have high oxidative capacity, low glycolytic capacity and are associated with endurance-type activities.

SMOOTH MUSCLE: An involuntary muscle, such as that which lines blood vessels and the gastrointestinal tract.

SOMATIC NERVOUS SYSTEM: The voluntary nervous system, including both cranial and spinal nerves.

SOMATOGRAM: A chart on which somatotypes are plotted.

SOMATOTROPHIC HORMONE (STH): A growth hormone (or GH) released by the pituitary gland that influences growth.

SOMATOTYPE: The characterization of the body physique in an objective and systematic manner (e.g., ectomorph [thin], mesomorph [muscular] and endomorph [fat]).

SPECIFICITY OF TRAINING: Since physiological adaptations in response to physical training are highly specific to the nature of the training activity, training should be carefully matched to an athlete's specific performance needs.

SPEED OF MOVEMENT: Sum of reaction time and movement time to complete a body movement.

SPHYGMOMANOMETER: An instrument used to measure arterial blood pressure.

SPIROMETER: An instrument used to measure various lung volumes and dynamic lung function.

STATIC ACTION: An action in which a muscle contracts without moving, generating force while its length remains unchanged; also known as isometric action.

STEADY STATE HEART RATE: A heart rate that is maintained at submaximal levels of exercise when the rate of work is held constant.

STRENGTH: The ability of a muscle to exert force.

STROKE VOLUME: The volume of blood pumped per contraction of the ventricle.

SYMPATHETIC NERVOUS SYSTEM: A major division of the autonomic nervous system.

SYNAPSE: The junction between two neurons.

SYSTOLE: The contraction phase of the cardiac cycle.

SYSTOLIC PRESSURE: The greatest pressure in the vessels or heart during a cardiac cycle resulting from the systole.

TAPERING: A reduction in training intensity prior to a competition to give the mind and body a break from the rigors of a heavy training load.

TARGET CELLS: Cells that possess specific hormone receptors.

TENDON: Connective tissue that attaches muscle to bone.

TESTOSTERONE: The predominant male androgen.

THERMIC EFFECT OF ACTIVITY: The energy expended in excess of the resting metabolic rate to accomplish a given activity.

THERMORECEPTORS: Sensory receptors that detect changes in body temperature and external temperature and relay this information to the hypothalamus, which adjusts and maintains normal body temperature.

THRESHOLD: The minimal level required to elicit a response.

THYROID GLAND: An endocrine gland located at the base of the neck that produces several hormones regulating total body metabolism.

THYROID-STIMULATING HORMONE: A pituitary hormone that controls the thyroid gland's release of thyroxin.

THYROXIN: A hormone produced by the thyroid gland that assists in the control of total body metabolism.

TIDAL VOLUME: The amount of air inspired or expired during a normal breathing cycle.

TONUS: That quality of a muscle that gives it firmness in the absence of a voluntary contraction.

TOTAL LUNG CAPACITY: The sum of the vital capacity and the residual volume.

TRAINING HEART RATE (THR): A heart rate goal established by using a percentage of the heart rate equivalent to VO_2 max (e.g., selecting 70 percent of a person's maximum capacity as the THR).

TRIGLYCERIDES: A fat consisting of three fatty acids and glycerol.

VALSALVA MANEUVER: Increased intra-abdominal and intrathoracic pressure created by holding the breath and attempting to compress the contents of the abdominal and thoracic cavities.

VASOPRESSIN HORMONE: A pituitary hormone that controls blood vessel diameter.

VEIN: A vessel that transports blood back to the heart.

VELOCITY: The speed, or rate, of movement; distance divided by time.

VENTILATION: The movement of air into and out of the lungs.

VENTILATORY EQUIVALENT FOR OXYGEN: The ratio between the volume of air ventilated and the amount of oxygen consumed, indicating breathing economy.

VENTRICLE: A chamber of the heart that expels, or pumps, blood into the lungs (right ventricle) or into the systemic circulation (left ventricle).

VENULE: A small vein that provides the link between capillaries and veins.

VESTIBULAR RECEPTOR: A proprioceptor located in the ear.

VISCOSITY: The quality of a fluid that describes its flow characteristics (e.g., water has a low viscosity while honey has a high viscosity).

VITAL CAPACITY: The greatest volume of air that can be expired following the deepest possible inspiration.

WEIGHT TRAINING: Progressive resistance exercise using weights.

WIND CHILL: A combined cooling effect of temperature and wind.

WORK: Force times distance.

APPENDIX 7

Daily Training Log

You may find it extremely helpful to keep a training log to measure your progress. This can be motivational if you are persistent in efforts to maintain your brisk walking consistently. You may find it interesting to estimate calories burned on each walk and keep track in the column provided. To do this use the following guidelines:

Speed	Body Weight	Calories Burned/Hour
3 mph	100 lb.	210
4 $\frac{1}{2}$ mph	100 lb.	295
3 mph	150 lb.	320
4 $\frac{1}{2}$ mph	150 lb.	440
3 mph	200 lb.	450
4 $\frac{1}{2}$ mph	200 lb.	600

If you walk only half an hour, cut the values in half (or in proportion to your time). You may also interpolate as far as weight is concerned for an estimate—for example, if your weight is 175 pounds and you walk 4 1/2 mph, use a figure midway between 440 and 600 calories burned per hour, which equals 520.

Sample Daily Training Log

(for photocopying)

Date _____

Your goal _____

Week number _____

For miles walked this week _____

Resting pulse rate _____

Target pulse rate _____

Weight _____

	Mon.	Tues.	Wed.	Thurs.	Fri.	Sat.	Sun.
Weather conditions (temperature, wet, dry)							
Course (flat, hilly, surface type)							
Pace (normal, slow, brisk)							
Target pulse rate (time maintained)							

	Mon.	Tues.	Wed.	Thurs.	Fri.	Sat.	Sun.
Cooldown (time and type)							
Duration of walk and estimated distance							
Estimated calories burned							
Aches and pains							
How I felt (tired, peppy, relaxed, hungry)							
Days off							
Notes and comments							

U.S. Walking Clubs and Promoters

The people on this list are knowledgeable about competitive and noncompetitive walking events in their own states. This list is intended to serve as a helpful resource of walking organizations to networking walkers all over the United States in an effort to gain further participation in this low-injury, excellent and healthful aerobic activity. However, because changes in walking clubs happen so frequently, it is virtually impossible to have a completely up-to-date list. Therefore, it is as accurate as possible—current as of July 1996. My intention is to update the information periodically as various changes occur. If you know of any corrections, such as new additions or address changes, please write or call Bob Carlson at 2261 Glencoe Street, Denver, Colorado 80207-3834; (303) 377-0576; e-mail: Frwbcarlsn@aol.com.

(*Author's note on abbreviations:* RW = racewalking; IAAF Judge = international racewalking judge, the top racewalking officials in the United States; USATF = USA Track & Field, the governing body of racewalking in the United States; those people listed as "Chair" are in charge of racewalking in their own association.)

ALABAMA
Judi Allen, 6474 D Cedar Bend Court, Mobile, AL 36608; (334) 344-5264. (Alabama Assn. USATF RW Chair)

ALASKA
(Alaska Assn. USATF RW Chair—Vacant)

Lyle Perrigo, 1921 Congress Circle, #B, Anchorage, AK 99507; (907) 561-5339.

Lark Hackney, 600 Street Anns, #7, Douglas, AK 99824; (907) 364-2382.

ARIZONA
(Arizona Assn. USATF RW Chair—Vacant)

Arizona Walkers Club, c/o Gus Pappas, 812 West Port, Au Prince, Phoenix, AZ 85023; (602) 942-4007.

Dawn Walk Club, c/o Jo Ann Taylor, 18205 North 45th Avenue, Glendale, AZ 85308; (602) 978-1887.

Gail Smith, c/o AZ TAC Office, 8436 East Hubbell, Scottsdale, AZ 85257; (602) 949-1991. Home address: 2755 West 14th Street, Yuma, AZ 85364; (602) 782-6546.

Prescott Walkers, 1150 Smokie, Prescott, AZ 86301.

ARKANSAS
Paul Johnson, 3011 Jackson, Fort Smith, AR 72901; (501) 785-2912. (Arkansas Assn. USATF RW Chair)

W. Randy Taylor, Worthen Bank, Box 1681, Little Rock, AR 72203; (501) 224-2823.

CALIFORNIA
(Central California Assn. of USATF—USATF RW Chair—Vacant; contact 105 East University Avenue, Fresno, CA 93704; [209] 266-0340)

Age Group Walkers, c/o Dave Japs, 2250 West Chestnut, Space 84, San Bernadino, CA 92410; (714) 888-6192.

Woody Benton, 1245 South Orange Grove Boulevard, Pasadena, CA 91105; (813) 799-1978. (RW Official)

Bob Bowman, 51 Chatsworth Court, Oakland, CA 94611; (415) 531-1427. (IAAF Judge, Chairman of IAAF Racewalking—Top RW Official in the World)

Ron Daniel, 1289 Balboa Court, #149, Sunnyvale, CA 94086; (415) 964-3580. (Pacific Assn. USATF RW Chair and IAAF Judge)

Easy Striders Walking Club, c/o Jim Coots, 2611 Voorhees, #E, Redondo Beach, CA 90278; (310) 542-5048. (RW Coach)

Wayne Glusker, 2449 Lehigh Avenue, San Jose, CA 95124. (RW Coach)

Golden Gate Walkers, c/o David Moore, newsletter editor, 1750 San Luis Road, Walnut Creek, CA 94596; (510) 937-6778.

Myron "Tad" Godwin Jr., 1811 Novato Boulevard, #25, Novato, CA 94947.

Ozzie Gontang, 2903 29th Street, San Diego, CA 92104-4912; (619) 281-7447.

Jim Hanley, 3346 South Allegheny Court, Westlake Village, CA 91362.

Robert A Hickey, 2217 Montrose Avenue, #6, Montrose, CA 91026; (818) 541-1447. (IAAF Judge)

Therese Ikonian, 544 Columbia Avenue, San Jose, CA 95126; (408) 297-3376. (Editor of USATF Newsletter)

Inland Empire Racewalkers, c/o Dave Snyder, 11878 Holly Street, Grand Terrace, CA 92324; (714) 824-2336, or Mel Grantham (714) 877-3548.

Marin Racewalkers, P.O. Box 21, Kentheld, CA 94914-0021; (415) 461-6843.

Lori Maynard, 2821 Kensington Road, Redwood City, CA 94061; (415) 369-2801. (IAAF Judge)

Monterrey Walk, Walk, Walk, c/o S. Sorenson, 870 Park Avenue, #311, Capitola, CA 95010-2334, or Buzz Schulte, President, 268 Hamilton Avenue, Suite A, Campbell, CA 95008; (408) 655-8190.

National Masters News, c/o Al Sheehan, Editor, P.O. Box 2372, Van Nuys, CA 91404.

North American Racewalking Foundation, c/o Elaine Ward, P.O. Box 50312, Pasadena, CA 91115-0312; (818) 577-2264.

Pacific Racewalkers Association, c/o Dick Petruzzi, P.O. Box 513, Carmichael, CA 95609; (916) 483-2917.

San Diego Track Club, c/o Lizzy Kemp Salvato, 12903 Pimpernel Way, San Diego, CA 92129; (619) 275-9255. (San Diego-Imperial Assn. USATF RW Chair)

San Diego Walkers, c/o Jaye Hanley, 9025 Hillary Drive, San Diego, CA 92126.

Santa Barbara Sport Walkers Club, c/o Jim Baltes, General Research, Box 6770, Santa Barbara, CA 93160; (805) 966-5865.

Sierra Racewalkers, P.O. Box 13203, Sacramento, CA 95813; (916) 483-2917

Walkers Club of Los Angeles, c/o Richard Oliver, 11431 Sunshine Terrace, Studio City, CA 91604; (818) 985-9854.

Southern California Racewalking News, c/o Elaine Ward, 1000 San Pasqual, #35, Pasadena, CA 91106-3393; (818) 577-2264. (Southern California Assn. USATF RW Chair and Southern California Walkers Club)

Walk for Life Club, c/o Kim McCreary, 6310 Nancy Ridge Drive, Suite 101, San Diego, CA 92121.

COLORADO

American Racewalk Association, c/o Viisha Sedlak, P.O. Box 4, Paonia, CO 81428; (970) 527-4557. (RW Coach)

Dr. Bill Byrnes, 2957 11th Street, Boulder, CO 80304; (303) 492-5301. (Researcher on RW at University of Colorado Human Performance Laboratory)

Front Range Walkers, c/o Bob Carlson, 2261 Glencoe Street, Denver, CO 80207-3834; (303) 377-0576. (Colorado Assn. USATF RW Chair)

Paula Hall, 2521 Ridgecrest Road, Fort Collins, CO 80524; (303) 221-0293. (Co-Coordinator North Colorado Section of Front Range Walkers)

Dan Pierce, 1617 Sixth Avenue, Longmont, CO 80501; (303) 678-9861. (RW Coach for High Altitude Racing Team and Vice President USATF RW Committee)

Sally Richards, 1153 Evergreen Parkway, Suite 224, Evergreen, CO 80439; (303) 674-4428. (Masters athlete, coach and trainer for Walking Beyond, Inc.)

Lonnie Schreiner, 2515 Tupelo Drive, Loveland, CO 80538; (970) 669-3488. (Co-Coordinator North Colorado Section of Front Range Walkers)

John Spuhler, P.O. Box 111243, Aurora, CO 80042-1243; (303) 753-4212. (Athlete and Director of Focus for Athletes)

CONNECTICUT

Abraxas TC, c/o Rich and Maryanne Torrellas, 28 Marion Lane, Clinton, CT 06339; (203) 669-4572. (Rich is a RW Coach and Maryanne is an athlete.)

Bruce L. Douglass, 14 Willow Lane, Ledyard, CT 06339; (203) 536-1309. (National USATF RW Chairman)

Bill Mongovan, 1169 Hope Street #B-4, Stamford, CT 06907; (203) 322-1964. (Connecticut Assn. USATF RW Chair)

New York Masters Club, c/o Dr. Jack Boitano, Fairfield College, Fairfield, CT 06430-7524.

Brian Savilonis, 41 Sherwood Circle, Manchester, CT 06040; (203) 642-1849.

DELAWARE

(Falls under Mid-Atlantic USATF—See Pennsylvania)

Delaware Healthwalkers, c/o Freida Holland; (302) 737-7400. (No Address Available)

Edward Morrill, 1303 Delaware Avenue, Wilmington, DE 19806.

DISTRICT OF COLUMBIA

(Falls under Potomac Valley Assn. USATF—See Potomac Valley Walkers under Virginia)

FLORIDA

Boca Raton Road Runners—Walking Division, c/o Alan Ronolfsky, 9200 SW Third Street, #110, Boca Raton, FL 33428; (407) 483-2992. (Judge Coordinator and Coach)

Central Florida Walkers, c/o Rod Larson, 104 111th Avenue, Windemere, FL 34786; (407) 876-4467.

Florida Athletic Club Walkers (South Florida), c/o Bob Cella, 7199 NW 49th Place, Fort Lauderdale, FL 33319; (954) 372-4392.

Greater Fort Lauderdale Road Runners Club (South Florida), c/o Betsy Nelson, 266 NW 65th Terrace, Plantation, FL 33317; (305) 791-1402.

Miami Runners Club—Walkers Division (South Florida), c/o Don Matuzsak, 7920 SW 40th Street, Miami, FL 33155; (305) 436-6967.

Jacksonville J-Walkers Walking Club (North Florida), c/o Bob Robertson, Jacksonville, FL; (904) 786-6888 or (904) 384-7541 (W).

Henry H. Laskau, 3232 Carambola Circle South, Coconut Creek, FL 33066; (305) 975-3385. (IAAF Judge Emeritus and RW Coach)

Naples Walking Club (West Coast), c/o Dick Bruce, 360 Goodlette Road South, Naples, FL 33940; (813) 947-5958.

Palm Beach Walkers (South Florida), c/o Joan Marineau Cadmus, 115 Timber Run East, West Palm Beach, FL 33407; (407) 848-3867.

Linda Stein, 9500 NW 32 Court, Sunrise, FL 33351; (954) 748-9679 or (954) 724-2108 (W). (Florida Assn. USATF RW Chair and RW Coach)

HAWAII
John Chanin, 707 Richards, Suite 728, Honolulu, HI 96813; (808) 261-2635.

Eugene Kitts, 98-1247 Kaahumanu Street, Suite 115, Honolulu, HI 96701; (808) 487-9999. (Hawaii Assn. USATF RW Chair)

Fit 'n Fast Walking Club, c/o Barbara Steffens, 1521 Puna Hou Street, Honolulu, HI 96822.

IDAHO
(Snake River Assn RW Chair—Vacant)

George Beall, 7820 Gary Lane, Boise, ID 83703; (208) 338-1010.

Treasure Valley Fitness Walkers, c/o Gundy Kaupips, P.O. Box 8432, Boise, ID 83707; (208) 344-3586.

ILLINOIS
Chicago Walker's Club, c/o Augie Hirt, 767 Bluff, #101, Carol Stream, IL 60188; (312) 828-6022.

Diane Graham-Henry, 442 West Belden, Chicago, IL 60614; (312) 327-4493 (phone & fax). (Illinois Assn. USATF RW Chair)

Walking Circuit, 259 Nicholson Street, Joliet, IL 60435.

INDIANA
Sam Bell, Assembly Hall, Indiana University, Bloomington, IN 47401; (812) 339-5978

Indiana Racewalker Club, c/o Patricia Walker, 3537 South State Road 135, Greenwood, IN 46143; (317) 535-5150.

Mike McGuire, 8997 Cinnabar, Indianapolis, IN 46228; (317) 872-5933.

Dennis Withem, 64 Chesterfield Drive, Noblesville, IN 46060; (317) 773-4288.

Bruce Williams, 8120 Georgia Street, Merrillville, IN 46410; (219) 465-7396. (Indiana Assn. USATF RW Chair)

IOWA
(Iowa USATF Assn. RW Chair—Vacant)

Gina Allard, 2843 East Locust Street, Davenport, IA 52803.

Ron Corey, 133 West Third, Tama, IA 52339.

Paul Schneider, Siouxland YMCA, 722 Nebraska Street, Sioux City, IA 51101; (515) 252-3276.

Randy Van Zee, RR #2, Box 33, Rock Valley, IA 51247.

Mike Wiggins, 1714 Avenue North, Hawarden, IA 51023.

KANSAS
(Falls under Missouri Valley Assn.)

Heartland Racewalkers, c/o Judy Strickland, P.O. Box 11141, Shawnee Mission, KS 66207; (913) 451-2228.

KENTUCKY
Patsy Caswell, 565 Southern Parkway, Louisville, KY 40214; (502) 456-6854.

Gil Clark, P.O. Box 36452, Louisville, KY 40233; (502) 456-8160. (Kentucky Assn. USATF RW Chair)

Gene Harrison, 3502 Illinois Avenue, Louisville, KY 40213.

LOUISIANA
Donna Boecher, 256 Walter Road, River Ridge, LA; (504) 737-7409. (Southern Assn. USATF RW Chair)

Dottie Clemmer, 830 Foucher, New Orleans, LA 70115; (504) 899-4902.

Cajun RRC, c/o Brian Papania, P.O. Box 30332555, Lafayette, LA 70593.

Agnes Courtney, 2261 Northbrook, Gretna, LA 70056; (504) 394-7535.

New Orleans Track Club, Box 52003, New Orleans, LA 70152-2003; (504) 482-6682.

MAINE
Western Maine Racewalkers, c/o Tom Eastler, RR#1, Box 1043, Farmington, ME 04938; (207) 778-6703. (Maine Assn. USATF RW Chair)

Maine Walkers, c/o Moshe Myerowitz, 1570 Broadway, Bangor, ME 04401; (207) 945-5559.

MARYLAND
(Falls under Potomac Valley USATF—See Potomac Valley Walkers under Virginia)

Beth Alvarez, 16000 Pointer Ridge Road, Bowie, MD 20716.

Sam MeerKreebs, 5509 Greystone, Chevy Chase, MD 20815.

MASSACHUSETTS
Mark Fenton, Racewalking Editor for *Walking* magazine, 9-11 Harcourt Street, Boston, MA 02116; (617) 266-3322. (RW Coach and USATF Sports Sciences)

Justin Kuo, 39 Oakland Road, Brookline, MA 02146-6700; (617) 731-9889 or (617) 354-3000 (W). (New England Assn. USATF RW Chair and National Records Chairman)

Needham Track Club, c/o John Hrones, 53 Coulton Park, Needham, MA 02192; (617) 449-4954.

New England Walkers, c/o Ken Mattson, 164 Cushing Street, Cambridge, MA 02138-4582; (617) 576-9331.

North Medford Club, c/o Philip McGaw, Shirley MA 02174; (617) 698-1806.

Reebok Shoe Co., c/o Kathy Smith, 100 Technology Drive, Stoughton, MA 02072; (617) 341-5000.

Rockport Shoe Co., c/o Frank Carroll, 220 Donald Lynch Boulevard, Marlboro, MA; (508) 485-2090.

Steve Vaitones, P.O. Box 1905, Brookline, MA 02146; (617) 566-7600.

MICHIGAN
Kalamazoo Valley Walkers, c/o Mark Kerstetter, 2201 Quail Run Drive, Kalamazoo, MI 49009.

Pegasus Walkers, c/o Frank Soby, 3907 Bishop, Detroit, MI 48224; (313) 881-5458. (RW Coach and Michigan Assn. USATF RW Chair)

Urban Walkers, Flint, MI. (No Address Available)

Wolverine Pacers, c/o Frank Alongi, 26530 Woodshire Avenue, Dearborn Heights, MI 48127; (313) 277-6060. (RW Coach and IAAF Judge Emeritus)

MINNESOTA
Fern Anderson, 3152 Kentucky Avenue South, St. Louis Park, MN 55426.

Mary Howell Langlie, 109 Third Avenue North, Albert Lee, MN 56007; (507) 377-8954.

Walk Sport Minnesota, Brad Struve, 817 Osceola Avenue, St. Paul, MN 55105.

Gary Westlund, 3054 NE Arthur Street, Minneapolis, MN 55418; (612) 782-9620. (Minnesota Assn. USATF RW Chair)

MISSISSIPPI
(Falls under Southern Assn. of USATF—See Louisiana)

No known contacts.

MISSOURI
Dr. Wayne Armbrust, 3604 Grant Court, Columbia, MO 65203; (314) 445-6675. (Missouri Valley Assn. USATF RW Chair)

Kansas City Walkers, c/o Anita Hermach, 5615 Wornall, Kansas City, MO 64113-1216.

Casey Meyers, 19712 Highway 169N, St. Joseph, MO 64505; (616) 662-4375. (Walking Author)

RW Club of St. Louis, c/o Ginger Mulanax, 11975 Gist Road, Bridgeton, MO 63044; (314) 298-0916. (Ozark Assn. USATF RW Chair)

Rob Sweetgall, 8230 Forsythe Boulevard, #209, Clayton, MO 63105; (314) 721-3600. (Endurance Walker, Author, President—Walking Wellness)

MONTANA
Dale Arthun, 207 Birchwood Drive, Billings, MT 59102.

Marjory McClaren, 1418 Sixth Avenue West, Kalispell, MT 59901; (406) 755-6007. (Montana Assn. USATF RW Chair)

NEBRASKA
Tim Klein, 10523 Hanson Avenue, Omaha, NE 68124; (402) 393-6395. (Nebraska Assn. USATF RW Chair)

Ruth White, 3333 D Street, Lincoln, NE 68510; (402) 423-4345.

NEVADA
Jim Bentley, P.O. Box 96804, Las Vegas, NV 89193. (RW Coach)

Roberta Hatfield, 2747 Crown Ridge Drive, Las Vegas, NV 89134; (702) 256-6938. (Nevada Assn. USATF RW Chair)

Las Vegas Walkers, c/o Stan Howser, 4939 East Owens Avenue, Las Vegas, NV 89110; (702) 452-7308.

Reno Track Club, 65 Date Palm Drive, Sparks, NV 89436; (702) 674-2011.

NEW HAMPSHIRE
(In New England USATF Assn.—See Massachusetts)

Wayne Nicoll, Ragged Mountain Club, Andover, NH 03216; (603) 735-5721. (Course Measurement Expert and Masters Athlete)

NEW JERSEY
Ray Funkhouser, 1471 Arapahoe Court, Tom's River, NJ 08753; (908) 341-7386. (Masters Athlete and USATF Official)

New Jersey Striders, c/o Ed Koch, P.O. Box 742, Madison, NJ 07940.

Jeff Salvage, 86 Five Crown Royal, Marlton, NJ 08053; (609) 983-8248. (Mid-Atlantic Assn. USATF RW Chair and RW Coach)

Shore AC, c/o Elliott Denman, 28 North Locust Avenue, West Long Branch, NJ 07764; (201) 222-9213. (New Jersey Assn. USATF RW Chair and IAAF Judge)

NEW MEXICO
Peter Armstrong, 141 Mesilla NE, Albuquerque, NM 87108; (505) 880-7104. (New Mexico Assn. USATF RW Chair)

Gene & Audrey Dix, 2301 El Nido Ct., Albuquerque, NM 87104.

Mataji Graham, 2701 Altez NE, Albuquerque, NM 87112; (505) 296-2873.

Las Cruces Walkers, c/o Pete Culbertson, 2025 Jordan, Las Cruces, NM 88001.

New Mexico Racewalkers, c/o Judy Clymer, P.O. Box 6301, Albuquerque, NM 87197.

NEW YORK
Helene Britton, 677 West End Avenue, #3D, New York, NY 10025; (212) 866-5647.

Marv Eisenstein, P.O. Box 23378, Rochester, NY 14692; (716) 334-2533. (Niagara Assn. USATF RW Chair)

Richard Goldman, 36 West 20th Street, Third Floor, New York, NY 10011; (212) 675-3021.

Bill Gorman, 1371 Kings Road, Schenectady, NY 12303.

Elaine Humphrey, 7048 Suzanne Lane, Schenectady, NY 12303; (518) 355-5138. (Adirondack Assn. USATF RW Chair)

John Izzo, 23 Beverly Drive, Brockport, NY 14420. (RW Coach)

Howard Jacobson, 510 East 86th Street, Suite 1-C, New York, NY 10028; (212) 424-9255. (Walkers Club of America, RW Coach)

Dave Lawrence, 94 Harding, Kenmore, NY 14217; (716) 875-6361. (RW Coach)

Bruce MacDonald, 39 Fairview Avenue, Port Washington, NY 11050; (516) 944-8905. (IAAF Judge Emeritus and RW Coach)

Natural Living Track Club, c/o Gary Null, 200 West 86th Street, #17A, New York, NY 10024.

Niagara Walkers, c/o Susan Brown, 101 Delaware Street, Tonawanda NY 14150.

Park Racewalkers USA, c/o Stella Cashman, 320 East 83rd Street, #2C, New York, NY 10028; (212) 628-1317. (Metropolitan Assn. USATF RW Chair and RW Coach)

Rob Picotte, 15 Knowles Terrace, Albany, NY 12203; (518) 459-0019.

Dave Talcott, RD 3, Box 152A, Oswego, NY 13827.

Walk USA, c/o Gary Westerfield, 350 Old Willets Path, Smithtown, NY 11787; (516) 979-9603. (IAAF Judge and RW Coach)

NORTH CAROLINA

Curt Clausen, 3004 Harriman Road, Durham, NC 27705; (919) 489-3419. (North Carolina Assn. USATF RW Chair and 1995–1996 National RW Team)

Mitch Craib, 64B Quail Hollow Road, Greensboro, NC 27410; (910) 292-6996. (Racewalking Sports Scientist)

Alvia Gaskill, Box 12527, Research Triangle P., NC 27709; (919) 544-1669. (Walking's Gadfly)

NORTH DAKOTA

Major Shirley J. Olgeirson, 142 Boise Avenue, Bismark, ND 58501; (701) 224-5189. (North and South Dakota Assn. USATF RW Chair)

OHIO

Edith Barrett, 3801 Shannon Road, Cleveland Heights, OH 44118.

Stanley Gorecki, 4409 West 140th Street, Cleveland, OH 44135; (216) 476-3968. (Lake Erie Assn. USATF RW Chair)

Ron Laird, 4706 Diane Drive, Ashtabula, OH 44004. (Longtime Athlete and RW Promoter)

Jim Janos, 4202 Archwood Avenue, Cleveland, OH 44104.

Tatiana Mejer, 151 East 233rd Street, Euclid, OH 44123; (216) 261-9263.

Miami Valley TC, c/o Vince Peters, 607 Omar Circle, Yellow Springs, OH 45387; (513) 767-7424. (Ohio Assn. USATF RW Chair)

Ohio Racewalker, c/o Jack Mortland, 3184 Summit Street, Columbus, OH 43202. (U.S. Racewalking's Bible)

Jim Snow, 4916 Hickory Woods Trail, Dayton, OH 45432; (513) 252-5590.

Catherine Sullivan, 10190 Pleasant Lake, #G-20, Parma, OH 44130; (216) 888-4868.

John White, 4865 Arthur Place, Columbus, OH 43220; (614) 459-2547.

OKLAHOMA

Loretta Hinkle, 5312 North Vermont, Oklahoma City, OK 73112; (405) 942-6733.

Tulsa Walkers, c/o Mike Hairston, 6706 South Quincy Avenue, Tulsa, OK 74136; (918) 492-5377. (Oklahoma Assn. USATF RW Chair)

OREGON
John Hanan, 74 Wheatherstone Court, Lake Oswego, OR 97035; (503) 697-2787.

Judy Heller, 3439 NE Sandy Boulevard, Suite 136, Portland, OR 97232; (503) 699-4266.

Oregon TC Masters, Box 10085, Eugene, OR 97440.

Racewalkers Northwest, c/o Doug Vermeer. (No Address Available)

Salem TC and Oregon Walking News, c/o Jim Bean, 4658 Fuhrer Street, Salem, OR 97385; (503) 393-1972. (Oregon Assn. USATF RW Chair)

PENNSYLVANIA
Leonard Jansen, 217 Maple Avenue, Hershey, PA 17033; (717) 533-2063. (Walking Biomechanics and RW Coach)

William Norton, RD 1, Box 360A, Freemansville Road, Reading, PA 19607.

Dr. Howard Palamarchuk, 800 Trenton Road, #95, Langhome, PA 19047. (Walking Sports Medicine)

H. William Phelps Jr., 73 Elmore Road, Pittsburgh, PA 15221; (412) 243-5504. (Three Rivers Assn. USATF RW Chair)

Phast Philadelphia Area Striders, c/o Thomas Zdrojewski; (302) 998-0720. (No Address Available)

Prevention Walking Club, c/o Maggie Spilner, Prevention Magazine, 33 East Minos, Emmaus, PA 18098; (215) 967-5171.

Dave Yukelson, Ph.D., 228 Bouke Building, Penn State University, University Park, PA 16802; (814) 865-0407. (USATF RW Sports Psychologist)

RHODE ISLAND
(Falls under New England USATF Assn.—See Massachusetts)

Joseph W. Light, 34 George Street, Westerly, RI 02891; (401) 596-3173.

SOUTH CAROLINA
John Snaden, 926 Sherwood Drive, Florence, SC 29501; (803) 665-4396. (South Carolina Assn. USATF RW Chair)

Ian Whatley, 240 Donington Drive, Greenville, SC 29615; (803) 268-5222. (RW Sports Scientist and 1995–1996 National RW Team)

SOUTH DAKOTA
(Falls under Dakotas USATF Assn.—See North Dakota)

Glen Peterson, 1906 South Hawthorn, Sioux Falls, SD 57105; (605) 336-3190.

Dr. C. S. Roberts, 1345 First Street, Brookings, SD 57006.

TENNESSEE
Bobby Baker, 318 Twin Hill Drive, Kingsport, TN 37660; (615) 349-6406 or (615) 229-4364 (W). (Tennessee Assn. USATF RW Chair)

Randall Brady, 2709 Linmar Avenue, Nashville, TN 37215; (615) 383-6733.

TEXAS
Tony Del Campo, 3707 North Stanton, El Paso, TX 79902.

Gary Chumbley, 15151 Diana Lane, Houston, TX 77062; (713) 488-8847.

Cheryl Cook, HC 63, Box 187, Big Spring, TX 79720; (915) 398-5254. (West Texas Assn. USATF RW Chair)

Richard Charles, 500 East Riverside Drive, #227, Austin, TX 78704; (512) 448-0118. (South Texas Assn. USATF RW Chair)

Dave Gwyn, 6502 South Briar Bayou, Houston, TX 77072; (713) 498-0027. (Gulf Assn. USATF RW Chair)

Howard Jones, 2110 Pebble Beach, League City, TX 77573; (713) 334-3367. (Youth Coach, Youth Camps)

Permian Basin Roadrunners, c/o Jim Bozell, P.O. Box 10483, Midland, TX 79702; (915) 682-9145.

River City Walkers, 2705 McCullough, Austin, TX 78703.

Southwestern Racewalkers, c/o Tracy Jo Wilson, 5950 Lindenshire, Dallas TX 75367-1372; (214) 661-WALK. (Southwestern Assn. USATF RW Chair)

Street Walkers of El Paso, c/o Ken Uecker, 10611 Havenrock Drive, El Paso, TX 79935-1514; (915) 598-8612. (Border Assn. USATF RW Chair)

Alex Woelper, 621 Cresta Alta, El Paso, TX 79912; (915) 584-8214.

UTAH
Floyd Ormsby, 4032 South 2700 East, Salt Lake City, UT 84121; (801) 277-9042. (Utah Assn. USATF RW Chair)

Paul Wick, 1490 Evergreen Lane, Salt Lake City, UT 84106; (801) 484-5134.

VERMONT
(Falls under New England USATF—See Massachusetts)

Don Collins, P.O. Box 303, Fairfax, VT 05454; (802) 849-2283.

VIRGINIA
Paul Cajka 5940 Blackpoole Lane, Virginia Beach, VA 23462-1433. (Virginia Assn. USATF RW Chair)

James Holdren, 1514 Westshire Lane, Richmond, VA 23233; (804) 740-1193.

Potomac Valley Walkers, c/o Sal Corrallo, 3515 Slate Mills Road, Sperryville, VA 22740; (540) 547-4355. (Potomac Valley Assn. USATF RW Chair)

Bob Ryan, 6055 Hollow Hill Lane, Springfield, VA 22152; (703) 569-3063. (RW Coach)

Jean Wood, 5302 Easton Drive, Springfield, VA 22151; (703) 941-4317.

WASHINGTON

Cindy Algeo, East 1208 42nd Avenue, Spokane, WA 99203; (509) 747-2486. (Inland Northwest Assn. USATF RW Chair)

Sharon Bowers, 23515 92nd Avenue West, Edmonds, WA 98020-5604; (206) 546-2296.

Stan Chraminski, 8036 Sunnyside North, Seattle, WA 98103; (206) 527-9393.

Comet Track Club, c/o Don Fountain, SE 125 South Street, Pullman, WA 99163; (509) 332-1435.

Darlene Hickman, 1960 Ninth Avenue West, Seattle, WA 98119; (206) 284-1028. (IAAF Judge)

Pacific Pacers, c/o Bev LaVeck, 6633 NE Windemere Road, Seattle, WA 98115; (206) 524-4721. (USATF Masters RW Record Keeper and Pacific Northwest Assn. USATF RW Chair)

Gwen and Lawrie Robertson, 255 Mount Quay Drive NW, Issoquah, WA 98027; (206) 392-1500.

Bill Roe, P.O. Box 2277, Bellingham, WA 98227; (206) 734-8892. (USATF Official)

Martin Rudow, 4831 NE 44th, Seattle, WA 98105; (206) 524-6081. (IAAF Judge and RW Coach)

Blake Surina, Exercise Science Center, 1101 Regents Boulevard, Tacoma, WA 98406; (206) 564-6050.

WEST VIRGINIA

West Virginia Racewalkers EW, c/o Nicholas and Natalie Winowich, 2003 Huber Road, Charleston, WV 25314; (304) 342-0996. (West Virginia Assn. USATF RW Co-Chairs)

WISCONSIN

Tom Colby, 6618 Piping Rock Road, Madison, WI 53711-3153; (608) 273-0989. (Wisconsin Assn. USATF RW Chair)

Mike Dewitt, 4230 27th Street, Kenosha, WI 53142; (414) 551-0142. (RW Coach at University of Wisconsin–Parkside)

Michael Doherty, 217 St. Paul, Suite B, Stevens Point, WI 54481; (715) 345-0471.

Larry K. Larson, 909 Ostergard Avenue, Racine, WI 53406; (414) 633-1943. (IAAF Judge)

Don and Debbi Lawrence, 1808 17th Avenue, Kenosha, WI 53140; (414) 551-9442.

WYOMING
(Wyoming Assn. USATF RW Chair—Vacant; contact Foot of the Rockies, 1740 Dell Range Boulevard, Cheyenne, WY 82009.)

Tina Braet-Thomas, P.O. Box 2294, Cody, WY 82414. (Sports Dietitian)

APPENDIX 9

Fat Percentage in Common Foods

The average American diet is loaded with almost 40 percent in fat calories. This is far too much fat consumption if a person desires to lead a healthy lifestyle. Fat overconsumption rates just below cigarette smoking as a primary risk factor to human health.

Use the following table as a guide to help you achieve a reasonable fat level in your diet. As you read the table, those foods with a rating of 14 percent and under pose no dietary risk; 15 to 29 percent = low risk; 30 to 49 percent = high risk; 50 to 100 percent = very high risk. A very strict diet, such as the one developed by the late Nathan Pritikin, calls for 10 percent fat in the diet. This level, however, is difficult to conform to for most people except strict vegetarians. A more reasonable and more easily reachable healthy goal would be an average of 20 percent, but never exceeding 30 percent.

Raw fruits, vegetables and natural grains are very nutritious and extremely low in fat calories. Essentially, the more natural the food eaten the better. It is the highly processed foods with the most additives that cause problems with excess fat content in addition to all those fatty meats.

When shopping, pay attention to the Food and Drug Administration's required nutrition labels on processed food packages under it's 1994 Food Labeling Law. The law's definitions follow:

FREE—Product contains an inconsequential amount.
CALORIE FREE—Fewer than 5 calories per serving.
SUGAR OR FAT FREE—Less than 0.5 grams per serving.
SODIUM FREE OR SALT FREE—Less than 5 mg. of sodium per serving.
CHOLESTEROL FREE—Less than 2 mg. per serving and 2 grams or less of saturated fat per serving.
LOW—Foods that can be eaten frequently without exceeding dietary guidelines.
LOW FAT—3 grams or less per serving.
LOW IN SATURATED FAT—1 gram or less of saturated fat per serving and no more than 15 percent of total calories.
LOW SODIUM—Less than 140 mg. per serving.

VERY LOW SODIUM—35 mg. of sodium or less per serving.

LOW CALORIE—10 calories or less per serving.

LOW IN CHOLESTEROL—20 mg. or less per serving and 2 grams or less of saturated fat per serving.

REDUCED—Contains 25 percent less than regular product. ("LIGHT" or "LITE" means reduced by at least 33 percent and by more than 40 calories.)

REDUCED SODIUM—Less than half of that found in the regular product plus reduced more than 14 mg. of sodium per serving.

REDUCED FAT—No more than 50 percent of the fat in the regular product; must be a reduction of greater than 3 grams per serving to be consequential.

REDUCED SATURATED FAT—A reduction of at least 50 percent from the regular product, and a reduction of more than 1 gram of saturated fat per serving.

REDUCED CHOLESTEROL—Reduced at least 50 percent from the regular product and reduced more than 20 mg. of cholesterol per serving.

The following table gives you a good idea of the relative fat contents of the various foods we eat.

FOOD NAME	PERCENTAGE OF FAT CALORIES
ALMONDS	76
APPLE	3
APRICOT	3
ARTICHOKE	3
ASPARAGUS	6
AVOCADO	81
BACON	74
BAGEL	1
BANANA	2
BEANS—Lima	5
Red Kidney	5
BEAN SPROUTS	4
BEEF—Ground	66
Chuck Roast, Braised	69
Sirloin, Lean Broiled	37
T-Bone, Lean Broiled	45
Tenderloin, Lean Broiled	62
BEER	0
BEET	3
BEVERAGE—Soft Drink	0
BISCUIT, Made with Whole Milk	26
BLACKBERRIES	10
BLUEBERRIES	10
BOLOGNA	75

BRAN FLAKES	4
BRAN MUFFIN	35
BRAZIL NUTS	92
BREAD—Wheat	11
White	11
BROCCOLI	9
BROWNIES—With Nuts	55
BRUSSELS SPROUTS	7
BUTTER	99
CABBAGE—Red	2
White	7
CAKE—Angel Food	0
Devil's Food	44
Pound	57
White	57
CANTALOUPE	3
CARROT	3
CASHEW NUTS	69
CAULIFLOWER	5
CELERY	4
CHEESE—American	76
Bleu	72
Brie	76
Cheddar	71
Cottage, Low-Fat 2%	18
Cottage, Regular	76
Cream	92
Monterey Jack	76
Parmesan, Grated	76
Swiss	67
CHERRIES	3
CHICKEN—Dark Meat, No Skin	46
Dark Meat with Skin	50
Light Meat, No Skin	18
Light Meat with Skin	42
CHICKEN AND NOODLES	44
CHOCOLATE—CANDY	55
With Nuts	59
CLAMS	15
COCONUT	86
CODFISH	30
COOKIES—Chocolate Chip	60
Lemon Bar	41
Oatmeal with Raisins	68
Peanut Butter	44
Sugar	50

CORN	9
CORN CHIPS	58
CORN MUFFIN	28
CORNED BEEF	63
CRACKERS—Graham	20
Saltine	26
CRANBERRIES	13
CREAM—Half and Half	90
Whipping	100
Whipping (Aerosol)	90
CREAMER—Nondairy	90
CROISSANT	45
CUCUMBER	5
DATES	1
DOUGHNUTS—Plain	43
DUCK—Roasted, No Skin	47
Roasted with Skin	75
EGG—Boiled	64
Fried with Butter	69
Poached	62
EGGPLANT	8
ENGLISH MUFFIN—Plain	1
FISH STICKS—Breaded	46
FLOUR—White	3
FRANKFURTER	81
FRENCH TOAST	51
GELATIN DESSERT	0
GRAPEFRUIT	2
GRAPEFRUIT JUICE	2
GRAPE JUICE	0
GRAPES	4
HALIBUT	18
HAM	74
HAMBURGER	39
HAZEL NUTS	90
HONEY	0
HONEYDEW MELON	7
ICE CREAM—Regular, 10% Fat	48
Rich, 16% Fat	62
ICE MILK	26
LAMB—Chops	74
Leg, Roasted	36
LEMON	6
LEMONADE	5
LENTILS	0
LETTUCE	10

LIVER	43
LOBSTER—Without Butter	15
MACADAMIA NUTS—Oil Roasted	97
MACARONI	3
MACARONI AND CHEESE	46
MARGARINE	99
MARSHMALLOW	0
MAYONNAISE—Imitation	79
Real	98
MILK—Chocolate	27
1% Fat	36
2% Fat	57
Whole	48
MILKSHAKE—Vanilla	23
MUSHROOMS	8
NECTARINE	0
OATMEAL—Cooked	16
OIL—All Types	100
OLIVE	92
ONION	2
ORANGE	1
ORANGE JUICE	3
OYSTER	23
PANCAKE	28
PEACH	3
PEANUT	76
PEANUT BUTTER	72
PEAR	6
PEAS	5
PECAN	87
PEPPER—Green	6
Red	8
PICKLE—Dill	11
PIE—Apple	58
Custard	46
Lemon Meringue	56
Pecan	50
Pumpkin	47
PINEAPPLE	3
PINEAPPLE JUICE	2
PISTACHIO NUTS	76
PIZZA—Cheese	36
Pepperoni	48
PLUM	0
POPCORN—Air-Popped	4
Popped with Oil	46

POPOVER	40
PORK CHOPS	74
POTATO—Baked Plain	1
French Fried	46
POTATO CHIPS	62
PRETZELS	8
PRUNES	0
PUDDING—Chocolate	21
PUMPKIN	7
RADISH	4
RAISIN	1
RASPBERRIES	7
RICE—White	1
ROLL—Hard	11
SALAD DRESSING—Bleu Cheese	95
French	80
Italian	91
Thousand Island	91
SALMON	35
SAUSAGE—Pork	77
SCALLOPS—Fried	39
SHERBET—Orange	13
SHRIMP—Breaded and Fried	49
Cooked	10
SOUP—Chicken Noodle	24
Chicken Vegetable	29
Cream of Chicken	54
Cream of Mushroom	62
Split Pea with Ham	19
Tomato	24
Vegetable	25
SOUR CREAM	85
SOY BEANS	22
SPAGHETTI—Plain	4
With Meat Sauce	32
SPINACH	10
SQUASH—Winter	6
STRAWBERRIES	10
SUGAR	0
TANGERINE	4
TARTAR SAUCE	95
TOMATO	6
TOMATO JUICE	3
TORTILLA CHIPS	61
TROUT	21
TUNA—Light, Packed in Water	15

Maximum Oxygen Uptake (VO$_2$ Max) Test on a Track

Estimation of VO$_2$ Max Based on a 1-Mile Walk Test

The best method is to walk on a 400-meter or 440-yard track. A 400-meter track is a little over 7 feet short of 440 yards or a little under 29 feet short for the four laps. It should be noted that experiments have indicated that normal everyday walking is more efficient than the racewalking technique at speeds less than 13 minutes per mile. This means that racewalking requires more oxygen at these slower speeds but is a far better workout at whatever speed because of increased muscle use. It should also be noted that normal walking cannot be done faster than approximately 12 minutes per mile, and that the racewalking technique must be employed at speeds exceeding this to be considered walking by definition.

Time to Walk 1 Mile (min./sec.)	Estimated VO$_2$ Max (ml/kg/min.)
7:00 and faster	75
7:01 – 7:30	71
7:31 – 8:00	67
8:01 – 8:30	62
8:31 – 9:00	58
9:01 – 9:30	55
9:31 – 10:00	52
10:01 – 11:00	49
11:01 – 11:30	46
11:31 – 12:00	44
12:01 – 12:30	41

Time to Walk 1 Mile (min./sec.)	Estimated VO$_2$ Max (ml/kg/min.)
12:31 – 13:00	39
13:01 – 13:30	37
13:31 – 14:00	35
14:01 – 14:30	33
14:31 – 15:00	32
15:01 – 15:30	31
15:31 – 16:00	30
16:01 – 16:30	29
16:31 – 17:00	28
17:01 – 17:30	27
17:31 – 18:00	26

Estimation of VO$_2$ Max Based on a 12-Minute Walking Test

A standard test for fitness for runners has been set up for running 12 minutes on a 400-meter or 440-yard track to measure approximate O$_2$ levels. I have correlated the running speed to walking speed to give the approximations in the following table.

Distance in Miles	Laps on $1/_4$-Mile Track	Estimated VO$_2$ Max (ml/kg/min.)
0.75	3	< 25
0.817	3 1/4	29
0.875	3 1/2	34
0.937	3 3/4	39
1.00	4	41
1.065	4 1/4	44
1.125	4 1/2	46

Distance in Miles	Laps on $1/_4$-Mile Track	Estimated VO$_2$ Max (ml/kg/min.)
1.187	4 3/4	48
1.25	5	50
1.317	5 1/4	52
1.375	5 1/2	54
1.437	5 3/4	57
1.50	6	60
1.565	6 1/4	63
1.625	6 1/2	66
1.687	6 3/4	68
1.75	7	70
1.817	7 1/4	72
1.875	7 1/2	74
1.937	7 3/4	76
2.00	8	78

U.S. Traditional Racewalks

Unbeknownst to practically everyone in the United States, there have been unpublicized traditional racewalks held in various parts of our country for many years. The great running boom of the 1970s and early 1980s have made running a very prominent part of the American scene. Hidden beneath all the hoopla of the fitness craze dominated by aerobics and running has been a dedicated, small group of racewalkers who have kept the sport alive by holding some of their low-attendance events over the years. Whenever an Olympiad was coming up, there was some flurry of activity, but, overall, Americans could not compete on an equal basis with Europeans, Mexicans and other excellent foreign athletes who systematically trained in racewalking. Therefore, the field of U.S. competitive racewalking has maintained a significant yet quiet following with its own active competitors and its own competitions. The names of specific contacts are listed at the end of this appendix.

Current U.S. Traditional Racewalks (Ten Years or More Consecutively)

Coney Island 10-Mile Racewalk. The granddaddy of all U.S. traditional racewalks. Held in early November since 1911 by Walkers Club of America, headquartered in New York City. Oldest traditional walk in the United States. Almost as old as the modern Olympics and the Boston Marathon. (Contact: Jacobson)

Millrose Games Racewalk in New York City. 1- or 2-mile invitational as part of a large invitational indoor track meet in February. Held since the mid-1930s. (Contact: Jacobson)

Taunton, Massachusetts 20K Racewalk (but short course of under 12 miles). Held around mid-July since 1958. (Contact: Vaitones)

***Los Angeles Times* Indoor 1-Mile Race.** Held as part of an invitational indoor track meet. Held on the second weekend in February since 1960. (Contact: Hanley)

Rose Bowl 10-Mile Handicap Racewalk in Pasadena, California. Held on the third weekend in January since 1963. (Contact: Hanley)

National 40K Championships at Brookfield College in Linfield, New Jersey. Held in September since 1963. (Contact: Denman)

Polar Bear 10-Miler at Asbury Park, New Jersey Boardwalk. Held on the last Sunday in December since 1963. (Contact: Denman)

Mt. Sac Relays Racewalk in Los Angeles. Held since 1964, starting out as a 2-miler and changing to 10K in 1968. Held on the third weekend in April as part of a huge track meet. (Contact: Hanley)

Seaside Heights, New Jersey 10-Miler. Held in mid-May since 1964. (Contact: Denman)

Lake Takanassee, New Jersey 5K Racewalks. held on Monday evenings for 12 straight weeks from the second Monday in June through the summer since 1964. (Contact: Denman)

Ron Zinn Memorial 10-Miler in Asbury Park, New Jersey Boardwalk. Held on last Sunday in April since 1966. (Contact: Denman)

Ron Zinn Memorial 10K Racewalk in Kenosha, Wisconsin. Started in Chicago in 1966 and moved to Wisconsin in 1983. Held on the first weekend in June. (Contact: Dewitt)

Lakewood, New Jersey 9-Miler. Held on last Sunday in May since 1967. (Contact: Denman)

Doc Tripp 5K/10K Memorial Racewalk. Held in August at Broomfield, Colorado, since 1972. (Contact: Carlson)

Fall Festival 5-Mile Racewalk at Central Park in New York City. Held in October since 1974. (Contact: Jacobson)

Mother's Day 5K/10K Walk at Central Park in New York City. Held in May since 1975. (Contact: Jacobson)

Father's Day 5K/10K Walk at Central Park in New York City. Held in June since 1977. (Contact: Jacobson)

St. Patrick's Day 20K Racewalk in Long Beach, California. Held on weekend closest to St. Patrick's Day since 1978. (Contact: Coots)

Casmiro Alongi Memorial 20K/10K/5K Racewalk in Dearborn Heights, Michigan. Only traditional international racewalking event in the United States. Held in late September since 1978. (Contact: Genzingler)

Henry Laskau 5K Racewalk in Westbury on Long Island. Held in early October since 1978. (Contact: Jacobson)

Julie Partridge 10K Racewalk at San Francisco State University. Held in late April since 1980. (Contact: Siitonen)

Todd Scully 10K Racewalk at Lake Takanassee, New Jersey. Held on second Sunday in December since 1980. (Contact: Denman)

Contacts

Bob Carlson, 2261 Glencoe Street, Denver, CO 80207.
Jim Coots, 2611 Voorhees, #E, Redondo Beach, CA 90278.
Elliott Denman, 28 North Locust Avenue, West Long Branch, NJ 07764.
Mike Dewitt, 4230 27th Street, Kenosha, WI 53142.
Vance Genzlinger, 5700 Crooks Road, Suite 212, Troy, MI 48098.
Jim Hanley, 3346 South Allegheny Court, Westlake Village, CA 91362.
Howie Jacobson, 510 East 86th Street, Suite 1C, New York, NY 10028.
Harry Siitonen, 106 Sanchez Street, #117, San Francisco, CA 94114.
Steve Vaitones, 90 Summit Street, Waltham, MA 02154.

APPENDIX 12

Starting a Walking Club

There are currently hundreds of running clubs in the United States, but comparatively few walking clubs. For this reason there may not be a walking club in your immediate area. In that case it may be desirable to start one yourself so that you can reap the joys of getting and staying in shape along with others of a like mind.

Starting your own club is a major challenge that takes significant initiative, but it can be done. If it is possible to assemble a group of four or more enthusiastic walkers who want to help establish a club, so much the better. Active clubs make walking more of a social and learning occasion and ultimately a more enjoyable activity for everyone. If you live in an area with few potential walkers in the immediate future because walking hasn't received its deserved publicity, you may be better off trying to add a walking division to the local running club—which would add to their overall membership. This way you can use their already established visibility, newsletter and race equipment to get off the ground. When the sport gets more visible after a year or two, you can split off and set up a viable separate club of your own. Come up with a catchy name for the club that will draw people interested in walking. In my opinion, the term "racewalking" in the club title should be initially downplayed or avoided until the organization is well known in the community. The term is often intimidating to health and fitness walkers who have not yet learned the great benefits to be derived from the technique of racewalking. However, this is not an absolute must since by the latter part of the 1990s the sport will surely become as popular as jogging or any other current aerobic sport.

As in almost all clubs of this type, it is the small core of officers that will help get the club off the ground. Dedicated organizers should divide up the duties according to their interests and abilities. Some things that should be addressed are: membership, promotion, finances, publicity, training and instruction, events (social and athletic) and newsletter and secretarial duties. The club will only succeed if each organizer puts in the necessary energy to get a viable club up and running. When the club has become somewhat successful, more volunteer help will likely become available.

In the case of my own club, Front Range Walkers, in Denver, Colorado, we assembled a list of over 1,000 people who we knew to be interested in either fitness walking or racewalking. A large local corporation, Wood Brothers Homes and their marketing director Joe Louis Barrow Jr., joined forces with the American Lung Association of Colorado in putting on walking clinics and low-key 5K races, as well as a national 5K racewalking championship. Subsequently, over 300 paying members were inducted into our new Front Range Walkers Club in about 23 months. In 1996 the number is currently about 400 dues-paying members.

Finding Members

Enroll members of all ages. My experience has found that young women take to the sport far more readily than young men. However, from age 35 and up, both sexes seem to join equally. In some parts of the United States there will be few competitive athletes who want to race, and the bulk of the club will be built around fitness walkers who are in it purely for the enjoyment. Look for runners who have become hurt in their injury-prone sport and who don't want to lose their conditioning. You'll need some members who are willing to teach the efficient technique of racewalking and extol its benefits in a logical manner to others. Remember that walking is potentially the best family-oriented sport there is. The 80-year-old great-grandfather can have a ball walking with his 6-year-old great grandchild; that is, of course, if the elder of the two has embraced an active physical life.

Publicity

Out of all the various tasks of starting a club previously mentioned, the publicity officer is probably the biggest key to a club's success. It is essential that word of a new walking club is heard by people everywhere in order to gain new members. This can be accomplished various ways. Put out flyers in athletic clubs, schools, recreation centers and YMCAs as well as parks, libraries and athletic shoe stores. Many referrals to our club come from doctors' and chiropractors' offices. In our area, some offices have one of our newsletters in the waiting rooms along with their magazines. Print schedules of upcoming events and put them in the local newspapers. Make a concentrated effort to get your events listed with the running events in the local newspaper and athletic publication (if one is published locally) and place low-cost classified ads if it becomes feasible. Talk race directors and/or sponsors into putting walking divisions in their races to add to the field of participants. Set up free periodic workouts and instructional clinics at scheduled times and locations and get the word out. Free instructional clinics will usually draw interested folks to the event if they know about them. Have them in a central location or in different parts of town to make them convenient for as many as possible. High school and university tracks and parks make good meeting locations. Print cards with pertinent information on them and hand them out to people on the sidewalk. If you see someone out walking briskly, give them a card and tell them of the fine new organization you are forming.

Provide a real public service by offering to take as members cardiac rehabilitation patients and recovering alcoholics from the local AA. The Front Range Walkers instituted a blind program in which we lead the unsighted on our fitness walks with volunteer guides. Try to gain the reputation of being an organization that is trying to improve the health and well-being of its members at a low cost. Remind them that the door to their health club is their own front door leading to the great outdoors, and that their only real expense is for a decent pair of walking shoes.

Financing

You will need some operating funds to get started and to remain afloat. Charge a reasonable amount for yearly membership dues such as $10 per year per individual and $15 per family. Try to play up the family aspect of the activity. The dues money, however, may not pay for all the mailings and newsletters and incidental expenses. Ideally, a sponsor should be found—many times new members that enroll have excellent contacts with businesses. Our club is a nonprofit educational organization because we hold free educational meetings on walking-related subjects each month. Our excess funds are channeled into a scholarship that can be used to help young athletes get into the sport of racewalking. Because of our nonprofit status, a large corporation agreed to print our monthly newsletter free of charge. Our monthly expenses are thus cut by about $200 per month. We make modest profits from various events we conduct during the year and sell our club T-shirts, fanny packs, duffle bags and hats with the club logo embroidered on them for $1 more than they cost us.

Charge race directors a fee for including a copy of their upcoming race blanks in your newsletter. Put a business's name on your T-shirt if they will donate the cost of them. Have a contest to find the best club logo to put on the shirts and newsletter. Some clubs assemble donated items and have raffles and yard sales. Charge an entry fee of about twice the cost of the individual awards and other expenses for competitive events and pump the profits into the club treasury. Set up a free fitness walking series open to the general public to get them acquainted with your club. Sometimes members come up with some very imaginative ideas, so take advantage of them.

Exchange newsletters with other clubs throughout the country or even within your own metro area. You will get a lot of helpful hints and ideas from doing this and thus make your club more interesting to the members. Work for steady attendance at workouts, meetings and fitness walks. Have a calling committee that can set up a phone tree to contact members—that way each person may only have to call 10 members or so. You will find that older persons and single persons will have more time to attend regularly due to fewer family and business commitments.

Lending Encouragement

Always encourage new members no matter how out of shape or nonathletic they may seem in the beginning. We have seen remarkable improvements in just a few months by people who have been motivated enough to stick to a steady program. Stress personal fitness and tell everyone at workouts how to measure their progress as time goes by (e.g., pulse rate, body fat, etc.).

As for competition, it is often best to have a handicap series in which contestants race against their own ability and speed standards. The slower contestants are given the appropriate head start based on previous times. The winner will be the one who does the best against his or her own handicap, or you can have a "predict" event in which the one coming closest to their predicted time is the winner. Another idea is to use the age-graded table in appendix 4 and base the awards upon age-graded performance. Perhaps your club could recruit a computer expert who would be willing to set up a database on the members so you can keep track of their progress. If your club reaches a membership of 50 or more, it is very helpful to keep track of everyone's progress on a computer database in any event.

Company Programs

Many companies all across the country are now organizing company clubs that walk during the lunch hour and after work. Many of them form company teams to walk in events such as those put on by the MS Society, March of Dimes, United Negro College Fund, etc. Some companies will absorb the cost and make it entirely free for employees because they realize that such an activity is a benefit for both the employees and the company. Many large companies already have established a running club, and walkers have persuaded them to start a walking division so they can share in an established group.

Planning Social Events

Walkers, in my experience, seem to have a camaraderie more pronounced than in almost any other activity. Perhaps this is because it is less competitive and stressful than running and other sports, and everybody seems to want others to improve just as they have. It is truly a family-oriented activity. Capitalize on this aspect by having noncompetitive social events from time to time, such as potlucks and picnics, so that the fast walkers have a chance to get better acquainted with the slower ones. At our fitness walks, we always have an out and back course and set a time to turn around and go back to the starting point—normally 45 minutes to an hour. This allows walkers of certain speeds to walk and converse together, and everyone gets back about the same time for a free refreshment party at the end. The fast fitness walkers or racewalkers might cover twice the distance of the very slow ones, but everyone enjoys the sociability of one another at the end. Stress the good fellowship and leave the highly competitive efforts to the dedicated athletes in the club. Use the athletes as role models to show that most people can get in really good shape if they persist in their efforts to improve.

Don't be afraid to spend a lot of time and energy to get a club going. As time goes by and your membership grows, more and more members will recommend the club to their friends and a "snowballing effect" will occur. A successful club is the source of a great amount of satisfaction, and you will be doing yourself and others a great service in promoting health awareness in your community.

Bibliography of Walking Books, Videos and Other Publications

RW = Useful information on racewalking.

Primary Resources on Walking

Alongi, Frank. *Introduction to Racewalking*. Order directly from author: 26530 Woodshire, Dearborn, MI 48127. $5 pb, RW.

Balboa, Deena, and David Balboa. *Walk for Life*. New York: Perigree Books, 1990. $9.95 pb, RW.

Bowman, Bob. *U.S. Racewalking Handbook*. To order, write c/o USA Track & Field, Box 120, Indianapolis, IN 46206. Published yearly, $12 (includes postage & handling) pb, RW.

Bob Carlson. *Front Range Walkers News*. Subscribe directly from author: 2261 Glencoe Street, Denver, CO 80207. Published monthly, $10/year, RW.

____. *Walking for Heath, Fitness and Sport*. Golden, Colo.: Fulcrum Publishing, 1996. $15.95 pb, RW.

Carlson, Bob, and O. J. Seiden, M.D. *HealthWalk*. Golden, Colo.: Fulcrum, Inc., 1988. $12.95 pb, RW.

Dix, Gene. *Racewalking and Fitness Walking Manual*. 1985. Order directly from author: 2301 El Nido Court NW, Albuquerque, NM 87104. $7 pb, RW.

____. *Youth Racewalking Manual*. 1989. Order directly from author: 2301 El Nido Court NW, Albuquerque, NM 87104. $7 pb, RW.

Gray, John. *Racewalking for Fun and Fitness*. New Jersey: Prentice-Hall, 1985. $16.95 hb, $7.95 pb, RW.

Hopkins, Julian. *Racewalking*. Order directly from author: Wimsey House, Box 33182, Granada Hills, CA 91344. $6.95 pb, RW.

Ikonian, Therese. *Fitness Walking*. Champaign, Ill.: Human Kinetics, 1995. P.O. Box 5076, Champaign, IL 61825-5076. $14.95 pb.

Jacobson, Howard. *Racewalk to Fitness*. New York: Simon & Schuster, 1980. Also may order directly from author: 510 East 86th Street, New York, NY 10028. $9.95 pb, RW.

Kashiwa, Anne, and James Rippe, M.D. *Fitness Walking for Women*. New York: Perigree Books, 1987. $8.95 pb.

Kiesling, Stephen, and E. C. Frederick, Ph.D. *Walk On: A Tool Kit for Building Your Own Walking Fitness Program*. Emmaus, Pa.: Rodale Press, 1986. $7.95 pb.

Kuntzleman, Charles T. *The Complete Book of Walking*. New York: Simon & Schuster, 1978. $10 hb, $3.50 pb.

Laird, Ron. *The Art of Fast Walking*. Self-published. 1986. Order directly from author: 4706 Diane Drive, Ashtabula, OH 44004. $27.50 pb, RW.

Meyers, Casey. *Aerobic Walking*. New York: Vintage, 1987. $7.95 pb, RW.

———. *Walking: The Complete Guide to the Complete Exercise*. New York: Random House, 1992. $12 pb, RW.

Ohio Racewalker. Jack Mortland, ed. Monthly newsletter with worldwide racewalking news and articles. Subscribe directly from editor: 3184 Summit Street, Columbus, OH 43202. $10/year, RW.

Racewalking Judging Handbook, c/o USA Track & Field, Box 120, Indianapolis, IN 46206. $4 pb, RW.

Rudow, Martin. *Advanced Racewalking, Fourth Ed*. Seattle, Wash.: Technique Productions, 1994. 4831 NE 44th, Seattle, WA 98105. $11.50 (plus $1.50 postage & handling) pb, RW.

———. *Maximum Walking*. Seattle, Wash.: Technique Productions, 1995. 4831 NE 44th, Seattle, WA 98105. $11.50 (plus $1.50 postage & handling) pb, RW.

Strangman, Denis. *An Annotated Bibliography of Racewalking and Related Subjects with Particular Reference to the Young Athlete*. Order directly from author: Australian Sports Commission, 10 Corrodus Street, Fraser, A.C.T. Australia (Write for current price) pb, RW.

Stride Magazine. New magazine in 1996 covering lower extremity health by editors of *BioMechanics*; a good source of information on foot care. 4604 Chicago Avenue South, Minneapolis, MN 55407-3513. Published quarterly, $12.95/6 issues.

Sweetgall, Rob, and Robert Neeves, Ph.D. *Walking for Little Children*. Clayton, Mo.: Creative Walking, 1986. Box 50926, Clayton, MO 63105. $5 pb.

———. *Walking Wellness Student Workbook*. Clayton, Mo.: Creative Walking, 1986. Box 50926, Clayton, MO 63105. $5 pb.

———. *Walking Wellness Teacher's Guide*. Clayton, Mo.: Creative Walking, 1986. Box 50926, Clayton, MO 63105. $13 pb.

Waddell, Peter. *Racewalking in Australia: An 80-Year History*. 1991. Order directly from author: P.O. Box E175, Canberra 2600, Australia. (Write for current price) pb, RW.

Walking Magazine. National magazine with articles of interest to all walkers. P.O. Box 56561, Boulder, CO 80322-6561. $14.95/yr, RW.

Wallace, Gordon. *Racewalking in America: Past and Present*. Doctoral diss. Handled through North American Racewalking Foundation, P.O. Box 50312, Pasadena, CA 91115. (Write for current price; may be $25), RW

———. *The Valiant Heart: From Cardiac Cripple to World Champion*. Pasadena,

Calif.: North American Racewalking Foundation. 1982. P.O. Box 50312, Pasadena, CA 91115. $14.70 (Including postage & handling) hb, RW.

Ward, Elaine B. *Introduction to the Technique of Racewalking.* Pasadena, Calif.: North American Racewalking Foundation, 1990. P.O. Box 50312, Pasadena, CA 91115. $7 pb, RW.

____. *Masters Racewalking.* Pasadena, Calif.: North American Racewalking Foundation, 1995. P.O. Box 50312, Pasadena, CA 91115. $14.95 (plus $2 postage & handling) pb, RW.

____. *Mobility Exercises for Racewalking.* Pasadena, Calif.: North American Racewalking Foundation, 1995. P.O. Box 50312, Pasadena, CA 91115. $7 pb, RW.

____. *Southern California Racewalking News.* Subscribe directly from author: 1000 San Pasqual, #35, Pasadena, CA 91106. Published monthly, $8/year, RW.

____. *Walking Wisdom for Women.* Pasadena, Calif.: North American Racewalking Foundation, 1995. P.O. Box 50312, Pasadena, CA 91115. $12.95 (plus $2 postage & handling) pb, RW.

Videotapes

The Basic Technique of Racewalking. North American Racewalking Foundation, c/o Elaine Ward, P.O. Box 50312, Pasadena, CA 91115-0312. VHS 32:39 min., 1993, RW.

The Health Walking Technique. East Action, c/o Henry Laskau, P.O. Box 783, Cooper Station, New York 10278. VHS 27 min., 1987, RW.

Ian and Dave's Low Budget Video. Ian Whatley and Dave McGovern, 240 Donington Drive, Greenville, SC 29615. VHS 30 min., $20.95 (including postage & handling), 1994, RW.

Keys to Weight Training for Men and Women. KTWT, P.O. Box 767, Palmer Lake, CO 80133; 1-800-333-1307. VHS 80 min., $29.95.

Maximum Walking. Technique Productions, c/o Martin Rudow, 4831 NE 44th, Seattle, WA 98105. VHS 28 min., 1995, RW.

Racewalking: A Lifetime Sport. Viisha Sedlak, P.O. Box 18323, Boulder, CO 80308. VHS 18 min., $29.95, 1991, RW.

Racewalking Technique. Technique Productions, c/o Martin Rudow, 4831 NE 44th, Seattle, WA 98105. VHS 19 min., 1988, RW.

Stretching: The Video. (Companion to book by Bob Anderson.) Spanish version available. P.O. Box 767, Palmer Lake, CO 80133; 1-800-333-1307. VHS 57 min., $29.95.

USA Track & Field, TAC USA's Guide to Racewalk Officiating. One Hoosier Dome, Suite 140, Indianapolis, IN 46225. VHS 16 min., 1990, RW.

Walk America. Creative Walking, Inc., c/o Rob Sweetgall, P.O. Box 50296, Clayton, MO 63105. VHS 22 min., 1986.

Walking Off Weight. Creative Walking, Inc., c/o Rob Sweetgall, P.O. Box 50296, Clayton, MO 63105. VHS 22 min., 1990.

Walking Workout. Good Times Home Video Corp., 402 Fifth Avenue, New York, NY 10016. VHS 30 min., 1988, RW.

YMCA *Healthy Back Video*. Human Kinetics, P.O. Box 5076, Champaign, IL 61825-5076. VHS 30 min., 1994.

Other Suggested Reading

Alter, Michael J., M.S. *Sport Stretch*. Champaign, Ill.: Human Kinetics, 1990. P.O. Box 5076, Champaign, IL 61825-5076. $15.95 pb.

American College of Sports Medicine. *ASCM Fitness Book*. Champaign, Ill.: Human Kinetics, 1992. P.O. Box 5076, Champaign, IL 61825-5076. $11.95 pb.

Anderson, Bob. *Stretching*. Bolinas, Calif.: Shelter Publications, Inc., 1980. Order directly P.O. Box 767, Palmer Lake, CO 80133; 1-800-333-1307. $12.00 pb, spiral bound.

Bland, Jeffrey Ph.D. *Nutraerobics*. San Francisco, Calif.: Harper & Row, 1983. $16.95 hb.

Castleman, Michael. *Healing Herbs*. Rodale Press, 33 East Minor Street, Emmaus, PA 18098.

Clark, Nancy, M.S., R.D. *Nancy Clark's Sport Nutrition Guide Book*. Champaign, Ill.: Human Kinetics, 1990. P.O. Box 5076, Champaign, IL 61825-5076. $14.95 pb.

Dishman, Rod K., Ph.D. *Advances in Exercise Adherence*. Champaign, Ill.: Human Kinetics, 1994. P.O. Box 5076, Champaign, IL 61825-5076. $39.00 hb.

Feltman, John. *Hands-On Healing*. Emmaus, Pa.: Rodale Press, 1989. 33 East Minor Street, Emmaus, PA 18098. $29.95 hb.

Gavin, James, Ph.D. *The Exercise Habit*. Champaign, Ill.: Human Kinetics, 1992. P.O. Box 5076, Champaign, IL 61825-5076. $14.95 pb.

Hanna, Thomas. *Somatics*. Menlo Park Calif.: Addison-Wesley, 1988. $10.95 pb.

Inglis, Brian, Ph.D., and Ruth West, M.A. *The Alternative Health Guide*. New York: Alfred Knopf, 1983. $19.95 hb.

King, Robert K. *Performance Massage*. Champaign, Ill.: Human Kinetics, 1993. P.O. Box 5076, Champaign, IL 61825-5076. $15.95 pb.

Kronhausen, Eberhard, Ed.D., and Phyllis Kronhausen, Ed.D., with Harry B. Demopoulos., M.D. *Formula for Life*. New York: William Morrow & Co., 1989. $20.95 hb.

Livingston, Michael K., J.D. *Mental Discipline: The Pursuit of Peak Performance*. Champaign, Ill.: Human Kinetics, 1989. P.O. Box 5076, Champaign, IL 61825-5076. $22.00 pb.

Mackinnon, Laura Traeger, Ph.D. *Exercise and Immunology*. Champaign, Ill.: Human Kinetics, 1992. P.O. Box 5076, Champaign, IL 61825-5076. $18.00 pb.

MacPherson, Barry, Ph.D. *Sport and Aging*. Champaign, Ill.: Human Kinetics, 1986. P.O. Box 5076, Champaign, IL 61825-5076. $36.00 pb.

Martens, Rainer, Ph.D., Yealey, Robin S., Ph.D., and Damon Burton, Ph.D. *Competitive Anxiety in Sport*. Champaign, Ill.: Human Kinetics, 1990. P.O. Box 5076, Champaign, IL 61825-5076. $24.00 pb.

Niedeffer, Robert M., Ph.D. *Psyched to Win*. Campaign, Ill.: Human Kinetics, 1992. P.O. Box 5076, Champaign, IL 61825-5076. $14.95 pb.

Noble, Bruce J., Ph.D., and Robert J. Robertson, Ph.D. *Perceived Exertion*. Champaign, Ill.: Human Kinetics, 1996. P.O. Box 5076, Champaign, IL 61825-5076. $34.00 hb.

Orlick, Terry, Ph.D. *In Pursuit of Excellence, Second Ed*. Champaign, Ill.: Human Kinetics, 1990. P.O. Box 5076, Champaign, IL 61825-5076. $14.95 pb.

Padus, Emrika. *Your Emotions and Your Health*. Emmaus, Pa.: Rodale Press, 1986. 33 East Minor Street, Emmaus, PA 18098. Hb.

Piscatella, Joseph. *Controlling Your Fat Tooth*. New York: Workman, 1991. 708 Broadway, New York, NY 10003. $22.95 hb.

Roberts, Glyn C., Ph.D. *Motivation in Sport and Exercise*. Champaign, Ill.: Human Kinetics, 1992. P.O. Box 5076, Champaign, IL 61825-5076. $24.00 pb.

Santillo, Humbart, M.H., N.D. *Food Enzymes: The Missing Link to Radiant Health, Second Ed*. Prescott, Ariz.: Hohm Press, 1993. Box 2501, Prescott, AZ 86302. $5.95 pb.

Sharkey, Brian, Ph.D. *New Dimensions in Aerobic Fitness*. Champaign, Ill.: Human Kinetics, 1991. P.O. Box 5076, Champaign, IL 61825-5076. $18.00 pb.

Shepherd, Roy J., M.D., Ph.D., D.P.E. *Aerobic Fitness and Health*. Champaign, Ill.: Human Kinetics, 1994. P.O. Box 5076, Champaign, IL 61825-5076. $48.00 hb.

Shepherd, Roy J., M.D., Ph.D., D.P.E., and Per-Olof Astrand, M.D., Ph.D., eds. *Endurance in Sport*. Champaign Ill.: Human Kinetics, 1992. P.O. Box 5076, Champaign, IL 61825-5076. $54.00 hb.

Sleamaker, Rob, M.S. *Serious Training for Serious Athletes*. Champaign, Ill.: Human Kinetics, 1989. P.O. Box 5076, Champaign, IL 61825-5076. $15.95 pb.

Sommer, Bobbe, Ph.D., with Mark Falstein. *Psycho-Cybernetics 2000*. Englewood Cliffs, N.J.: Prentice Hall, 1993. $19.95 hb.

Spirduso, Waneen W., Ph.D., and Helen M. Eckert, Ph.D., eds. Physical Activity and Aging. Champaign, Ill.: Human Kinetics, 1989. P.O. Box 5076, Champaign, IL 61825-5076. $22.00 pb.

Tribole, Evelyn, M.S., R.D. *Eating on the Run, Second Ed*. Champaign, IL: Human Kinetics, 1984. P.O. Box 5076, Champaign, IL 61825-5076. $14.95 pb.

Vartabedeân, Roy E., M.D., and Kathy Matthews. *Nutripoints*. New York: Harper & Row, 1990. 10 East 53rd Street, New York, NY 10022. $19.95 hb.

Weinberg, Robert S. Ph.D., and Daniel Gould, Ph.D. *Foundations of Sport and Exercise Physiology*. Champaign, Ill.: Human Kinetics, 1995. P.O. Box 5076, Champaign, IL 61825-5076. $49.00 hb.

Wilmore, Jack H. Ph.D. and David L. Costill, Ph.D. *Physiology of Sport and Exercise*. Champaign, Ill.: Human Kinetics, 1994. P.O. Box 5076, Champaign, IL 61825-5076. $49.00 hb.

——. *Training for Sport and Activity, Third Ed.* Champaign, Ill.: Human Kinetics, 1988. P.O. Box 5076, Champaign, IL 61825-5076. $27.00 hb.

YMCA *Healthy Back Book*. Champaign, Ill.: Human Kinetics, 1994. P.O. Box 5076, Champaign, IL 61825-5076. $10.95 pb.

Index

About the Author

Bob Carlson has had an interest in physical exercise all his life. A veteran of the famed 10th Mountain Division of World War II and a former architect, he gave up his profession in the mid-1970s to devote his life to health promotion and physical fitness. He started as a marathon runner in 1967, but since 1982 has gravitated to walking, especially racewalking, as a far more sensible form of staying in excellent shape. Bob has won many racewalking regional championships and a national one in the 60 to 64 age group, normally doing the 5K in 29 to 30 minutes. He has done extensive writing and teaching on the benefits of walking as the best exercise for the most people. In 1985 Bob founded the Front Range Walkers Club in Denver, Colorado, continually promoting the steady growth of walking for health, fitness and sport. In 1988 he cowrote the book *HealthWalk* with O. J. Seiden, M.D. (Fulcrum Publishing, Golden, Colorado) and was one of the ten most prominent walking leaders in the United States by the Rockport Walking Institute in 1989.

About the Author